LAB MANUAL for

A+ Guide to Software: Managing, Maintaining, and Troubleshooting

2nd Edition

Jean Andrews, Ph.D.

THOMSON
★
COURSE TECHNOLOGY™

Australia • Canada • Mexico • Singapore • Spain • United Kingdom • United States

THOMSON
™
COURSE TECHNOLOGY

Lab Manual for A+ Guide to Software: Managing, Maintaining, and Troubleshooting, 2nd Edition

is published by Course Technology.

Senior Editor:
Lisa Egan

Product Manager:
Donna Gridley

Associate Product Manager:
Tim Gleeson

Editorial Assistant:
Nick Lombardi

Marketing Manager:
Jason Sakos

Developmental Editor:
Donna Gridley

Production Editor:
Catherine G. DiMassa

Executive Editor:
Jennifer Locke

Senior Editor:
William Pitkin III

Composition:
GEX Publishing Services

Text Designer:
GEX Publishing Services

Manuscript Quality Engineers:
Nicole Ashton, Ashlee Welz,
Marc Spoto, Christian Kunciw

Manufacturing:
Trevor Kallop

Cover Designer:
Julie Malone

TABLE OF CONTENTS

PREFACE

This Lab Manual is designed to be the very best tool on the market to help you get the hands-on practical experience you need to learn to install, troubleshoot, and repair the operating systems used by personal computers. It is designed to be used along with *A+ Guide to Software: Managing, Maintaining, and Troubleshooting, 2nd Edition,* by Jean Andrews. It has more than 70 labs, each of which target a very practical problem you are likely to face in the "real world" when supporting PC operating systems. You will learn to use the command prompt and learn to support Windows 98, Windows NT Professional, Windows 2000 Professional, and Windows XP Professional. In addition, you will be introduced to the Mac and Linux operating systems. Each chapter contains labs that are designed to provide the structure needed by the novice, as well as labs that challenge the experienced and inquisitive student.

This book helps prepare you for the 2003 A+ Certification Operating System Technologies examination offered through the Computer Technology Industry Association (CompTIA). Because the popularity of this certification credential is quickly growing among employers, obtaining certification increases your ability to gain employment, improve your salary, and enhance your career. To find more information about A+ Certification and its sponsoring organization, CompTIA, go to the CompTIA Web site at *www.comptia.org*.

Whether your goal is to become an A+ certified technician, or become a PC operating system support technician, the *Lab Manual for A+ Guide to Software, 2nd Edition*, along with the *A+ Guide to Software: Managing, Maintaining and Troubleshooting, 2nd Edition* textbook, will take you there!

FEATURES

In order to ensure a successful experience for both instructors and students, this book includes the following pedagogical features:

- **Objectives**—Every lab opens with learning objectives that set the stage for students to absorb the lessons of the lab.
- **Materials Required**—This feature outlines all the materials students need to complete the lab successfully.
- **Activity Background**—A brief discussion at the beginning of each lab provides important background information.
- **Estimated Completion Time**—To help students plan their work, each lab includes an estimate of the total amount of time required to complete the activity.

Activity—Detailed, numbered steps walk students through the lab. These steps are divided into manageable sections, with explanatory material between each section.

- **Review Questions**—Exercises at the end of each lab help students test their understanding of the lab material.
- **Web Site**—For updates to this book and information about other A+ and PC Repair products, go to www.course.com/pcrepair.

ACKNOWLEDGMENTS

I would like to give special thanks to Donna Gridley for her persistence, patience, and support throughout this entire project.

I would also like to extend my sincere appreciation to Lisa Egan, Laura Hildebrand, Tim Gleeson, Nick Lombardi, Catherine DiMassa, Nicole Ashton, Ashlee Welz, Marc Spoto, and Christian Kunciw. And to all the good folks at Course Technology for the super support you cheerfully gave in developing this lab manual. You're a great team to work with.

Many thanks to Nadine Schreiter of Lakeshore Technical College who served as technical editor of the manual and classroom-tested most of the labs. Nadine, your work, done with such excellence, helped shape the manual and you are appreciated. Thank you to Scott Johns for your invaluable experience and for help in developing many of the labs. This book is dedicated to the covenant of God with man on the earth.

— Jean Andrews, Ph.D.

CLASSROOM SETUP

Lab activities have been designed to progressively explore several operating systems so that you can install and use Windows 98, followed by Windows NT Professional, Windows 2000 Professional and Windows XP. Lastly, you will take a brief look at the Mac and Linux operating systems.

Most labs take 30 to 45 minutes; a few may take a little longer. For several of the labs, your classroom should be networked and provide access to the Internet. When access to the Windows setup files is required, these files can be provided on the Windows installation CD or on a network drive made available to the PC.

The minimum hardware requirements for Windows 98 are:

- 90 MHz or better Pentium-compatible computer
- 24 MB of RAM
- 195-MB hard drive

The minimum hardware requirements for Windows NT Professional are:

- 90 MHz or better Pentium-compatible computer
- 16 MB of RAM
- 125-MB hard drive

Additional setup notes on Windows NT Professional:

- Install Windows NT Professional on a FAT partition and provide an additional NTFS partition for data.
- You will need a user account with administrative privileges

The minimum hardware requirements for Windows 2000 are:

- 133 MHz or better Pentium-compatible computer
- 64 MB of RAM
- 2-GB hard drive

Additional setup notes on Windows 2000 Professional:

- You will need a user account with administrative privileges

The minimum hardware requirements for Windows XP are:

- 233 MHz or better Pentium-compatible computer (300 MHz preferred)
- 64 MB of RAM (128 MB preferred)
- 1.5-MB hard drive (2-GB preferred)

Additional setup notes on Windows XP:

- You will need a user account with administrative privileges
- An NTFS partition that might or might not be the partition where Windows XP is installed

A few of the labs focus on special hardware. For example, one lab requires a CD-ROM drive, sound card and speakers be installed and another lab uses a PC camera, a sound card, microphone and speakers. Also, one lab requires a modem and a working phone line, and another lab requires a parallel cable.

LAB SETUP INSTRUCTIONS

Configuration Type and Operating Systems

Each lab begins with list of required materials. Before beginning a lab activity, verify that each student group or individual has access to the needed materials. Then, make sure that the proper operating system is installed and in good health. Note that in some cases, it is not necessary that an operating system be installed. When needed, the Windows setup files can be provided on the Windows CD, on a network drive, or, in some cases, on the local hard drive.

Protect Data

In several labs, it is possible that data on the hard drive might get lost or corrupted. For this reason, it is important that valuable data stored on the hard drive is backed up to another media.

INTRODUCING AND COMPARING OPERATING SYSTEMS

LAB 1.1 DETERMINE HARDWARE COMPATIBILITY WITH WINDOWS XP

Objectives

The goal of this lab is to help you determine if your hardware is compatible with Windows XP. After completing this lab, you will be able to:

➤ Use Windows to identify system components

➤ Find and use the Microsoft Hardware Compatibility List (HCL)

Materials Required

This lab will require the following:

➤ Windows 9x or Windows 2000 operating system

➤ Internet access

Activity Background

You can't always assume your operating system will support your hardware. This is especially true of older devices, because software developers need to focus on supporting the most capable and popular devices. You can verify that Microsoft software supports your hardware by checking Microsoft's Hardware Compatibility List (HCL). The HCL, which can be found at *www.microsoft.com/hwdq/hcl/* includes only devices whose drivers were written by Microsoft, or devices whose drivers have been tested and approved by Microsoft. In this lab you will use Device Manager to inventory some devices in a system. Then you will check the HCL to see if the system's devices are supported by Windows XP.

Estimated completion time: **30 minutes**

ACTIVITY

To use Device Manager to inventory your system, follow these steps:

1. Open the **Control Panel** and then double-click the **System** icon.

2. For Windows 9x, select the **Device Manager** tab. (For Windows 2000, select the **Hardware** tab and then click the **Device Manager** button.) The Device Manager window opens.

3. In Device Manager, devices are arranged by categories. To see what kind of video adapter is installed on your system, click the + sign to the left of "Display Adapters."

4. Select your video adapter and then click the **Properties** button. Information about the adapter's model and manufacturer appears. Record that information here.

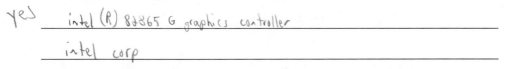

yes   intel (R) 82865 G graphics controller

      intel corp

5. Use Device Manager to find similar information for your network adapter, modem card, or sound card and record that information here.

yes.   Intel (R) PRO/1000 MT Network connection   yes   Sound max integrated Digital avd

       Intel   analog Devices

Now that you have a list of devices installed on your system, check the HCL to determine if these devices are supported by Windows XP. Web sites change often, so know that the steps listed below might have to be adjusted slightly in order to accommodate changes in the Microsoft site. If you have difficulty following the steps due to Web site changes, see your instructor for help. Otherwise, follow these steps:

1. Open your browser and go to *www.microsoft.com/hwdq/hcl/*. Click the link **Continue to original HCL**.

2. Click the text box, and replace "All Products" with the specific information about your video adapter that you learned from Device Manager. If you don't find your adapter, try again using a more general description of the adapter. For example, for one video adapter, you might type "Intel 82810E". If that doesn't return a result, try just typing "Intel".

3. Click the **In** list arrow and select the correct category in the drop-down list.

4. Click **Search Now**. A list of devices appears.

5. Verify you have found your device by verifying that the correct manufacturer is listed.

6. Look to the right to see if the device has an XP logo symbol or a compatible symbol under the XP column. Either one indicates that the device is compatible with XP.

7. Add a note to your list of devices above indicating whether or not the device is compatible with Windows XP.

8. Check the other devices in your list, and note whether they are compatible with Windows XP.

Review Questions

1. Explain how to compile a list of devices installed on your system.

go to control panel, system, system Properties, device manager, write down what you have./ open the case and look inside.

2. How are devices grouped in Device Manager?

by type or connection

3. What does "HCL" stand for?

hardware compatability list.

4. If a device is not listed in the HCL, what are your options when installing Windows XP? List at least two possibilities.

go to the manufacturer of device, is there a device driver. install as a test to see if it's compatable

5. Does the hardware in your system qualify for Windows XP? If it doesn't qualify, explain why.

Yes.

LAB 1.2 EXAMINE FILES AND DIRECTORIES

Objectives

The goal of this lab is to use different methods to examine files and directories. After completing this lab, you will be able to:

➤ Use the command line to view information about files and directories

➤ Use My Computer to view information about files and directories

➤ Display information about files and directories in other ways

Materials Required

This lab will require the following:

➤ Windows 9x or Windows 2000 operating system

Activity Background

You can access information about the file structure of a PC in several ways. From the command line, you can use the DIR command to list files and directories. In Windows, you can use Explorer or My Computer to view the same information. In the following activity, you will practice using the DIR command and My Computer.

Estimated completion time: **30 minutes**

ACTIVITY

Follow these steps to access file information via the command line:

1. For Windows 9x, click the **Start** button on the taskbar, point to **Programs**, and then click **MS-DOS Prompt**. (For Windows 2000, click the **Start** button on the taskbar, point to **Programs**, point to **Accessories**, and then click **Command Prompt**.)

2. The command line window opens with the current directory indicated by the prompt. Type **DIR** and press **Enter**.

3. A detailed list of files and directories within the current directory appears. If there are many files and directories, only the last several will be visible on the screen. Try these variations of the DIR command and explain how the information is displayed:

   DIR/P

   DIR/W

   DIR/P gives you one page at a time.

   DIR/w gives wide list page.

4. Examine the results of the DIR command. The results vary with versions of Windows, but each listing should include the following information:

   ▪ The date and time the file was created.

   ▪ The directory markers. Directories do not include an extension. Instead, they are indicated by a <DIR> tag.

   ▪ The size of the file, in bytes.

- The name of a file or directory. Most files have an extension.
- A summary including the number of files and directories within that directory, the number of bytes used by those files, and the number of bytes of free space on the drive.

To print this file information, you can copy the contents of the Command Prompt window to the Windows Clipboard, open the Notepad program, paste the file information into Notepad, and then use Notepad's Print command. To try that technique now, follow these steps:

1. Click the **MS-DOS Prompt** icon (for Windows 9x) or the **Command Prompt** icon (for Windows 2000) located on the title bar.
2. Point to **Edit**, and then click **Mark**. A blinking cursor will appear at the top of your Command Line window.
3. Left-click and drag over the information you would like to copy to the clipboard; you will notice the information is highlighted. It may be necessary for you to scroll the window to capture all necessary information.
4. Once you have highlighted all the information you wish to copy, click the **MS-DOS Prompt** icon (for Windows 9x) or the **Command Prompt** icon (for Windows 2000) located on the title bar again.
5. Point to **Edit**, and then click **Copy**.
6. Click **Start**, point to **Programs**, and then point to **Accessories** and select **Notepad**.
7. Click **Edit**, and then click **Paste**.
8. Click **File**, and then click **Print**. Use the print options to print your document.
9. Close the Command Prompt window and Notepad without saving the file.

In addition to the Command Prompt Window, you can also use My Computer to examine files and directories. My Computer can display information in a variety of ways. Before you view files and directories using this tool, you'll first change some settings to control how the information is displayed. In Windows 9x, follow these steps:

1. From the Windows 9x desktop, double-click the **My Computer** icon. The My Computer window opens.
2. Click **View** on the menu bar, and then click **Folder Options**. The Folder Options window opens.
3. Click the **General** tab (if necessary), click the **Custom, based on settings you choose** option button and then click the **Settings** button.
4. In the "Browse Folders as Follows" section, click the **Open each folder in its own window** option button and then click **OK**. The Custom Settings window closes.
5. Click **Apply** and then click **OK** to close the Folder Options window.

To change settings in Windows 2000, follow these steps:

1. From the Windows 2000 desktop, double-click the **My Computer** icon. The My Computer window opens.

2. Click **Tools** on the menu bar and then click **Folder Options**. The Folder Options dialog box opens.

3. In the Folder Options window, click the **View** tab (if necessary), check **Show hidden files and folders** and uncheck **Hide file extensions for known file types**.

4. Click **Apply** and then click **OK** to close the Folder Options window.

Now that you have changed the way information is displayed, you are ready to use My Computer to access specific information about your system's files and directories. Complete the following for both Windows 9x and Windows 2000:

1. Maximize the My Computer window and then click the icon representing drive C.

2. How much free space is available?

   7.04 GB

   _____

3. How much space is used?

   2.64 GB

   _____

4. Double-click the icon for drive C:. How are folders represented in this window?

   Large icons

   _____

5. Windows uses a different icon for different types of files. Describe three different icons and the files they represent.

   folder = file folder.

   dos window = Dos files.

   trash can = recycle Bin

6. Click **View** on the My Computer menu bar and then click **Details**. Notice that this command displays the same information as the DIR command.

7. Close all open windows.

Review Questions

1. What command displays a list of files and directories at the command line?

   Dir

2. Does Windows display file extensions by default?

   Yes

3. How can you change the way Windows displays file extensions?

   view from the C folder and click folder options, view tab then Hide the extensions for known file types.

4. What tool other than My Computer can you use to explore a file structure graphically?

   explore

5. In My Computer, what type of graphic displays information about a drive?

   The pie

6. How does Windows graphically distinguish between different file types?

   different icons

LAB 1.3 COMPARE WINDOWS VERSIONS USING THE MICROSOFT WEB SITE

Objectives

The goal of this lab is to search the Microsoft Web site in order to compare different Windows versions. After completing this lab, you will be able to:

➤ Look up information on Windows on the Microsoft Web site (*www.microsoft.com*)

➤ Use Microsoft's search feature to find information on different versions of Windows

➤ Determine which version of Windows is compatible with the most types of hardware

1

Materials Required

This lab will require the following:

➤ Internet access

Activity Background

The Microsoft Web site is an excellent source of information on all Microsoft products. In this lab you will explore the site to gain an idea of what kind of information is available. Then you will focus specifically on information regarding the Windows product line.

Estimated completion time: **30 minutes**

ACTIVITY

1. Open your browser and go to *www.microsoft.com.*

2. What Product Families are listed?

   windows, office, mobile devices, servers and then some.

3. Point to **Support** and then click **Knowledge Base**.

4. The "Search the Knowledge Base" page appears. The Microsoft Knowledge Base is a collection of information (grouped into articles) about different products or common errors. Study the page. As you can see, the first step on this is selecting a Microsoft product. Follow the general directions below, remembering that specific directions on using the Web site cannot be given, as the site sometimes changes. If you have difficulty following the steps due to Web site changes, see your instructor for help. Otherwise, follow these steps:

5. Choose to search on **Windows 98** by selecting it from the "Select a Microsoft Product" drop-down list.

6. The Knowledge Base page asks you what you would like to search for. In the **Search for...** text box, type **FAT32.**

7. Next, you need to specify some search options. If necessary, select **All of the words entered** on the drop-down menu.

8. Leave all other options as they appear by default. Click **Go**.

9. List the titles of the first three articles that appear as a result of your search.

   Post a question to the MS windows 98 newsgroup.

   windows 98 support center.

   description of the Fat 32 File system.

10. Take a look at any of the articles. When you are finished examining the articles, return to the Microsoft home page at *microsoft.com*.

11. Click the **Windows** link (under "Product Families"). What versions of Windows are listed in the upper left-hand corner of the page?

    XP, server 2003, small Business server 2003, 2000, embedded mobile, previous versions.

12. Click **Previous Versions**. What "Previous Versions of Windows" do you see listed?

    me, 98, 95, NT workstation, NTserver

look it up.

13. Click **Windows 95**, click the **Get the latest info.** link, and then click the **Windows 95, Installations, Frequently Asked Questions** link.

14. Locate the **Windows 95 Installation Requirements (Q138349)** article.

15. Print the page information on the system requirements for Windows 95 by clicking the **Print** button on the browser toolbar (or by clicking **File** on the menu bar and then clicking **Print**.) Next verify that the correct printer is selected and then click **OK** or **Print** (depending on which version of Windows you are using).

16. Search for and print the system requirements for Windows XP.

17. Go to the Hardware Compatibility List (HCL) at *www.microsoft.com/hwdq/hcl/*. Leave "All Products" in the Search for the following text box.

18. Click the **In** list arrow, scroll down the list, click **Display** and then click **Search Now**. According to the list on this page, which version or versions of Windows support the most display adapters? Which support the least?

    windows 2000 = most.

    windows. XP 64 Bit = least.

Review Questions

1. What information is available in the HCL?

   Compatabile hardware.

2. What are the minimum system requirements for Windows XP?

300 MHz processor

128 Meg ram

1.5GB hard drive

3. Name two Product Families offered by Microsoft (besides Windows). What are these Product Families used for?

Servers = server services, IIS etc.

games and XBOX = games.

4. Based on your knowledge of Windows, what do you think is the most recent Windows OS that Microsoft now describes as a "previous version"?

windows 2000

LAB 1.4 INVESTIGATE LINUX

Objectives

The goal of this lab is to find information about Linux. After completing this lab, you will be able to:

➤ Research Linux on the Linux Web site (*www.linux.org*)

➤ Compare Linux with other operating systems

➤ Use the Linux tutorial on the Linux Web site

Materials Required

This lab will require the following:

➤ Internet access

Activity Background

In this lab, you will search the *www.linux.org* site for general information on Linux. You will also survey the Linux tutorial.

Estimated completion time: **60 minutes**

ACTIVITY

1. Open your browser and go to *www.linux.org*. Spend a few minutes exploring the site on your own and then return to the main page.

2. Click the **General Info** link (on the navigation bar). Using the information on the "What is Linux" page, answer the following:

   - What is the current, full-featured version of Linux?

     2.4

   - Who is credited with inventing the Linux kernel?

     Linus Torvalds.

   - How is Linux licensed? Read the GNU General Public License. Give a brief description of the terms and conditions of this license.

     General Public license.

     freely-distributed

   - How much does Linux cost?

     its free.

In order for an operating system to be really useful, there must be applications written specifically for it. For instance, suppose a small business is interested in using Linux on its desktop computers. Will this business be able to run common business-type applications on its Linux desktops? To find out, click the **Applications** link (on navigation bar). The various types of applications are listed by category. Search this page and its links to answer the following questions:

1. Will the business be able to send faxes from a Linux machine?

   yes

2. List two Web browsers suitable for Linux.

   Emacs/w3   web wader

3. How many anti-virus software packages are available for Linux? List at least two.

   12

   Antivir   A MAVES

4. Searching under "Office" and "Word Processor", list at least three word-processing applications that are available for Linux.

Led It

abizpdf.

Aik Saurus

5. How many accounting applications are available for Linux? List at least two and tell where you found them.

_52_

_GC+B_

SQL - Ledger

Now you can continue exploring the Linux Web site. Follow these steps to compare Linux to other operating systems:

1. Click the **Documentation** link on the navigation bar.

2. Read about the Linux Documentation Project.

Use the information displayed on the Linux Web site to answer the following questions:

1. Give a brief description of the Linux Documentation Project.

they are trying to write How-to's and guides for linux

2. Who is responsible for writing the documentation for the Linux Operating System?

volunteers.

Next, you will explore the site's Linux tutorial. Follow these steps:

1. Return to the Home page, scroll down to display the heading **Linux 101** and then click **more** at the bottom of that section.

2. Scroll down, and then click **Getting Started with Linux**. Browse through this tutorial and answer the following questions.

3. What are the distributions (flavors) of Linux and how are they categorized?

4. Can you install Linux on a computer that has another operating system already installed? Print the Web page supporting your answer.

_____

5. When preparing to install Linux, what is a good computer-use practice?

_____

_____

Continue exploring the Web site by completing the following:

1. Click the **Distributions** link. Notice that a link to the source code for Linux kernels is available on this page. Also notice the Distribution search area. When searching for a distribution of Linux, if you do not narrow your search, you will return a large number of distributions.

2. Select **English** from the **Language** drop-down list.

3. Select **Mainstream/General Public** from the **Category** drop-down list.

4. Select **Intel compatible** from the **Platform** list and click **Go**. How many distributions do you see listed?

_____

5. Browse through the list of distributions, looking specifically for Caldera Systems, Linux Mandrake, and Red Hat. Which one claims it is the most popular distribution? What user level is it geared for?

_____

_____

6. Can Linux be used on systems other than those that run Intel-compatible processors? Print the Web page supporting your answer.

_____

Review Questions

1. What is the least amount of money that you will pay for Linux?

_____

2. Why do you think a company might not want to use Linux on its desktop computers?

_____

_____

_____

3. What is one advantage of using Linux on a desktop rather than a Windows operating system?

_____

_____

_____

4. Based on what you learned from the Linux Web site, how do you think companies that provide Linux make the most profit?

_____

_____

_____

LAB 1.5 EXPLORE THE MACINTOSH WORLD

Objectives

don't spend much time on this

The goal of this lab is to familiarize you with the Macintosh operating systems and the hardware it supports. After completing this lab, you will be able to:

➤ Describe the various Apple operating systems, hardware, and applications

➤ Research Apple technology on the Apple Web site (*www.apple.com*)

Materials Required

This lab will require the following:

➤ Internet access

Activity Background

The Macintosh operating systems are designed to be used only on Macintosh (or Mac) computers; they cannot be used on PCs. In addition, many developers (including Apple, the company that created the Macintosh computer) have developed Macintosh applications. The Apple Web site (*www.apple.com*) is the best source of information about the Macintosh products. In this lab, you will investigate Macintosh operating systems, hardware and applications. Now that you've had some practice exploring Web sites in the Labs 1.3 and 1.4, you should be able to find information on the Apple Web site on your own. To encourage you to explore the Web site on your own, this lab provides less direction about exactly which links to use than the preceding two labs.

Estimated completion time: **30 minutes**

ACTIVITY

1. Open your browser and go to *www.apple.com*. Spend a few minutes exploring the site on your own and then return to the main page. Use the various links on the Apple Web site to answer the following questions.

2. What versions of the Mac operating system currently come preinstalled on the iMac?

   _____

   _____

3. What's the cost of upgrading your operating system from OS 9 to OS X?

   _____

4. At the time of this writing, there are four different iMacs (The New iMac) for sale on the Apple Web site. What are the current speeds or frequencies of the iMac processors?

   _____

5. How much does the iMac (classic design) cost?

   _____

   _____

6. What software comes bundled with "The new iMac"?

   _____

   _____

   _____

7. What is an iBook?

_____

_____

8. How much does the most expensive iBook cost?

_____

9. What features are included with the least expensive iBook?

_____

_____

10. Describe the features of the Apple Pro Mouse.

_____

_____

11. What is the function of an AirPort card?

_____

12. What Apple computer can use the AirPort card?

_____

13. What is the purpose of QuickTime software?

_____

_____

14. Describe what the AppleWorks software does.

_____

_____

15. Describe the purposes of iMovie software.

_____

Review Questions

1. What is one advantage of using an Apple computer compared to using a PC?

_____

2. What type of user do you think the Apple applications are intended for?

   _____

3. Why do you think it is easier for Apple to provide compatibility between hard-ware and the operating system than it is for Microsoft or Linux to provide com-patibility between their operating systems and hardware on which they run?

   _____

   _____

4. What type of user is the iMac intended for?

   _____

   _____

CHAPTER TWO

HOW AN OPERATING SYSTEM WORKS WITH HARDWARE AND OTHER SOFTWARE

Labs included in this chapter

➤ Lab 2.1 Examine System Resources with Device Manager

➤ Lab 2.2 Use Shareware to Examine a Computer

➤ Lab 2.3 Create a Windows 98 Startup Disk

➤ Lab 2.4 Use Microsoft Diagnostics with Windows

➤ Lab 2.5 Install Windows Components

➤ Lab 2.6 Convert Numbers

LAB 2.1 EXAMINE SYSTEM RESOURCES WITH DEVICE MANAGER

Objectives

In Lab 1.1, you were introduced to Window's Device Manager. In this lab, you will learn more about this tool. After completing this lab, you will be able to use Device Manager to:

➤ Determine what components are installed on a system

➤ Examine system resource allocation

➤ Print a system summary

Materials Required

This lab will require the following:

➤ Windows 9x or Windows 2000 operating system

Activity Background

Windows 9x, Windows 2000, and Windows XP provide a powerful configuration tool called Device Manager, which you can use to view and print a system's hardware configuration. Windows NT does not have Device Manager. Device Manager is more powerful than MSD, but not quite as good as some third party utilities. (You will examine one of these third party utilities in Lab 2.2.) Note that Windows 9x and Windows 2000 offer slightly different Device Managers, so as you complete this lab be sure to follow the directions for your version.

> Estimated completion time: **30 minutes**

ACTIVITY

To access Device Manager in Windows 9x, follow these steps:

1. Click the **Start** button on the taskbar, point to **Settings**, and then click **Control Panel**. The Control Panel window opens.

2. Double-click the **System** icon.

3. In the System Properties dialog box, click the **Device Manager** tab.

To access Device Manager in Windows 2000, follow these steps:

1. Click the **Start** button on the taskbar, click **Settings**, and then click **Control Panel**. The Control Panel window opens.

2. Double-click the **System** icon.

3. In the System Properties dialog box, click the **Hardware** tab, and then click the **Device Manager** button.

In both Windows 9x and Windows 2000, Device Manager appears similar to Figure 2-1. You can right-click an item in the list and then select Properties from the shortcut menu to view information about that item, or you can view the item's Properties by double-clicking the item. When you click the + sign to the left of an item, a list of the installed devices for that item appears beneath the item. To see how this works, follow these steps:

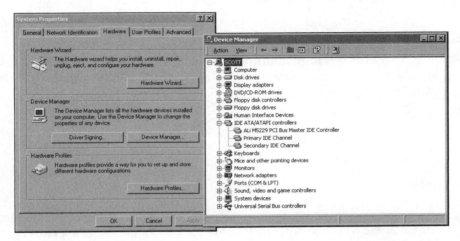

Figure 2-1   Windows 2000 Device Manager can be accessed from System Properties window

1. Click the sign next to "Network Adapters."
2. Double-click on a device listed under Network adapters. A Properties dialog box opens.
3. Click the **Resources** tab. This tab shows all resources used by the selected device.

Use the Resources tab in the Properties dialog box to complete the following:

1. What IRQ is assigned to the network adapter?

_____

2. What is the I/O range of the network adapter?

_____

3. What Memory Addresses are available to the network adapter?

_____

4. Close the Properties window.

Device Manager also allows you to view resources in other ways.

To view resources in Windows 9x:

1. In Device Manager, click the **View resources by connection** option button and observe that the groupings change.

2. Click the plus sign next to Plug and Play BIOS to view the devices managed by the Plug and Play BIOS.

To view resources on Windows 2000:

1. Click **View** on the Device Manager menu bar and then click **Resources by type**. Note that information is now grouped into four categories.

2. Click the **plus sign** next to "Interrupt Request (IRQ)" to see which device is assigned to each IRQ line.

Device Manager lets you print information about individual devices or device categories. You can also print a system summary. To print a system summary follow the directions for your version of Windows.

To print a system summary for Windows 9x:

1. Click the **Print** button.

2. Click the **System summary** option button and click **OK**.

To print a system summary for Windows 2000:

1. Click **View** on the Device Manager menu bar and then click **Print**.

2. Click the **System summary** option button and then click **Print**.

Review Questions

1. Name the Windows operating system that does not include Device Manager.

_____

2. How do you display individual devices under the group headings?

_____

3. What are two ways to view device properties in Device Manager?

_____

_____

4. What are the four types of system resources?

_____

_____

5. What three options are available for printing in Device Manager?

_____

_____

_____

LAB 2.2 USE SHAREWARE TO EXAMINE A COMPUTER

Objectives

The goal of this lab is to use SANDRA, Standard version to examine your system. After completing this lab, you will be able to:

➤ Download a file from the Internet

already downloaded.

➤ Install SANDRA

➤ Use SANDRA to examine your system

Materials Required

This lab will require the following:

➤ Windows 98

➤ Internet access

➤ Software such as WinZip to uncompress a zipped file

Activity Background

Good PC support people are always good investigators. This lab is designed to help you learn how to conduct an investigation via the Internet. As you will see, the Internet offers a wealth of resources to those who take the time to search, download, and investigate the possible uses of software available there. This exercise is designed to help you learn to be such an investigator. Follow these directions to find and download a shareware utility that you can use to diagnose PC problems. Then you will print a report from the downloaded software about the hardware and software on your computer.

Estimated completion time: **30 minutes**

ACTIVITY

1. Open your browser and go to *www.3bsoftware.com*.

2. Point to **Downloads** and click **SANDRA Trial Versions**.

3. Under SANDRA Standard, click the **Download STANDARD** button. You will be routed to C|Net Download.com.

4. When the File Download dialog box appears, save the file **san_897a.zip** to your PC Desktop. You can then disconnect from the Internet.

Note that if you cannot find SANDRA on the C|Net Web site, you can use a search engine to locate the shareware. Also, note that later versions of SANDRA might have different file names for the zip file.

Next, you can decompress the SANDRA file and install the utility on your PC. Follow these steps:

1. Uncompress the SANDRA zip file by double-clicking the **san_897a.zip** icon located on your desktop and then extracting all the files including Setup.exe with its components.

2. Run the setup program, **Setup.exe**, which creates a new program in your Program Group and adds an icon to your desktop.

3. Run the program **SiSoftware Sandra 2002**. You should see a screen similar to the one shown in Figure 2-2.

Figure 2-2   SiSoft SANDRA main window

2

You can execute each of the utilities, in turn, by double-clicking the icons, or you can create a composite report of the results of each selection. To learn more, complete the following:

1. Double-click the **System Summary** icon. The System Summary utility launches and gathers information about your system before displaying it in a format similar to Device Manager, with devices listed by type.

2. Click the Red **X** at the bottom of the System Summary utility or hit **Esc** on your keyboard to close the System Summary utility.

3. Open the **Windows Information** utility. Scroll down and note the information types that are listed. According to this utility, what version of Windows are you using?

   _____

4. What is the path to the Temporary Folder on your system?

   _____

5. Click the Red **X** at the bottom of the Windows Information utility or hit **Esc** on your keyboard to close the Windows Information utility.

6. Open the **Drives Information** utility. The utility begins to gather information regarding your drives. Do not move the mouse or touch the keyboard while in progress. How much Total Space does the hard drive contain? How much Free Space does the hard drive contain? What type of File System does the hard drive use?

   _____

   _____

7. Click the Red **X** at the bottom of the Drives Information utility or hit **Esc** on your keyboard to close the Drives Information utility.

8. Open the **DMA Settings** utility. Why are you unable to view the DMA Settings information?

   _____

   _____

9. Close the DMA Settings utility.

You can create a composite report of your system using SANDRA. To learn more, follow these steps:

1. On the SiSoft Sandra menu bar, click **File** and then click **Create a Report Wizard...**

2. In the wizard introduction window, click **Next**.

3. In the Step 1 of 8 window, click the **Clear All** button and then select the **System summary** checkbox. Click **Next** to continue.

4. In the Step 2 of 8 window, click the **Clear All** button and then click Next to continue.

5. In the Step 3 of 8 window, click the **Clear All** button and then click **Next** to continue.

6. In the Step 4 of 8 window, click the **Clear All** button and then click **Next** to continue.

7. In the Step 5 of 8 window, add any comments that you desire and click **Next** to continue.

8. In the Step 6 of 8 window, click the **Print it or Fax it** option button and then click **Next** to continue.

9. In the print dialog box, click **OK**.

10. Click **Finish** and then collect your report from the printer.

11. Continue to explore each utility in SANDRA, and then close SANDRA. You will use SANDRA again in later chapters, so don't uninstall it.

In this lab, you downloaded SANDRA from the C|Net Download.com Web site. But many popular utilities are available from multiple sources on the Internet. To see for yourself, follow these steps:

1. Attempt to find SANDRA at www.zdnet.com.

2. Is the program available through this avenue as well? Print the Web page or pages to support your answer.

Review Questions

1. What URL can you use to find a link to download SANDRA?

---

2. Is SANDRA capable of only hardware diagnostics?

---

3. What two of the four system resources are you not able to view with the version of SANDRA you downloaded and why?

_____

_____

_____

4. Based on your experience with the labs in this chapter, which do you think is better at analyzing your system, SANDRA or Device Manager? Why?

_____

_____

5. What type of software is SANDRA considered?

_____

LAB 2.3 CREATE A WINDOWS 98 STARTUP DISK

Objectives

The goal of this lab is to follow the process of creating a Windows 98 startup disk, then to examine its contents. After completing this lab, you will be able to:

➤ Create a Windows 98 startup disk

➤ Create a bootable floppy disk from the command line

➤ Examine each disk

➤ Compare the two disks you created

Materials Required

This lab will require the following:

➤ Windows 98 operating system

➤ Two blank floppy disks

➤ Path to Windows 98 setup files as provided by your instructor

Activity Background

Early versions of Windows provided no automated utility for creating a bootable disk with troubleshooting and set-up utilities. But with Windows 98 came a utility that does just that. The Windows Startup Disk contains configuration files and drivers that provide CD-ROM support. In this lab, you will make a bootable disk and a startup disk and examine the difference between the two.

Estimated completion time: **30 minutes**

ACTIVITY

To create a bootable floppy disk from the command line, follow these steps:

1. Click **Start**, and then click **Run**. For Windows 98, in the Run dialog box, type **Command** and click **OK**.

2. Label a floppy disk "Boot disk" then insert the floppy disk into the floppy drive.

3. Type **FORMAT A: /S** (with a space between the "T" and the "A" and a space between the colon and the forward slash) and then press **Enter**. This instructs the system to format the floppy disk. The /S switch instructs the system to copy to the floppy disk the system files required to boot the computer.

4. The system checks the existing file format of the disk and begins formatting the floppy disk, giving you a progress report as it proceeds. The system notifies you that format is complete and then begins copying system files to the floppy disk, notifying you again when that process is finished.

5. The system prompts you to enter a volume label if you wish or to press Enter to bypass this step entirely. Type **your last name** and then press **Enter**.

6. The system displays the format summary. Record the first three lines of the system summary here:

   _____

   _____

   _____

   _____

7. When asked if you want to format another disk, type **N** and then press **Enter**.

8. At the Command Prompt type: **DIR A:** to display a list of the files transferred to the floppy disk. Record the filename and file size here.

   _____

9. Compare the file size with the number of bytes used by the system in the summary you recorded in Step 6. Note that there seems to be a discrepancy. This is because three hidden files were copied to the disk.

10. Remove the floppy disk from the drive. Keep this floppy disk for future use.

To create a Windows 98 startup disk, follow these steps:

1. Open the Control Panel, and then double-click the **Add/Remove Programs** icon. The Add/Remove Programs window opens.

2

2. Click the **Startup Disk** tab and then click the **Create Disk** button.

3. When prompted to insert the Windows 98 CD-ROM, click **OK** without inserting the CD.

4. In the Add/Remove Programs Properties dialog box, type the correct path for the Windows 98 CD-ROM set-up files and click **OK**. Your instructor will supply you with this path or you can use the Windows 98 CD.

5. The system begins reading setup files. When prompted, label a floppy disk **Windows 98 Startup Disk**, insert it in drive A: and then click **OK**. The system begins copying files to the floppy disk.

6. When the copy operation is complete, launch Windows Explorer and examine the contents of the floppy disk. How many files have been copied to the floppy disk?

_____

CRITICAL THINKING

1. Using information learned from previous labs, how can you view the hidden files stored on this disk? List the steps below to display hidden files:

_____

_____

_____

_____

2. What are the three hidden files on this disk?

_____

3. Remove the floppy disk from the system.

Review Questions

1. When added to the Format command, what switch directs the system to copy system files?

_____

2. When formatting a disk, what should you do if you do not want to specify a volume label?

_____

3. What applet in the Control Panel is used to create a startup disk?

_____

4. What collection of files is required in order to make a disk bootable?

_____

LAB 2.4 USE MICROSOFT DIAGNOSTICS WITH WINDOWS

Objectives

The goal of this lab is to observe the boot process. After completing this lab, you will be able to:

➤ Use the Microsoft Diagnostics (MSD) utility to examine your system

➤ Compare results of MSD using real mode and protected mode

Materials Required

This lab will require the following:

➤ Windows 98 operating system

➤ Bootable floppy disk from Lab 2.3 or startup disk from Lab 2.3

➤ Path to Windows 98 setup files as provided by your instructor

Activity Background

The Microsoft Diagnostics (MSD) utility, which is included with both DOS and all versions of Windows, examines your system and displays useful information about ports, devices, memory, and the like. The program file for Microsoft Diagnostics, MSD.EXE, can be found in the Tools/OldMSDOS directory on your Windows 98 installation CD. In this lab you will install and use MSD.

```
Estimated completion time: 30 minutes
```

ACTIVITY

Before you can begin using MSD, you need to copy the program file to your hard disk.

1. Insert the Windows 98 installation CD into your CD-ROM drive or access the setup files at another location as provided by your instructor.

2. Copy the file **MSD.EXE** from the Windows 98 Tools/OldMSDOS directory to your hard drive, storing it in a folder named **\Tools**.

Now that you have copied the necessary program file to your hard disk, you can launch MSD. Follow these steps to use MSD in a real mode environment:

1. Reboot your computer using the bootable floppy disk from Lab 2.3 or a Windows 98 startup disk from Lab 2.3, which will boot your PC into real mode and provide a command prompt.   Point to **Start**, click **Shut Down**, and then click **Restart Computer in MS-DOS mode**.

2. At the command prompt, type **C:\TOOLS\MSD.EXE** and then press **Enter**. Note that this is a way to execute a program file located in a different directory from the one you are working in. You told the computer the exact path, called an absolute path, to the file you wanted to execute. At this point, your screen should look similar to Figure 2-3.

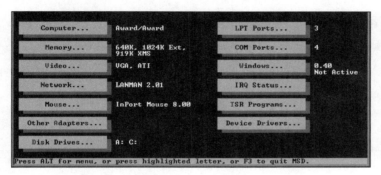

Figure 2-3   The MSD utility

Study all the MSD menu options and answer the following questions about your system:

1. What categories of information are available in MSD?

_____

_____

2. What version of the operating system are you running?

_____

3. What COM ports are available on the system?

_____

4. What IRQ and Port Address are associated with COM1?

_____

5. How far does the MEMORY map extend?

_____

_____

6. What is the Address Range at 1024K?

_____

_____

Save the information you noted so that you can compare it with the information you will obtain from MSD in the next set of steps. Now you are ready to close MSD.

1. Click **File** on the MSD menu bar and then click **Exit**.

2. Remove the floppy disk and reboot your PC to the Windows desktop.

3. Using Windows Explorer, double-click the **MSD.EXE** file to start it again.

With MSD open, answer the following questions again:

1. What categories of information are available in MSD?

_____

_____

2. What version of the operating system are you running?

_____

3. What COM ports are available on the system?

_____

4. What IRQ and Port Address are associated with COM1?

_____

5. How far does the MEMORY map extend?

_____

6. What is the Address Range at 1024K?

_____

Compare the information obtained the first time you used MSD with the information you obtained the second time, and then answer these questions:

1. How does your first set of answers compare to your second set of answers?

_____

_____

2. How do you explain the differences?

_____

3. What key can you press to exit MSD?

_____

You are finished with the MSD now, so you can close it.

Review Questions

1. In what categories would you look to find information on COM ports?

_____

2. What message did you see when you started MSD from within Windows?

_____

3. What category gives information on the type of network installed?

_____

4. What is an advantage of saving MSD.EXE to the hard drive?

_____

5. What is the absolute path to MSD.EXE on the Windows 98 setup CD?

_____

6. What Windows tool is similar to MSD?

_____

7. As a PC repair technician, when would you use MSD?

_____

_____

Lab 2.5 Install Windows Components

Objectives

The objective of this lab is to add an optional component to Windows. After completing this lab, you will be able to:

➤ Use the Add/Remove Programs utility

➤ Install desktop wallpaper

➤ Select a wallpaper for your desktop

Materials Required

This lab will require the following:

➤ Windows 98 operating systems

➤ Path to the Windows 98 setup files as provided by your instructor

Activity Background

Windows includes many optional features that can be installed either when you install the operating system itself, or at some later time, after the operating system has already been installed. In this lab you will install optional Desktop Wallpapers on a computer that already has Windows 98 installed.

```
Estimated completion time: 30 minutes
```

Activity

1. Open the Control Panel and double-click the **Add/Remove Programs** icon.

2. Click the **Windows Setup** tab. In the Components field you should see several categories of Windows components listed.

3. Click **Accessories** and then click the **Details** button. A window opens displaying Windows components in the Accessory category.

4. Select the **Desktop Wallpaper** checkbox and then click **OK** to close the window.

5. Click **Apply**.

6. When prompted, click **OK**, type the path to the Windows setup files and then click **OK** again.

2

7. Windows installs the files containing the new desktop wallpaper. When the installation is complete, click **OK** to exit the Add/Remove Programs utility.

8. In the Control Panel, double-click the **Display** icon.

9. Click the **Background** tab and then browse through the various wallpapers. Experiment with the Tile, Center, and Stretch options in the dropdown menu. Observe the preview of your wallpaper selections in the Background tab.

10. Select a background combination you like, click **Apply**, and then click **OK** to close the Display utility.

11. Close any other open windows and observe your new desktop wallpaper.

Review Questions

1. What collection of files is necessary to install a new Windows component?

_____

2. Which utility is used to install new Windows components?

_____

3. What category of components is Desktop Wallpaper part of?

_____

4. What utility did you use to select a wallpaper for your system?

_____

5. Is it necessary to apply the Display properties before you see what a wallpaper will look like?

_____

LAB 2.6 CONVERT NUMBERS

Objectives

The objective of this lab is to practice converting numbers between decimal, binary and hexadecimal forms. After completing this lab, you will be able to:

➤ Convert decimal numbers to hexadecimal and binary form

➤ Convert hexadecimal numbers to binary and decimal form

➤ Convert binary numbers to decimal and hexadecimal form

Materials Required

This lab will require the following:

➤ Pencil and paper and/or Windows Calculator

➤ Appendix C (The Hexadecimal Number System and Memory Addressing) from the textbook, *A+ Guide to Software*

➤ Windows 98, Windows 2000, or Windows XP

Activity Background

You will sometimes want to know what resources are being reserved for a device. This information is often displayed on a computer in hexadecimal (or hex) numbers, which is shorthand for the binary numbers that computers actually use. Often, you will want to convert these into the more familiar decimal numbers. This will give you a better picture about which resources are reserved for a device.

Estimated completion time: **45 minutes**

ACTIVITY

1. Convert the following decimal numbers to binary numbers using either a calculator or the instructions provided in Appendix C (The Hexadecimal Number System and Memory Addressing) from the textbook, *A+ Guide to Software*. (To access the Windows Calculator, click **Start** on the taskbar, point to **Programs**, point to **Accessories**, and then click **Calculator**.)

   ▪ 14 = _____

   ▪ 77 = _____

   ▪ 128 = _____

   ▪ 223 = _____

   ▪ 255 = _____

2. Convert the following decimal numbers to hexadecimal notation:

   ▪ 13 = _____

   ▪ 240 = _____

   ▪ 255 = _____

   ▪ 58880 = _____

   ▪ 65535 = _____

3. Convert the following binary numbers to hexadecimal notation:

   ▪ 100 = _____

   ▪ 1011 = _____

2

- 111101 = _____
- 11111000 = _____
- 10110011 = _____
- 00000001 = _____

4. Hexadecimal numbers are often preceded with "0x." Convert the following hex numbers to binary numbers:

- 0x0016 = _____
- 0x00F8 = _____
- 0x00B2B = _____
- 0x005A = _____
- 0x1234 = _____

5. For Windows 98, click the **Start** button on the taskbar, click **Run**, type **winipcfg** and click **OK**. In the IP Configuration window, click the **More Info** button. [For Windows 2000/XP, to open a Command window, click **Start** on the taskbar, point to **Programs** (for Windows XP, **All Programs**), point to **Accessories**, and then click **Command Prompt**. At the command prompt, type **ipconfig /all**.] A network card is assigned an address that identifies the card on the network. For Windows 98, the address is called the Adapter Address, and for Windows 2000/XP, the address is called the Physical Address. Either way, the address assigned to the network card is expressed in a series of paired hexadecimal numbers separated by dashes. Convert each pair to a binary number.

- Adapter address in hexadecimal form: _____
- Adapter address in binary pairs: _____

6. Convert the following hexadecimal numbers to decimal:

- 0x0013 = _____
- 0x00AB = _____
- 0x01CE = _____
- 0x812A = _____

7. Referring to Figure 2-4, convert the numbers in the network adapter's memory range and determine how many bytes, expressed in a decimal number, are in its memory address range.

_____

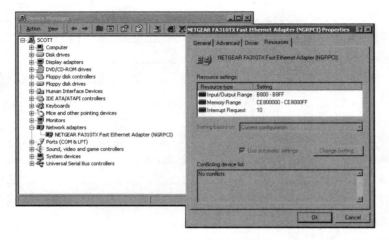

Figure 2-4   Memory Range and Input/Output Range expressed as hex numbers

8. Convert the following binary numbers to decimal:

- 1011 = _____
- 11011 = _____
- 10101010 = _____
- 111110100 = _____
- 10111011101 = _____
- 11111000001111 = _____

Review Questions

1. Computers actually work with _____ numbers.

2. Computers often express numbers in _____ format, which is a base-sixteen number system.

3. Most people are more comfortable when working within a _____, or base-ten number system.

4. In hex, what decimal value does the letter A represent?

_____

5. Hexadecimal numbers are often preceded by _____ so that a value containing only numerals is not mistaken for a decimal number.

3
UNDERSTANDING THE BOOT PROCESS AND MS-DOS MODE

Labs included in this chapter

➤ Lab 3.1 Learn to Work from the Command Line

➤ Lab 3.2 Examine Windows Configuration Files

➤ Lab 3.3 Modify Configuration Files and Observe the Results

➤ Lab 3.4 Learn File Naming Conventions

➤ Lab 3.5 Examine and Adjust CMOS Settings

Lab 3.1 Learn to Work from the Command Line

Objectives

The goal of this lab is to introduce you to some commands used when working from the command line. You will change and examine directories and drives, and you will perform a copy operation. You will also learn to use the DOS Help feature and how to read the Help information. In later labs, you will learn to perform more advanced operations from the command line. After completing this lab, you will be able to:

➤ Create a file and folder with Notepad and My Computer

➤ Examine directories

➤ Switch drives and directories

➤ Use various commands at the command prompt

Materials Required

This lab will require the following:

➤ Windows 9x, Windows 2000 or Windows XP operating system

➤ Blank formatted floppy disk

Activity Background

In Lab 1.2 you were introduced to the command line environment when you used the DIR command to explore file structure. Most people work from the command line only when troubleshooting or performing some specific task. For most tasks, you'll rely on a graphical interface such as My Computer, in Windows. In this lab, you will use My Computer to create a new folder and a new file. Then, you will delete that file from the command line. In this lab it is assumed that Windows is installed on drive C:. If your installation is on a different drive, substitute that drive letter in the steps below.

Estimated completion time: **30 minutes**

Activity

To create a new folder and text file from within My Computer, follow these steps:

1. From the Windows desktop, double-click **My Computer**, and then double-click the drive **C:** icon. Note that if you are using Windows XP, the My Computer icon might not be on the desktop. In this case, click **Start** and click **My Computer**.

2. Right-click anywhere in the blank area of the drive C: window, select **New** in the shortcut menu, then click **Folder**. A new folder icon appears with "New Folder" highlighted, ready for you to rename it.

3. Type **Tools** and press **Enter** to rename the folder "Tools."

4. To create a file in the Tools folder, double-click the **Tools** folder icon and then right-click anywhere in the blank area of the Tools window. Select **New** in the shortcut menu, and then click **Text Document**. A new file icon appears in the Tools window with "New Text Document.txt" highlighted, ready for you to rename it.

5. Double-click the **New Text Document.txt** icon in \Tools. The file opens in Notepad.

6. Click **File** on the Notepad menu bar, and then click **Save As...**.

7. In the Save As dialog box, name the file **Deleteme**, and make sure the **Save as type:** is **Text Documents**. Click **Save** to save the file.

8. Close Notepad.

9. Right-click **New Text Document.txt** and then click **Delete** in the Shortcut menu. Click **Yes** to confirm the deletion. The file is deleted.

10. Close all open windows.

To practice using the command line environment, perform these steps:

1. To open the command line window in Windows 9x, click **Start** on the taskbar, point to **Programs**, and then click **MS-DOS Prompt**. To open the command line window in Windows 2000, click **Start** on the taskbar, point to **Programs**, point to **Accessories**, and then click **Command Prompt**. To open the command line window in Windows XP, click **Start** on the taskbar, point to **All Programs**, point to **Accessories**, and then click **Command Prompt**.

2. A command line window opens. The title bar of this window differs with different versions of Windows. Below the title bar, a command prompt like the following appears in Windows 9x:

C:\WINDOWS>

In Windows 2000, the following command prompt appears instead:

C:\>

The Windows XP command prompt depends on the user name of the person currently logged in, for example:

C:\Documents and Settings\Jean Andrews>

The command prompt indicates the working drive (drive C) and working directory (either the \Windows directory, the root directory indicated by the backslash, or the Documents and Settings directory of the current user). Commands issued from this prompt apply to this folder unless you indicate otherwise.

3. Type **DIR** and press **Enter**. Remember that DIR is the command used to list the contents of a directory. You should see a list of files and directories in the command line window. The list may be too large to fit within one screen, in which case you will see only the last entries. This list contains the names of both files and directories. For example, Config.sys is a single file. Entries with the label <DIR> indicate that they are directories (folders), which can contain files or other directories. Also listed for each entry is the time and date it was created and the number of bytes it contains. (This information will display differently depending on which version of Windows you are using.) The last two lines in the list give a summary of the number of files and directories in the current directory, as well as the space consumed and the free space available on the drive.

As you'll see in the next set of steps, there are two ways to view any files that are not displayed due to the length of the list and the size of the window. To learn more about displaying lists of files in the command line environment, perform the following steps:

1. Type **DIR /?** and then press **Enter** to display Help information for the directory command. You can obtain Help information for any command by entering the command followed by the **/? switch**.

2. Type **DIR /W** and then press **Enter**. What happened?

_____

_____

3. Type **DIR /P** and then press **Enter**. What happened?

_____

_____

4. Type **DIR /OS** and then press **Enter**. What happened?

_____

_____

5. Type **DIR /O-S** and then press **Enter**. What happened? What do you think the hyphen between O and S accomplishes?

_____

_____

6. Insert a blank disk into the floppy drive. Type **A:** and then press **Enter**. The resulting prompt should look like this: A:\>

3

7. What does the A: indicate?

_____

8. What do you think you would see if you executed the DIR command at this prompt?

_____

_____

9. Type **DIR** and press **Enter**. Did you see what you were expecting?

_____

10. Change back to the C: drive by typing **C:** and pressing **Enter**.

11. Type **DIR C:\Tools** and press **Enter**. This tells the computer to display a list of the contents of a specific directory without actually changing to that directory. In the resulting file list, you should see the file you created earlier, Deleteme.txt.

12. Type **DEL Deleteme.txt** and press **Enter** to instruct the computer to delete that file. You will see a message indicating that the file could not be found. This is because the system assumes commands refer to the working directory unless a specific path is given. What command do you think you could use to delete the file without changing to that directory?

_____

_____

13. Type **CD** and press **Enter**. The resulting prompt is C:\> for Windows 9x, Windows 2000, and Windows XP. The \ in the command you typed indicates the root directory.

14. Type **CD Tools** and then press **Enter**. The prompt now ends with "Tools>," (indicating that Tools is the current working directory).

15. Now type **DEL Deleteme.txt /p** and press **Enter**. You will be prompted to type in "**Y**" for **Yes** or "**N**" for **No**. If you do not enter the **/p switch** to **Prompt for Verification**, the file is deleted automatically without a confirmation message. It is a good practice to use the **Prompt for Verification switch**, especially when deleting multiple files with wildcard characters. Also, when you delete a file from the command line, the file does not go to the Recycle Bin, as it would if you deleted it from Windows Explorer or My Computer, therefore making it more difficult to recover accidentally deleted files.

16. Type **Y** to delete the Deleteme.txt file. You are returned to the Tools directory.

To display certain files in a directory, you can use an asterisk (*) or a question mark (?) as wildcard characters. Wildcard characters are placeholder characters that represent other unspecified characters. The asterisk can represent one or more characters. The question mark represents any single character. The asterisk is the most useful wildcard, and for that reason it is the one you'll encounter most often. To learn more, follow these steps:

1. Return to the root directory. What command did you use?

   _____

   _____

2. Type **DIR *.*** and press **Enter**. How many files are displayed?

   _____

   _____

3. Type **DIR C*.*** and press **Enter**. How many files are displayed?

   _____

   _____

4. Explain why the results differed in the previous two commands.

   _____

   _____

CRITICAL THINKING (additional 30 minutes)

Do the following to practice using additional commands at the command prompt:

1. Copy the program file **notepad.exe** from the \Windows directory in Windows 98 (or the \WINNT or \Windows directory in Windows 2000/XP) to the **\Tools** directory. What command did you use?

   _____

   _____

2. Rename the file in the \Tools directory as **Newfile.exe**. What command did you use?

   _____

   _____

3. Change the attributes of **Newfile.exe** to make it a hidden file. What command did you use?

_____

_____

4. Type **DIR** and then press **Enter**. Is the Newfile.exe file being displayed?

_____

5. Unhide **Newfile.exe**. What command did you use?

_____

6. List all files in the \Windows or \WINNT directory that have an .exe file extension. What command did you use?

_____

7. Create a new directory named **\New** in \Windows or \WINNT and copy **Newfile.exe** to the \New directory. What commands did you use?

_____

_____

8. Using the /p switch to prompt for verification, delete the **\New** directory. What commands did you use?

_____

_____

Review Questions

1. What command/switch can you use to view Help information for the DIR command?

_____

2. What do you add to the DIR command to list the contents of a directory that is not the current working directory?

_____

3. What command can you use to change directories?

_____

4. What command can you use to delete a file?

_____

5. What command can you use to switch from drive A: to drive C:?

_____

LAB 3.2 EXAMINE WINDOWS CONFIGURATION FILES

Objectives

The goal of this lab is to introduce you to the Autoexec.bat and Config.sys configuration files. After completing this lab, you will be able to:

➤ Use Windows Explorer to examine your system's file structure

➤ Locate configuration files

➤ View configuration files using Notepad

Materials Required

This lab will require the following:

➤ Windows 9x or Windows 2000/XP operating system

➤ Windows 9x startup disk created in Lab 2.3

Activity Background

Two files in DOS and Windows 9x that can be used to configure a system each time it boots are Autoexec.bat and Config.sys. These files are used to load real-mode programs and drivers and to set environmental variables. In this lab, you will examine these files using Windows Explorer to locate the files on the startup disk and examine their contents.

Windows Explorer is a good tool for browsing through a system's file structure. Whenever you are instructed to find a file in this manual, the instructions will assume that you are using Windows Explorer unless otherwise specified. Although there are other ways to browse for files, such as in the My Computer window, Windows Explorer has some key advantages. In Windows Explorer, the left pane shows a hierarchical view of the file structure. If you click a folder in this pane, the contents of the folder are then displayed in the right pane.

Estimated completion time: **15 minutes**

ACTIVITY

To use Windows Explorer to open the Autoexec.bat and Config.sys files, follow these steps:

1. Click the **Start** button on the taskbar, point to **Programs**, and then click **Windows Explorer** (or right-click the **Start** button on the taskbar and then click **Explore**).

2. Insert the startup disk you created in Lab 2.3.

3. In the left pane of Windows Explorer, click the icon for **drive A:**. The drive is highlighted in the left pane, and the right pane displays a list of folders and files stored on the floppy disk.

4. If necessary, scroll down the right pane until you can see the Autoexec.bat file.

5. Right-click **Autoexec.bat**, and then click **Edit** on the shortcut menu. The file opens in a text editor (usually Notepad by default), ready for you to modify it. Autoexec.bat is a batch file that contains a list of commands for tasks that you want the system to execute each time it starts up. Your system might contain other batch files, but only Autoexec.bat is run by default each time the system boots.

6. Look for entries in the Autoexec.bat file (similar to the entry shown in Figure 3-1) that instruct the OS where to look for executable files. Virus protection software and any drivers that are loaded for DOS compatibility can also be referenced in Autoexec.bat.

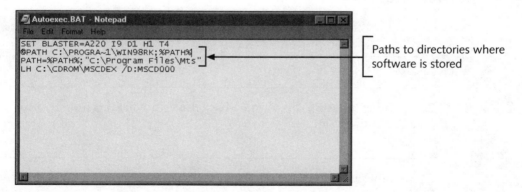

Paths to directories where software is stored

Figure 3-1   The Autoexec.bat file tells the OS where to look for executable files, virus protection software, and DOS-compatible drivers

7. Close the file. If you had made any changes, you would be asked whether you wanted to save them. Do not save any changes at this time.

8. In Windows Explorer, locate the Config.sys file on the A: drive, right-click **Config.sys**, click **Open With...** on the shortcut menu. The Open With dialog box appears.

9. In the Open With dialog box, scroll down and select **Notepad**, deselect the **Always use this program to open this file** check box, and then click **OK**. Config.sys opens in Notepad.

10. Note that the Config.sys file contains configuration instructions as well. An example is shown in Figure 3-2. Yours may have instructions for loading device drivers to high memory to free up conventional memory for DOS applications.

Figure 3-2   A Config.sys file

11. Close Config.sys. If you made any changes, do not save them.

Review Questions

1. What is the purpose of configuration files?

_____

_____

2. On either a startup disk or on a hard drive, in what directory are Autoexec.bat and Config.sys located?

_____

3. Are other batch files besides Autoexec.bat automatically processed during the boot process?

_____

4. Which configuration file can contain a path statement?

_____

5. Which configuration file can instruct DOS drivers to load in high memory?

_____

3

LAB 3.3 MODIFY CONFIGURATION FILES AND OBSERVE THE RESULTS

Objectives

The objective of this lab is to learn to use configuration files that affect the MS-DOS command line environment. Specifically, you will load drivers that make it possible to use a mouse in the command line environment. You will also learn to use utilities executed at the command line. After completing this lab, you will be able to:

➤ Create a bootable floppy disk

➤ Copy files to a floppy disk

➤ Modify configuration files

Materials Required

This lab will require the following:

➤ Windows 9x operating system

➤ File provided by your instructor needed to load a 16-bit generic mouse driver (for example, Mouse.com or Mouse.sys)

➤ Location provided by your instructor of the Windows and DOS utility programs, Msd.exe and Edit.com.

➤ Blank floppy disk

Activity Background

In this lab you will boot to a command prompt by using a bootable floppy disk. As you will see, normally a command prompt environment does not allow you to use the mouse. Once the PC is booted, you will use Microsoft Diagnostics Utility (MSD), a program that displays information about the hardware environment, to verify that the PC does not provide mouse support. Then you will add mouse support by adding a configuration file to your system that loads a mouse driver. The mouse driver file normally comes on a floppy disk bundled with a mouse, but your instructor might provide an alternate location. Finally, you will reboot the PC, run MSD again, and verify that mouse support has indeed been enabled.

Estimated completion time: **30 minutes**

ACTIVITY

Follow these steps on a Windows 9x PC to create a bootable floppy disk and to copy a file to the disk.

1. Click **Start** on the taskbar, point to **Programs**, and then click **MS-DOS Prompt**.

2. Insert a blank floppy disk.

3. Type **FORMAT A: /S** and press **Enter**.

4. The following prompt appears: "Insert new diskette for drive A: and press Enter when ready." Press **Enter** to start formatting the disk.

5. Watch as the floppy disk is formatted and the system files are transferred to the floppy disk.

6. When prompted, type a volume name if you wish and press **Enter** (or simply press **Enter** to bypass this step entirely).

7. When asked if you want to format another disk, type **N** and then press **Enter**. (Note that if your disk was already formatted, you could have used the SYS A: command to copy system files to the disk.)

Now that you have created a boot disk, follow these steps to copy some configuration files to the boot disk.

1. Insert the Windows 9x CD into the CD drive, type **Copy D:\tools\ oldmsdos\msd.exe A:** and then press **Enter**. (If you don't have access to the Windows 9x CD, your instructor might give you an alternate location for the file. If your CD has a drive letter other than D, substitute the appropriate drive letter.)

2. Repeat Step 1 for the mouse driver file and the text editor, Edit.com, in the location specified by your instructor. The mouse driver file will be named Mouse.com, Mouse.sys or a similar name.

3. Close the Command Prompt window and shut down the system.

At this stage, the boot disk contains the necessary configuration files. Next, you will boot the PC using the boot disk and verify that the mouse is not available.

1. With the floppy disk still in the drive, boot the system. An A prompt displays on your screen.

2. To use the Microsoft Diagnostic Utility, at the command prompt, type **MSD.EXE** and then press **Enter**.

3. Move the mouse around. Does the mouse work as you would expect?

_____

4. Press **F3** to exit MSD.

You will now use the Edit program to create and edit an Autoexec.bat file.

1. At the A prompt, type **Edit Autoexec.bat**. The Edit window opens and the Autoexec.bat file is created.

2. Enter the command to load the mouse driver, using the file name of the driver such as Mouse.com.

3. To exit the editor, save your changes, press the **Alt** key and use your arrow keys to select **Exit** on the **Exit** menu.

4. When asked if you want to save your changes to the file, select **Yes**.

Now you will test your floppy disk to see if it provides mouse support.

1. With the boot disk still in the floppy drive, reboot.

2. Run the MSD program. Did you observe any change when you moved the mouse?

_____

3. Click **Exit** on the File menu to close MSD. Remove the floppy disk and reboot the PC.

Review Questions

1. When formatting a disk, what command can you use to make the floppy disk a boot disk?

_____

2. If you have a formatted floppy, what command other than **Format a: /s** can you use to transfer the system files to the floppy disk?

_____

3. Which configuration file did you modify to cause the mouse to be automatically supported?

_____

4. Did you notice a difference in the boot process after you changed a configuration file?

_____

5. When booting from a floppy disk, how would you automatically load a program to provide support for your CD-ROM drive?

_____

_____

LAB 3.4 LEARN FILE NAMING CONVENTIONS

Objectives

The goal of this lab is to teach you about file naming conventions. After completing this lab, you will be able to:

➤ Describe the 8.3 convention

➤ Describe long filenames

➤ Observe long filename conversion in an 8.3 environment

Materials Required

This lab will require the following:

➤ Windows 9x operating system

Activity Background

In Windows 9x, you can use filenames of up to 255 characters. DOS, however, only recognizes filenames that use the 8.3 convention—that is, filenames that are up to eight characters long, followed by a period, followed by up to three characters. The last three characters after the period are referred to as the file extension. The file extension usually defines the file type; for instance, the extension "txt" indicates a text file. If you use DOS on your Windows 9x computer, DOS will convert any long filenames to the 8.3 format. In this lab you will create several files within Windows, assigning them file names of various lengths. Then you will display these file names at the command prompt (that is, from within DOS) and note any changes to the long file names.

Estimated completion time: **30 minutes**

ACTIVITY

By default, file extensions are not displayed within Windows. So before you can examine file extensions in Explorer, you need to display them. Follow these steps:

1. Open Windows Explorer, click **Tools** on the menu bar and then click **Folder Options**.

2. On the View tab, deselect the **Hide file extensions for known file types** check box, click **Apply** and then click **OK**. The Folder Options dialog box closes.

3. In Explorer, browse through several folders and note the file extensions. Table 3-1 lists common file extensions with their corresponding file types. Note that in Windows, files with the same extension are represented by the same icon.

Table 3-1   File Extensions with Corresponding File Types

File Extension	File Type
.txt	Text
.exe	Executable
.com	Command
.sys	System
.cab	Cabinet (contains compressed installation or setup files)

3

Now you will use a DOS command window (DOS box) to create a directory on the hard drive and store a file in it using the DOS naming convention. Do the following:

1. Open a command prompt window. Change directories to the root of the C: drive.

2. Type **MD Test** and press **Enter**. The MD command instructs the system to make a directory, in this case one called Test.

3. Use the **DIR /AD /P** command to verify that this new directory exists.

4. Type **CD Test** to change to the Test directory.

5. Type **Edit Test.txt** and press **Enter**. This edit command opens a DOS text editor called Edit, and creates a file named Test.txt. Using this program, you can create and edit text files.

6. Type **This is a test. This file was created with Edit.**

7. Press **ALT+F+S** to save the file.

8. Press **ALT+F+X** to exit Edit. Leave the command window open.

Now that you have created a file using the DOS naming convention, you will use Notepad to create a file with a long file name. Follow these steps:

1. In Windows Explorer, find the Test folder and double-click **Test.txt**. (Note that this fairly short filename is identical in Explorer and in the command prompt environment.) The file opens in Notepad, which is the default text editor for Windows.

2. In Notepad, click **File** on the menu bar and then click **New**. Type **This is a test. This file was created in Notepad with a long filename.**

3. Click **File** on the menu bar, click **Save as...**, name the file **Longnametest.txt** and then click **Save**. Do not close Notepad.

4. Look at the filename in Explorer. Note that the name appears exactly as you typed it in the Save As dialog box. Note also that the file is represented by the same icon as the Test.txt file. Next, you will see how DOS displays the long file name.

5. Return to the DOS command window, which should still have \Test as the current working directory. Type **DIR** and record the short names and long names of the files listed.

---

6. Now you're ready to create another file with a long file name. In Notepad, amend the text to read **This is the second file created in Notepad with a long filename.** and save this file as **Longnametestagain.txt**, using the same procedure as in Step 3.

7. In the command prompt window, execute another DIR command. You should now see two files other than Test.txt. These files are named Longna~1.txt and Longna~2.txt. As you can see, DOS changes long filenames to the 8.3 format by leaving the first six characters and adding a ~ (tilde) and a number indicating the alphabetical instance (beyond the sixth character) of that file. Compare the way the file Longnametest.txt was displayed earlier, when it was the only file other than Test.txt, and the way it is displayed now.

In DOS, directory names that are longer than eight characters are automatically abbreviated in the same way as long file names. It is possible, however, to use long directory names in DOS in some situations. To learn more, perform these steps:

1. At the command prompt, make the C: root the current directory and then type **DIR /O /P**. Note the way DOS lists the Program Files directory, which does not follow the 8.3 DOS naming convention for files and directories. The directory is listed by DOS as Progra~1.

2. From the C:\> prompt, type **CD Progra~1** and press **Enter**. This makes the Progra~1 directory the current directory.

3. If you want to use a long (that is, unabbreviated) directory name with the CD command, you need to enclose the directory name in quotation marks. To try this now, first type **CD** and then press **Enter**. This makes the C: root the current directory.

4. Type **CD "Program Files"** (including the quotation marks) and press **Enter**. Program Files is now the current directory.

Review Questions

1. What does 8.3 mean in the context of naming conventions?

---

2. How does Windows graphically depict file types?

_____

_____

3. What type of file ends in .exe?

_____

4. How is a long filename represented at the DOS prompt?

_____

_____

5. How can you use long names at the DOS prompt?

_____

_____

LAB 3.5 EXAMINE AND ADJUST CMOS SETTINGS

Objectives

The goal of this lab is to help you explore and modify CMOS settings. After completing this lab, you will be able to:

➤ Enter the CMOS setup utility

➤ Navigate the CMOS setup utility

➤ Examine some setup options

➤ Save changes to setup options

Materials Required

This lab will require the following:

➤ Lab PC designated for this lab

➤ SANDRA, Standard version, installed in Lab 2.2

Activity Background

When a system is powered up, the startup process is managed by a set of instructions called the BIOS. The BIOS, in turn, relies on a set of configuration information stored in CMOS that is continuously refreshed by battery power when the system is off. You can access and modify the CMOS setup information via the CMOS setup utility included in the BIOS. In this lab, you will examine the CMOS setup utility, make some changes, and observe the effects of your changes.

Setup utilities vary slightly in appearance and function, depending on manufacturer and version. The steps in this activity are based on the common Award Modular design. You might have to perform different steps in order to access and use the CMOS utility on your computer.

Estimated completion time: **30 minutes**

ACTIVITY

Before you access the BIOS on your computer, you will record the exact date and time as indicated by your computer's internal clock. (You will use this information later, to confirm that you have indeed changed some CMOS settings.) After you record the date and time, you will determine which version of the BIOS is installed on your computer. To do this, you will use the SANDRA utility, which you installed in Lab 2.2. Follow these steps:

1. Using Windows, double-click the clock on the taskbar and record the time and date.

   _____

   _____

2. Close the Date/Time Properties window.

3. Start **SANDRA**, and then double-click the **CPU & BIOS Information** icon.

4. Select **System BIOS** in the **Device** field.

5. Record the manufacturer and version information for your BIOS:

   _____

6. Close SANDRA.

Now that you know what BIOS your computer runs, you can determine how to enter the setup utility. In general, to start the setup utility, you need to press a key or key combination as the computer is booting up. To learn more about entering the setup utility on your particular computer, follow these steps:

1. Using the information recorded in Step 5 above, consult Table 3-2 to find out how to enter your system's setup utility. (Alternately, you can look for a message on your screen when you first turn on the PC, which might read something like "Press F2 to access setup.")

Table 3-2   Methods for entering CMOS setup utilities, by BIOS

BIOS	Method for entering CMOS setup
AMI BIOS	Boot the computer, and then press the Delete key.
Award BIOS	Boot the computer, and then press the Delete key.
Older Phoenix BIOS	Boot the computer, and then press the Ctrl + Alt + Esc or Ctrl + Alt + S key combination.
Newer Phoenix BIOS	Boot the computer, and then press the F2 or F1 key.
Dell Computers with Phoenix BIOS	Boot the computer, and then press the Ctrl + Alt + Enter key combination.
Older Compaq computers like the Deskpro 286 or 386	Place the diagnostics disk in the drive, reboot the system, and choose Computer Setup from the menu.
Newer Compaq computers like the Prolinea, Deskpro, DeskproXL, Deskpro LE, or Presario	Boot the computer, wait for two beeps, then, when the cursor is in the upper-right corner of the screen, press the F10 key.
All other older computers	Use the setup program on the floppy disk that came with the PC. If the floppy disk is lost, contact the motherboard manufacturer to obtain a replacement.

3

Note: For Compaq computers, the CMOS setup program is stored on the hard drive in a small, non-DOS partition of about 3MB. If this partition becomes corrupted or the computer is an older model, you must run setup from a diagnostic disk. If you cannot run setup by pressing F10 at startup, it's likely that a damaged partition or a virus is taking up space in conventional memory.

Now you are ready to enter the CMOS setup utility included in your BIOS. Follow these steps:

1. If a floppy disk is necessary to enter the CMOS setup utility, insert it now.

2. Restart the computer.

3. When the system restarts, enter the setup utility using the correct method for your computer.

4. Notice that the CMOS utility groups settings by function. For example, all the power management features will be grouped together in a Power Management window.

5. The main screen usually has a Help section describing how to make selections and exit the utility. Typically, you can use the Arrow Keys or Tab key to highlight options. Once you have highlighted your selection, you usually need to press the Enter key, Page Down key, or the Spacebar. The main screen may or may not display a short summary of the highlighted category. Look for and select a category called something like **Standard CMOS Setup**.

6. In the Standard CMOS Setup screen, you should see some or all of the following settings. List the current setting for each of the following:

- Date: _____

- Time: _____
- For IDE hard drives, a table listing drive size and mode of operation, cylinder, head and sector information:

   _____

   _____

- Floppy drive setup information, including drive letter and type:

   _____

- Halt on error setup (the type of error that will halt the boot process):

   _____

- Memory summary (summary of system memory divisions):

   _____

- Boot sequence (drives the BIOS searches for an OS):

   _____

7. Exit the Standard CMOS setup screen and return to the main page. Select a section called something like **Chipset Features Setup**.

8. Record settings for the following, as well as any other settings in this section:

- RAM setup options:

   _____

   _____

- AGP setup options:

   _____

   _____

- CPU-specific setup options:

   _____

   _____

- Settings for serial and parallel ports:

- Provisions for enabling/disabling onboard drive controllers and other embedded devices:

Note: Most of the CMOS settings never need changing, so it isn't necessary to understand every setting.

9. Exit to the CMOS setup main screen. You may see options for loading CMOS defaults (which restores everything to factory settings and can be helpful in troubleshooting) as well as options for exiting with or without saving changes. There probably will be an option to set user and supervisor passwords as well as a utility to automatically detect IDE hard disk drives.

Now that you are familiar with the way the CMOS setup utility works, you will change the date and time settings. Then you will reboot the computer, confirm that the changes are reflected in the operating system, and then return the CMOS date and time to the correct settings.

1. Return to the Standard CMOS setup screen.

2. Highlight the time field(s) and set the time ahead one hour.

3. Move to the date field(s) and set the date ahead one year.

4. Return to the main CMOS setup screen and select an option named something like **Save Settings and Exit**. If prompted, verify that you do wish to save the settings.

5. Wait while the system reboots. Allow Windows to load.

6. At the desktop, check the time and date. Are your CMOS setup changes reflected in Windows?

7. Reboot the computer, return to CMOS setup and change to the correct time and date.

8. Verify that the changes are again reflected in Windows.

CRITICAL THINKING (additional 30 minutes)

Working with your team, do the following to practice troubleshooting problems with CMOS.

1. Propose a change that you could make to CMOS setup that would prevent a computer from booting successfully. What change do you propose?

_____

2. Have your instructor approve the change, because some changes might cause information written to the hard drive to be lost, making it difficult to recover from the problem without reloading the hard drive. Did your instructor approve the change?

_____

3. Now go to another team's computer and make the change to CMOS setup while they make a change to your system.

4. Return to your computer and troubleshoot the problem. Describe the problem as a user would describe it.

_____

_____

5. What steps did you go through to discover the source of the problem and fix it?

_____

_____

6. If you were to encounter this same problem in the future, what might you do differently to troubleshoot it?

_____

_____

Review Questions

1. Do all systems use the same method to enter CMOS setup? Can you enter CMOS setup after the system has booted?

_____

2. How are settings usually grouped in the CMOS setup utility?

_____

3. In what section will you usually find time and date setup located in the CMOS setup utility?

_____

_____

4. What type of options are shown on the CMOS setup main screen?

_____

5. What automatically happens after you exit CMOS setup?

_____

6. What tool in SANDRA can you use to find information on your version of the BIOS?

_____

_____

7. Why does a computer need CMOS?

_____

_____

8. When troubleshooting a computer, when might you have to enter CMOS setup? List at least three reasons.

_____

_____

_____

Installing and Using Windows 9x

Labs included in this chapter

Lab 4.1 Use Windows Keyboard Shortcuts

Objectives

The goal of this lab is to introduce you to some keyboard shortcuts. After completing this lab, you will be able to use the keyboard to:

➤ Display the Start menu

➤ Switch between open applications

➤ Launch utilities with the Windows logo key

Materials Required

This lab will require the following:

➤ Windows 9x operating system

Activity Background

Certain keys or key combinations (called keyboard shortcuts) allow you to perform repetitive tasks more efficiently. These shortcuts are also useful when the mouse is not working. In this lab you will learn to use some common keyboard shortcuts.

> Estimated completion time: **30 minutes**

Activity

The F1 key is the universal keyboard shortcut for launching Help. To learn more, follow these steps:

1. Open **Paint** and then minimize it.

2. Open the **Control Panel** and then minimize it.

3. Click the desktop and then press the **F1** key. Windows Help launches.

4. Close Windows Help. Restore Paint.

5. Press the **F1** key. Because Paint is the active window, Help for Paint launches. Close Help for Paint.

6. Restore the Control Panel and then press the **F1** key. Help for Control Panel launches.

You can activate many shortcuts by pressing the Windows Logo key in combination with other keys. An enhanced keyboard has two Windows logo keys, usually located between the Ctrl and Alt keys on either side of the space bar. Try the combinations listed in the table below and record the result of each key combination in the Result column. (Close each window you open before proceeding to the next key combination.)

Key or Key Combination	Result
1. Windows Logo	
2. Windows Logo + E	
3. Windows Logo + F	
4. Windows Logo + R	
5. Windows Logo + Break	
6. Windows Logo + M	

4

Suppose for some reason that your mouse is not working, and that you have to print a text file. In that case, you would have to use the keyboard to find, select, open, and print the document. To learn more, follow these steps:

1. Boot the computer, wait for the Windows desktop to appear, and then unplug the mouse.

2. Press the **Tab** key a few times until one of the desktop icons is highlighted.

3. Use the arrow keys to highlight **My Computer**.

4. Press **Enter**. My Computer opens.

5. Press the **Tab** key a few times until drive **A:** is highlighted.

6. Use the arrow keys again to select the **C:** drive, and then press **Enter** to open it.

7. Use similar methods to find, select, and open the **Test.txt** file (within the Test folder) that you created in Lab 3.4. You should see the contents of the file displayed in Notepad.

8. Notice on the Notepad window that one letter of each menu item is underlined. For example, in the File menu, the F is underlined. You can select menu options by holding down the Alt key while you press this underlined letter. For example, to open the File menu in Notepad, hold down the **Alt** key and press the **F** key. After the menu is open, you can use the arrow keys to move over the menu and select an option by pressing **Enter**, or you can type the underlined letter of a menu option. With the **Alt** key pressed down, press the **F** key. The File menu opens.

9. Press the **P** key to select Print. The print dialog box opens.

10. Verify that the correct printer is selected. (To select a different printer, use the arrow keys.)

11. To send the print job to the printer, use the tab key until the Print button is active and then press **Enter**. (Or you can press Alt and P.)

12. Practice editing text, using the following shortcuts for cutting, copying and pasting:

   ■ To delete one or more characters, move your cursor to the beginning of the text to delete, hold down the Shift key and use the arrow keys to highlight the text. (If you were using a mouse, you could hold down the left mouse button and drag the mouse until the entire block was highlighted.)

- With the text highlighted, hold down the **Ctrl** key and press the **X** key, then release both keys. This cuts the highlighted text from its original location and moves it to the clipboard. You can then paste it in another location if you wish.

- To copy a highlighted block of characters to the clipboard (without removing it from its original location), hold down the **Ctrl** key, press the **C** key, and then release both keys. A copy of the highlighted block of characters is placed on the clipboard. You can then paste it in another location if you wish.

- To paste text from the clipboard to a new location, move the cursor to the desired location, press and hold the **Ctrl** key, and press the **V** key, and then release both.

CRITICAL THINKING (additional 15 minutes)

Using the keyboard skills you have learned in this lab, perform the following steps and answer the questions without using the mouse:

1. Open Device Manager and view the resources for the mouse. What status does Device Manager report about the mouse?

   _____

2. What IRQ is used by the mouse?

   _____

3. According to Windows Explorer, how much space is available on the hard drive?

   _____

Review Questions

1. What key is universally used to launch Help?

   _____

2. How many Windows logo keys are usually included on an enhanced keyboard?

   _____

3. What shortcut combination can you use to paste a block of text?

   _____

4. What key combination can you use to switch between open applications?

   _____

5. Is it possible to open the Start menu by pressing only one key?

   _____

LAB 4.2 CUSTOMIZE YOUR DESKTOP

Objectives

The goal of this lab is to show you how to personalize your desktop. After completing this lab, you will be able to:

➤ Choose and apply a background for your desktop

➤ Modify Appearance settings to match the dominant color of the desktop background

➤ Rename My Computer

Materials Required

➤ Windows 9x operating system

Activity Background

Windows allows you to customize certain settings on your computer so that the desktop is set up exactly the way you want it. Once you create custom settings on a computer, those settings go into effect each time you log onto that computer. If another user logs onto that same computer, the system will configure the desktop according to that user's settings rather than yours. This ensures that each user has access to his or her own customized work environment. As you will see in the following steps, you customize the desktop via the Display Properties dialog box.

Estimated completion time: **30 minutes**

ACTIVITY

Perform the following steps to customize your desktop colors:

1. Boot the computer and take a moment to examine the Windows desktop. Note the color of the desktop itself, as well as any other features on the desktop.

2. Open the Control Panel and double-click the **Display Properties** icon or right-click the desktop and click **Properties**. The Display Properties dialog box opens.

3. Click the **Background** tab, and scroll through the list of backgrounds available to you.

4. Click a background in the list. A preview appears in the monitor graphic at the top of the dialog box, similar to the one in Figure 4-1.

Figure 4-1 The selected background is shown in the monitor graphic in the Display Properties window

5. If you wish, experiment with the Picture Display list arrow, selecting different background options.

6. When you find a background that you like, click **Apply** and note that the new settings have been applied to your desktop. (The Display Properties dialog box should remain open.) Note that some backgrounds require that Active Desktop be enabled. It's best not to use Active Desktop because it can slow down a system. If you see a message indicating that the background you selected requires Active Desktop, select a new background.

7. At this point, the color behind the text on the desktop might not match your background. You can adjust the color behind the text (which is considered the desktop color) via the Appearance tab.

8. Click the **Appearance** tab, click the **Item** list arrow, and note all the items whose color you could change if you wanted. For instance, you could select Active Title bar if you wanted to change the color of the title bar for the active application.

9. Click **Desktop** in the Item list (if necessary), click the **Color** list arrow, and then click the color you want to use as your desktop color. See Figure 4-2. You see a sample of the color you selected at the top of the dialog box, behind the various sample windows.

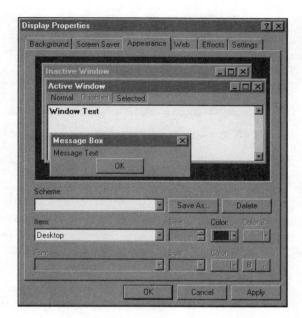

Figure 4-2   On the Appearance tab of the Display Properties window, you can change specific colors

10. Click **Apply**. The new color appears behind all the text on the desktop. (Note that if you hadn't already selected a background for your desktop, the entire desktop would change to the color you just selected. In this case, because you previously selected a background, the color change only affects the rectangles behind any text on the desktop.)

In addition to modifying desktop colors, you can change the name of My Computer. To learn how, follow these steps:

1. Right-click the **My Computer** icon (located on the Windows desktop) and then click **Rename**. The text below the My Computer icon is highlighted, ready for you to type a new name for the icon.

2. Type a new name for the My Computer icon, and then press **Enter**. You should be aware that this change does not affect the identity of the system for networking purposes. (You will learn more about a computer's name on a network in Chapter 12.)

3. Change the name back to **My Computer**, or remember that any mention of "My Computer" in this book refers to that icon.

Review Questions

1. What are two ways to open the Display Properties window?

   _____

   _____

2. What tab in the Display Properties window can you use to change the color of specific items in Windows?

   _____

3. What button must you click to make changes to your desktop take effect?

   _____

4. Describe how to rename My Computer. Does this change the name of your computer for networking purposes?

   _____

   _____

   _____

5. Can different users have different desktop settings on the same computer? How does Windows know which user is currently using the system?

   _____

   _____

LAB 4.3 UPDATE DRIVERS WITH DEVICE MANAGER

Objectives

The goal of this lab is to explore the functions of Device Manager. After completing this lab, you will be able to:

➤ Select your display adapter in Device Manager

➤ Update the driver for your display adapter from Device Manager

Materials Required

This lab will require the following:

➤ Windows 9x operating system

➤ Windows 9x CD or access to the setup files stored in a different location as designated by your instructor

Activity Background

Not only does Device Manager allow you to monitor resource use, it also allows you to update device drivers. If you find a new driver for a particular device, you can use Device Manager to select the device and update the driver. In this lab, you will use Windows 9x Device Manager to update the driver for your display adapter.

4

Estimated completion time: **30 minutes**

ACTIVITY

1. Open Device Manager and select your display adapter from the Display Adapters section.

2. Open the Properties window for your display adapter, and then click the **Driver** tab.

3. Click **Driver File Details**. Write down the path to the Driver files and then backup these files to a disk or another directory so you can backtrack if necessary.

4. Return to the Driver tab in Device Manager, and then click **Update Driver**. The Update Driver Wizard starts.

5. In the first wizard dialog box, click **Next**.

6. In the second wizard dialog box, click **Search for...** and then click **Next**.

7. In the next wizard dialog box, select the **Specify a location and CD** check box (if you are using the Windows 9x CD), deselect any other check boxes, and then click **Next**.

8. In the next wizard dialog box, type the location of the Windows CD installation file or use the **Browse** button to select a location designated by your instructor. After you have specified a location, click the **OK** button.

9. Windows searches the location and reports its findings. If the wizard indicates that it has found a file relating to the device you selected in Step 1 (that is, the display adapter), click **Next** to continue. If the wizard reports that it cannot find the file, verify you have correctly located the installation files.

10. After Windows locates the drivers, it copies the driver files. If a file being copied is older than the file the system is currently using, you will be prompted to confirm that you want to use the older file. Usually, newer drivers are better than older drivers. However, you may wish to use an older one if, after having recently updated drivers, you encounter problems. In this case, you may wish to reinstall the old driver that was not causing problems.

11. When the files have been copied, click **Finish** to complete the installation.

12. Restart the computer if prompted to do so.

CRITICAL THINKING (additional 30 minutes)

Use Device Manager to identify the display adapter installed. Search the Web site of the device manufacturer for new video drivers for this adapter. If you find drivers newer than the one currently in use, install the updated drivers.

Review Questions

1. Describe the steps required to access Device Manager.

_____

_____

2. How can you access a device's properties in Device Manager?

_____

_____

3. What tab in the Properties window will allow you to update a driver?

_____

4. Besides typing the path, what other option do you have to specify a driver's location?

_____

_____

5. Why might you wish to use an older driver?

_____

_____

LAB 4.4 EXAMINE THE WINDOWS 9X CD

Objectives

The goal of this lab is to familiarize you with the contents of the Windows 9x installation CD. After completing this lab, you will be able to:

➤ Find files on the Windows 9x installation CD

➤ Print a screen shot of some files on the Windows installation CD

Materials Required

This lab will require the following:

➤ Windows 9x operating system

➤ Windows 9x installation CD or access to a copy of the files on the CD at a
  location designated by your instructor

Activity Background

In this lab you will explore a Windows installation CD. (You can use the installation CD
for Windows 95, 98, or ME—whichever Windows CD you have access to.) The CDs for
the various versions of Windows differ in several ways, but the process of finding files on
the CDs is the same.

Estimated completion time: **30 minutes**

ACTIVITY

If you are using a CD, follow these steps and answer the questions:

1. Insert the CD into the CD-ROM drive. What happens after you inserted the CD?

   _____

   _____

2. On the Setup menu, click **Browse This CD**. Windows Explorer launches,
   showing the root directory of the CD. List the files at the root of the CD.

   _____

   _____

If you are using a copy of the CD files stored at a different location, follow these steps:

1. Start Explorer and browse to the location of the CD files.

2. List the files at the root of the main CD directory.

   _____

   _____

Continue exploring the installation files (whether on the CD or at another location), by
following these steps:

1. Open the **winXX** folder, where *XX* is your version of Windows.

2. What is the file extension of the majority of files in this folder? What does this file extension stand for?

_____

These compressed files contain all the files used to build Windows on the computer during the installation process. These files are also used when you decide to add another Windows component.

1. How many files in this folder have an .exe file extension? _____

2. How many files in this folder have a .com file extension? _____

Files with .exe and .com extensions are the program files that are used during installation. Some of these files are useful in other situations as well. For instance, the program Scandisk.exe will check file structure, file fragmentation, and the disk surface. Format.com is the program that you use to format a disk. These two files are useful when stored on a troubleshooting floppy disk. To learn more about other files, continue with these steps:

1. Double-click **Setup.txt**. The file opens in Notepad. What is this file's intended use?

_____

2. Print Setup.txt from Notepad. Close Notepad.

3. Another file called **Intl.txt** may also be included in the folder. Examine this file as well. What is this file's intended use?

_____

4. Close any open Notepad windows.

5. Return to the root of the CD in Explorer and then open the **Drivers** folder. List the categories of drivers contained in this folder.

_____

_____

_____

6. Double-click the **Readme.txt** file and then print this file. What URL is mentioned in this file?

_____

7. What does this URL provide?

_____

_____

8. Return to the root of the CD in Windows Explorer and then open the **Tools** folder.

9. Open the **Oldmsdos** folder. Both folders contain utilities that are useful on a troubleshooting floppy disk.

Sometimes it's helpful to create a hardcopy of a list of files on the installation CD. To do that, you paste a copy of the screen into Paint, and then print the Paint file. To learn more, follow these steps:

1. Click **Start** on the taskbar, point to **Programs**, point to **Accessories**, and then click **Paint**.

2. Minimize Paint.

3. Click the Windows Explorer title bar to make it the active window.

4. Hold down the **Alt** key and press the **Print Screen** key, which is usually located to the right of the F12 key. This copies the image of the active window (Windows Explorer) onto the clipboard. Throughout the rest of this lab manual, this process will be referred to as "taking a screenshot."

5. Restore Paint, click **Edit** on the menu bar, and then click **Paste**. (Note that you can also use the key combination Ctrl + V to paste the image of Windows Explorer from the clipboard into Paint.) You will probably be notified that the image is larger than the bitmap (the white square in the Paint window). See Figure 4-3.

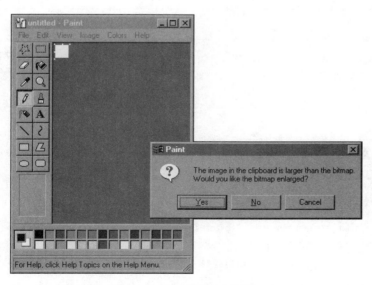

Figure 4-3   When prompted, expand the bitmap

6. Click **Yes** to expand the bitmap.

7. Print the screen shot and then close Paint without saving any changes.

8. Remove the CD from the CD-ROM drive, place it in its protection case, and store it in a safe location (or return it to your instructor).

Review Questions

1. What are files with .exe and .com extensions used for?

_____

2. List the steps to take and print a screenshot.

_____

_____

_____

_____

3. What type of information is contained in the Readme.txt file?

_____

4. Name two folders that contain useful utilities for a troubleshooting diskette.

_____

_____

5. What key combination is used to paste a screenshot from the clipboard into the Paint program?

_____

Lab 4.5 Perform a Custom Windows 98 Installation and Write Documentation

Objectives

The goal of this lab is to compare the differences between a Typical and Custom installation of Windows 98. After completing this lab, you will be able to:

➤ Perform a Custom installation of Windows 98

➤ Explain the differences between a Typical and Custom installation

➤ Explain when to use each type of installation

➤ Write documentation to install Windows 9x

Materials Required

This lab will require the following:

➤ Windows 98 operating system

➤ Windows 98 CD-ROM or access to the setup files on another location designated by your instructor

Activity Background

In the Case Project at the end of Chapter 4 in the textbook *A+ Guide to Software: Managing, Maintaining and Troubleshooting*, you performed a Typical installation of Windows 98. In this lab, you will perform a Custom installation and note the differences.

Estimated completion time: **60 minutes**

 ACTIVITY

 This project will erase everything on your hard drive. Do not do it if you have important data on the hard drive.

1. Prepare a hard drive for a clean install of Windows 98 by formatting the hard drive.

2. Copy files from the Windows 98 CD to a folder on the hard drive named C:\WIN98CD.

3. Perform a Custom installation of Windows 98 using the clean install method.

4. On another sheet of paper, as you are performing the installation, write User Documentation that would guide an individual step-by-step through the process of performing a Custom installation of Windows 98. Write the documentation as detailed as you think is necessary for a computer user who has never performed an operating system installation.

5. Record each decision you made and values that you entered during the setup process.

_____

_____

_____

_____

_____

_____

_____

_____

_____

6. Give your User Documentation to another student to perform a critique of it. Have the student enter the following information:

Student name: _____

Rate the documentation for:

- Clarity of each step:

_____

- What to do if problems occur:

_____

- How to respond to questions asked by setup:

_____

- Any other helpful comments:

_____

_____

_____

Review Questions

1. Compare your notes on the Custom installation you performed in this lab to the Typical installation you performed in the Case Project in Chapter 4 of the textbook *A+ Guide to Software: Managing, Maintaining and Troubleshooting*. What are the differences between a Typical and Custom installation? Be specific.

_____

_____

_____

_____

2. What added control do you have when performing a Custom installation compared to a Typical installation?

_____

_____

_____

_____

3. When would you recommend a Custom installation rather than a Typical installation?

_____

_____

_____

4

CHAPTER FIVE

SUPPORTING AND TROUBLESHOOTING WINDOWS 9x

Labs included in this chapter

➤ Lab 5.1 Manage Windows File Associations

➤ Lab 5.2 Update Windows

➤ Lab 5.3 Optimize Windows

➤ Lab 5.4 Modify System Configuration Files

➤ Lab 5.5 Save, Modify and Restore the Registry

➤ Lab 5.6 Critical Thinking: Sabotage and Repair Windows 98

LAB 5.1 MANAGE WINDOWS FILE ASSOCIATIONS

Objectives

The goal of this lab is to give you some experience managing Windows file associations. After completing this lab, you will be able to:

➤ Associate a default application with a file type

➤ Associate an additional application with a file type

Materials Required

This lab will require the following:

➤ Windows 9x operating system

Activity Background

In Windows, file extensions are associated with specific applications. For example, a file with a .doc file extension is associated with Microsoft Word. This means that when you double-click a file with the .doc file extension in Windows Explorer, the file opens in Word. (If Word is not yet open, it will open automatically and then display the file.) Often, when you install a new application, the installation process will specify which file extensions will be associated with that application.

It is possible to associate multiple applications with one file extension. However, you must specify a default application for that file type—that is, you must indicate which application you want to open automatically when you double-click a file with that file extension.

When you double-click any file in Windows Explorer, Windows will first attempt to find an application associated with it. If Windows fails to locate the associated application, Windows then gives you the opportunity to choose an application with which to open the file.

Keep in mind that file associations are sometimes lost when you remove an application from a system. This can be caused by poorly written uninstall software. It can also happen if you delete the application's files rather than using the application's uninstall option.

In this lab, you will create a new text file from Windows Explorer. You will check to see which application is associated with that file type and then associate a different application with that file type.

Estimated completion time: **30 minutes**

ACTIVITY

In the following steps you'll create a new file and then determine which application is associated with it:

1. Right-click the **Start** button and then click **Explore**. In Windows Explorer, open the **My Documents** folder, right-click a blank area in the right-hand pane, click **New** on the shortcut menu, and then click **Text Document**.

2. Name the new file **associ8.txt**.

3. Double-click **associ8.txt**. In what application does the file open?

_____ *notepad*

4. Close the application.

You can use Windows Explorer to view and change associations between applications and file types. Follow these steps:

1. If necessary, open Windows Explorer, click **Tools** on the menu bar, and then click **Folder Options**.

2. Click the **File Types** tab. Note that the Extension, Content Type (MIME), and the default application associated with a file type (Opens with) are displayed in the **File type details** section.

3. Scroll down the **Registered file types** list box and then click **Text Document**. What application opens this type of file by default? *notepad.*

_____

4. With Text Document highlighted, click **Edit**. The Edit File Type dialog box opens. Here you can modify all the information found on the File Types tab. Modifying the settings here changes how Windows handles interactions with this file type.

5. In the Actions list box, click **open** and then click the **Edit** button. The "Editing action for type: Text document" dialog box opens. Here you can specify which application to use to perform an action. If you don't know which one you're going to use or where it is located, you can browse for an application to associate with this file type.

6. Next to the **Application used to perform action** field, click the **Browse** button and open the **Program Files\Accessories** directory. Click **Wordpad.exe**, and then click the **Open** button. You return to the Editing action for type dialog box.

7. To associate this application with the selected file type, click the **Application used to perform action** text box, move the cursor after the close quotation mark, press the **space bar** once and then type **"%1"** including the quotation marks. See Figure 5-1. The "%1" is a temporary holding place used by COMMAND.COM, and tells Windows that Wordpad.exe is to be used to open files of type Text Document. Click **OK**. The Editing action for type dialog box closes and you return to the Edit File Type dialog box.

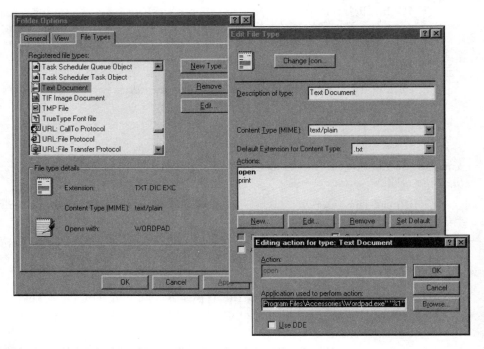

Figure 5-1   Change the application associated with a file type

8. Click **Close**. The Edit File Type dialog box closes and your changes are saved.

9. Click **Close** to exit the Folder Options dialog box.

You have finished changing the application associated with the .txt file extension. Now you can test the new association. Follow these steps:

1. In Windows Explorer, double-click **associ8.txt**. What application opens the file now?

   _____wordpad._____

2. Type a sentence in the associ8.txt file, save the change, and close the application window.

To change the file association back to its original setting, follow these steps:

1. In Windows Explorer, click **Tools** on the menu bar and then click **Folder Options**.

2. Click the **File Types** tab, scroll down the **Registered file types** list box, click **Text Document** and then click the **Edit** button. The Edit File Type dialog box opens.

3. In the **Actions** list box, click **open** and then click **Edit**. The Editing action for type dialog box opens.

4. Click the **Browse** button, browse to the **Windows** directory, click **notepad.exe** and then click **Open**. You return to the Editing action for type dialog box. Click **OK** to close the Editing action for type dialog box.

5. Click **Close**. The Edit File Type dialog box closes and your changes are saved.

6. Click **Close** to exit the Folder Options dialog box.

7. In Windows Explorer, double-click **associ8.txt**. What application opens the file now? Close the application that was launched.

_____ notepad _____

You saw earlier that you can double-click a file in Windows Explorer to open the file in the default application. Another way to open a file is to right-click the file and select Open from the shortcut menu. If you would like the option of using more than one application to open a particular file type, you can add a new entry to the shortcut menu. Follow these steps to add WordPad to the shortcut menu for text files:

1. Return to Windows Explorer and open the Folder Options dialog box. Select the **File Types** tab. In the Registered File Types field, double-click **Text Document**. The Edit File Type dialog box opens. Click **New**. The New Action dialog box opens.

2. In the New Action dialog box, click the **Action** text box and type **Open with WordPad**.

3. Click the **Browse** button, browse to the **Program Files\Accessories** directory, click **wordpad.exe** and then click **Open**. You return to the New Action dialog box.

4. Click the **Application used to perform action** text box, position the cursor after the close quotation mark, press the space bar once and type **"%1"** including the quotation marks.

5. Click **OK**. The Editing action for type dialog box closes. You return to the Edit File Type dialog box.

6. Click **Close**. The Edit File type dialog box closes and your changes are saved.

7. Close the Folder Options dialog box.

To test the new shortcut menu option, do the following:

1. In Windows Explorer, right-click **associ8.txt**, and then click **Open with WordPad**. The document opens in WordPad.

2. To remove the **Open with WordPad** option from the shortcut menu, return to the Edit File Types dialog box. In the Actions list box click **Open in WordPad**, and then click the **Remove** button. Click **Yes** to remove this action.

3. Click **Close** to close the Edit File Type dialog box and save your changes. Then close the Folder Options dialog box.

Review Questions

1. What Windows utility is used to manage associations between file types and applications?

   explorer

2. What tab in the Folder Options window lets you modify file associations?

   File types

3. In Windows, what indicates a file's type?

   the extension

4. Which text editor does Windows normally associate with .txt files?

   notepad.

5. How can you open a file in an application when the file's type is not associated with that application?

   create an association.

6. Why might you wish to add a second file association?

   to have more editing options.

7. Using the Internet, find the definition of MIME and give a brief explanation of its importance.

   it allows us to send more stuff over the internet as mail.

LAB 5.2 UPDATE WINDOWS

Objectives

The goal of this lab is to show you how to update Windows to keep current with the latest fixes and features. After completing this lab, you will be able to:

➤ Update Windows with the Critical Update Package

➤ Upgrade Internet Explorer to the latest version

Materials Required

➤ Windows 9x operating system

➤ Internet access

NOTE: Some educational institutions have polices applied to their Internet firewalls that prevent you from downloading Microsoft updates. If you cannot download the updates from your institution's lab PC, you might have to perform this lab at home.

Activity Background

Microsoft continuously updates many of its products to provide enhancements or repair newly discovered problems. You can take advantage of these improvements by installing these updates on your system. Keep in mind, however, that an update is not the same thing as an upgrade. Operating system updates typically make fairly minor changes to the existing version of Windows, whereas an upgrade installs a new version of Windows. It's important to update your Microsoft products regularly to ensure that they can take advantage of the most recent developments in technology. This is especially important with products like Internet Explorer, which interact regularly with many computers and other software. Such products will not work correctly without regular updates because they will lack the technology required to interact with more current systems. In this lab you will update your current version of Windows 9x to its most current state and upgrade Internet Explorer to the most recent version.

> Estimated completion time: **45 minutes (not including download time)**

ACTIVITY

Use the following steps to update Windows:

1. Open your browser and go to *windowsupdate.microsoft.com* and click the **Product Updates** link. You may receive a Security Warning asking if you want to install and run "Windows Update Control"; click **Yes** to install it. The browser displays a message indicating that Microsoft is examining your system and customizing the update selection for your system. Next, a list of available updates is displayed, with the Critical Updates Package selected.

2. Scroll through the available updates and notice that they are grouped into categories and include a brief description indicating the purpose of each update.

3. Click the **Download** link. Depending on your update package and how you are connected to the Internet (28.8 modem, DSL, cable modem, and so forth), downloading might take considerable time.

4. When prompted, confirm the update files you selected.

5. Click the **View Instructions** link and make a note of any special instructions not included in this lab.

6. Close the View Instructions window and click the **Start Download** link.

7. Your update may require you to accept an End User Licensing Agreement (EULA). If you are prompted to do so, accept the agreement.

8. A window appears indicating the download progress.

9. When the installation process is complete, you will be prompted to restart your computer. Click **Yes** to restart. When your system is in text mode, a message appears indicating that "setup will update configuration files." Next, you might see a message indicating that the update is complete. Windows will then continue to load to the desktop.

Follow these steps to upgrade to the latest version of Internet Explorer:

1. Open Internet Explorer, click **Help**, and then click **About Internet Explorer**. Make a notation of your current version of Internet Explorer.

2. Go to *www.microsoft.com/windows/ie/default.asp* and click the **Download Now** link to download the most current version of Internet Explorer.

3. You see a page describing the most current version of Internet Explorer. Verify that the correct language is selected in the **Select a Language** list box, and then click **Go**.

4. Directions for downloading and installing the new version of Internet Explorer appear. Read the directions carefully. Note that you can choose to download the file to your hard drive and execute the downloaded file later, or you can install the update from the Microsoft server. To save time, choose to install from the Microsoft Server across the Internet.

5. Click the link for downloading the latest version of Internet Explorer—for example, **Internet Explorer 6 Service Pack 1**—and then follow the installation directions.

6. If at any time during the process you see a warning about receiving files, select the **Always trust content from Microsoft** checkbox and then continue.

7. Windows asks whether you wish to save to disk or run from the current location. To indicate that you want to install the file from its current location, click **Open**.

8. The installation wizard launches, ready to guide you through the Internet Explorer upgrade. When the End User Licensing Agreement (EULA) appears click the **Agree** button to continue.

9. Next, click the **Install Now** option button and then click **Next**.

10. You are asked if you want to accept additional files to be downloaded as necessary. Click **Yes** to allow the download of additional files. The download process begins and you see a window indicating the progress of the download. When the download is complete, the installation process begins.

11. When the installation is complete, click **Finish** to restart the computer.

12. Start Internet Explorer and verify that the new version has been installed.

13. Close Internet Explorer.

CRITICAL THINKING

1. What is the specific version of Windows 9x you are using?

    Microsoft windows 98 second edition 4.10.2222A

2. Explain how you got your answer for Question 1.

    Right click My computer   general tab.

3. Assign a new name for My Computer on your desktop that includes your version of Windows. List the steps required to perform this task.

    Right click My computer click rename, give a new name click enter.

Review Questions

1. What types of changes are normally associated with an operating system update? What types of changes are associated with an operating system upgrade?

2. Why does Microsoft need to examine your system before displaying update files?

    to know what pertains to your system.

3. What is an EULA?

    end user license agreement.

5

4. What is the most current version of Internet Explorer?

what we have.   IE 6 sp 1

5. Did you load your new version of Internet Explorer over the Internet or did you save it to the hard drive and run it from there? Why did you choose this option?

I didn't load it.

LAB 5.3 OPTIMIZE WINDOWS

Objectives

The goal of this lab is to give you practice using common methods for optimizing Windows performance and security. After completing this lab, you will be able to:

➤ Enable and disable a screen saver with password protection

➤ Defragment a drive

➤ Improve the performance of Internet Explorer

Materials Required

This lab will require the following:

➤ Windows 9x operating system

➤ Internet Explorer version 6 or higher

Activity Background

As a result of normal use, your computer's performance will gradually deteriorate—perhaps not dramatically, but enough that you will eventually notice it. This slowing in performance is caused by a number of factors. For example, as files are copied, moved, and deleted, a drive will become fragmented, a condition in which segments of a file are scattered over the disk, prolonging read and write times.

Another potential problem relates to the fact that Internet Explorer caches (or stores) Web pages each time you visit them. Normally, this feature can speed up browsing if you return to the same pages often and the pages don't change much. (For example, if you go to a site that you have visited previously, half of the site's Web pages might already be stored in the cache; as a result, only half of the Web pages would have to be downloaded over the Internet, thereby increasing the speed with which the pages are displayed.) However, when this cache, called Temporary Internet Files, becomes very large, caching can have the opposite effect, and actually increase the time it takes to display Web pages. The reason for this is that your browser searches the cache every time you enter a URL (or click a link) in order to determine what Web pages it should get from the Internet and what is already in the cache. Searching a very large cache can take more time than simply downloading all Web pages over the Internet.

You can prevent problems like these, which arise as a result of normal use, by optimizing your system, using tools provided by Windows for just that purpose. In this lab, you'll have a chance to practice using some of these tools. You will start, however, by using a tool designed to protect your system from mischief—in particular, a special screen saver that activates password protection if you are away from your system for a specified amount of time. This does not completely prevent someone else from accessing your system, but it does make unauthorized access more difficult.

Estimated completion time: **30 minutes**

ACTIVITY

To enable a password-protected screen saver, follow these steps:

1. Right-click the desktop and then click **Properties** on the shortcut menu. (You can also open the Control Panel and then double-click the Display icon.) The Display Properties window appears.

2. Click the **Screen Saver** tab.

3. Click the **Screen Saver** list arrow, and then click a screensaver. You see a preview in the monitor at the top of the dialog box.

4. Try out several screen savers and choose one that you like.

5. Click the **Settings** button and customize the appearance of your selected screen saver. Then click **OK** to save the settings.

6. Click the **Preview** button. The screensaver appears on your monitor.

7. Press any key or move the mouse. You return to the Display Properties dialog box.

Now that you have selected a screen saver, you can assign a password to it:

1. Select the **Password protected** check box and then click **Change**. The Change Password dialog box appears, where you can specify a password.

2. Type the password, retype it to confirm it, and then click **OK**. This password can be, but does not have to be, the same as your Windows login password. You return to the Display Properties dialog box.

3. In the **Wait** field, you can specify how long the system will be inactive before the screen saver appears. Change this setting to **one minute**.

4. Click **Apply** to save your settings, then click **OK** and set aside the mouse and keyboard.

5. Wait one minute. The screen saver appears.

6. Move the mouse. A password dialog box appears.

7. Type your password and then click **OK**. The Windows desktop appears.

8. Re-open the **Display Properties** dialog box and list the required steps to disable the screen saver:

_____

_____

Next, you will practice defragmenting a hard drive. This process can take quite a while, so it is best done when you don't need your computer for a while and can walk away from it. Many people choose to run the utility during the night, when they are not using the computer. The Disk Defragmenter utility will have to start over if interrupted by a screen saver, so you will begin by disabling the screensaver you selected in the preceding steps. To defragment drive C: on your system, follow these steps:

1. Because the Disk Defragmenter utility will have to start over if interrupted by a screen saver or other tasks, disable the screen saver.

2. To open Disk Defragmenter, click **Start** on the menu bar, point to **Programs**, point to **Accessories**, point to **System Tools** and then click **Disk Defragmenter**.

3. Verify that drive C: is selected and then click **OK**.

4. Continue using Disk Defragmenter even if you see a message indicating that the drive is only slightly fragmented. (This message tells you that the drive doesn't really require defragmentation. But in order to practice using the Disk Defragmenter, you'll go ahead and defragment it anyway.)

5. A window appears displaying the progress of defragmentation. Click **Show Details**. A graphical illustration of the defragmentation progress appears.

6. Observe the progress window and answer the following questions while the drive is being defragmented:

   ■ What unit of division does each box represent?

   _____

   ■ What does a green box represent?

   _____

   ■ What does a red box represent?

   _____

- What does a box with a red slash through it represent?

_____

- What color represents Free Space?

_____

7. When defragmentation is complete, click **Yes** to exit Disk Defragmenter.

Follow these steps to clear temporary Internet files:

1. Open the **Control Panel**, and then open the **Internet Options** applet.

2. Click the **General** tab, and then, in the Temporary Internet Files section, click **Settings**. The Settings dialog box opens.

3. In the Amount of disk space to use section you can specify a size for the cache. The best size for your cache will depend on your surfing habits, but for a multi-Gig hard drive, it should never exceed 1% of the drive size. Over time, you'll want to experiment with this setting until you achieve the best performance for your system.

4. Click **View Files**. The Temporary Internet Files folder opens, and you can see a list of files in the cache.

5. Drag this window to the side but do not close it. The cache might contain many types of files. Examine the cache and list four file types found there.

_____

_____

6. Click **OK**. The Settings dialog box closes and you return to the Internet Properties dialog box.

7. To delete most files in the cache, click **Delete Files**. Click **OK** to confirm deletion.

8. Click the window that displays the Temporary Internet Files contents and press **F5** to refresh the window's display. The list of files is updated to reflect the fact that you just deleted files. Note that all the files have disappeared except for files with names similar to dave@abcnews.go(1).txt. These files are called cookies. Cookies are files that are created by Web servers when you visit a site. They are often used in a good way to help customize content to match your preferences when you revisit a page. However, cookies can also be used to invade your privacy and to secretly send private information from your computer to another computer. Periodically deleting cookies is a good idea if you value your privacy.

9. Click **Delete Cookies** in the Temporary Internet Files section of the Internet Properties dialog box.

10. Again click on the window displaying the Temporary Internet Files contents and then press **F5** to refresh. There should be no files visible in your Temporary Internet cache.

11. Click **OK** to close the Internet Options dialog box and to close the window displaying the cache.

Review Questions

1. Why should you disable your screen saver before defragmenting a drive?

   it will restart each time.

2. Why might a drive need defragmenting?

   it will run better if it is not fragmented.

3. What Control Panel utility allows you to enable the screen saver?

   display icon.

4. What is the name of the Internet Explorer cache that contains content from Web sites you have viewed?

   history

5. What factors might determine the size of your Internet cache?

   Personal preferences.

LAB 5.4 MODIFY SYSTEM CONFIGURATION FILES

Objectives

The goal of this lab is to familiarize you with working with Windows configuration files. After completing this lab, you will be able to:

➤ Use the System Configuration Editor to modify configuration files

➤ Edit Msdos.sys

Materials Required

This lab will require the following:

➤ Windows 9x operating system

Activity Background

Windows uses several configuration files when booting. In previous labs, you worked with two of these files, Autoexec.bat and Config.sys. In this lab you will work with the System Configuration Editor utility to examine and adjust several other configuration files. You will also edit one configuration file, Msdos.sys, from the command line.

> Estimated completion time: **30 minutes**

5

ACTIVITY

Follow these steps to edit MSDOS.SYS using the text edit, Edit.com:

1. Open a command prompt window.

2. To remove the hidden, system, and read-only status from the msdos.sys file, enter the command **attrib –h –s –r C:\msdos.sys** and then press **Enter**.

3. Type **Edit C:\msdos.sys** and press **Enter**. The msdos.sys configuration file opens in the command prompt window. msdos.sys can be modified to control where Windows files are located and how Windows boots. The [Paths] section indicates on what drive, and in which directory Windows system files can be found. The [Options] section controls how Window boots.

4. Notice the remarks (or comment lines), which begin with a semicolon, indicating that extra characters have been added in order to ensure that msdos.sys is greater than 1024 bytes in size.

5. Locate the line **Boot GUI=1**. You can think of the 1 as meaning yes and the 0 as meaning no. Thus, this line tells the system to load a graphical user interface (also known as a GUI). Change the 1 to a 0, so that it reads: **Boot GUI =0**. (Be sure to type a zero and not a capital letter "O".) What are you instructing the system to do the next time it boots?

_____

_____

6. Press and release the **Alt** key. This activates the menu options in the edit utility that you are using from within the command prompt window.

7. Press the **F** key. This activates the File menu.

8. Press the **S** key. The file is saved.

9. Press and release the **Alt** key again, and then press **F** to access the File menu and then press **X** to exit the edit utility.

10. Type **exit** and then press **Enter**. The command prompt window closes.

11. Restart Windows. Describe what happens. Was your prediction from Step 5 accurate?

_____

_____

Now you will make another change to the MSDOS.SYS file and observe the change. Follow these steps:

1. Open a command prompt window, type **edit msdos.sys**, and press **Enter**.

2. Change the **BootGUI** entry to **=1**.

3. Save your changes, exit, close the command prompt window and reboot, observing the boot process. What changed?

_____

Now you will make a third change to the MSDOS.SYS file and observe the change. Follow these steps:

1. Open the **msdos.sys** file for editing.

2. Place the cursor under the "D" in the Doublebuffer line and press **Enter**.

3. Press the up arrow to move the cursor to the new blank line and type **Logo=0** . (Again, be sure to type a zero and not a capital letter "O".) What do you think you just instructed the system to do?

_____

_____

4. Save your changes, exit, close the command prompt window and reboot, observing the boot process. What changed?

_____

_____

Next, you will practice working with files using the Sysedit utility, which is a Windows utility used to edit system files. You'll start by creating a new user called Test1 on your system. Follow these steps:

1. Restart your PC and log in as **Test1**, entering a password. Windows creates a new user, Test1, making entries in the \Windows\System.ini file and creating a new password file in the Windows folder named Test1.pwl.

2. Log out as **Test1** and then log back in as another authorized user on the computer (using your own name or whatever login you were using on the computer previously).

3. Next, you will use the System Configuration Editor utility to examine the Windows\system.ini file. Click **Start** on the taskbar, click **Run**, type **sysedit** and then click **OK**.

4. The System Configuration Editor utility opens, displaying five files. List these files here:

C:\windows\Protocol.ini

System.ini

win.ini

config.sys

autoexec.Bat

5. Click the title bar of the window showing the **C:\windows\system.ini** file bringing it to the front, and scroll down to the **[Password Lists]** section. In this section you see an entry for each user account on this computer.

6. Using the Delete or Backspace key, delete the entry for Test1. Do not delete anything other than the entry for Test1.

7. To save the changes to System.ini, with the Windows\system.ini window selected, click **File** on the menu bar and then click **Save**. Your changes are saved.

8. To examine the Win.ini file which is also opened by Sysedit, click the **Windows\win.ini file** window.

9. Click **Search** on the menu bar and then click **Find**.

10. In the Find dialog box, type **colors** and then click **Next**.

11. The Windows\win.ini file displays the **[colors]** section, with the word *colors* highlighted. After you specify a search item in the Find dialog box, you can use the F3 key to find the next instance of the search text (in this case, "colors").

12. Press **F3** to jump to the next instance of the word "colors." Was there another instance of the word "colors?" What message do you see?

can't find another

13. Exit the System Configuration Editor.

14. Log out and try to log back in as **Test1**.

15. Did you have to enter a password? _yes_

16. Did test1 show up in the users list? _yes_

Review Questions

1. What was the purpose of the Test1 entry in System.ini?

hold the password.

2. What utility can you use to modify the msdos.sys file?

edit

3. What is the minimum size of msdos.sys in megabytes?

_1025_

4. What are the five configuration files you can automatically edit with the System Configuration Editor?

See question 4 of previous section.

5. Of the five files you listed in Question 4, which two are used by MS-DOS and Windows in real mode?

config.sys

autoexec.Bat.

LAB 5.5 SAVE, MODIFY AND RESTORE THE REGISTRY

Objectives

The goal of this lab is to learn to backup, restore and modify the Windows 98 registry. After completing this lab, you will be able to:

➤ Modify the registry

➤ Observe the effects of a damaged registry

➤ Restore the registry

Materials Required

This lab will require the following:

➤ Windows 98 operating system

Activity Background

The registry is a database of configuration information stored in two files, system.dat and user.dat. Each time Windows boots it rebuilds the registry from the configuration files and stores it in RAM. When you need to modify the behavior of Windows, you should consider editing the registry as a last resort. Errors in the registry can make your system inoperable, and there is no way for Windows to inform you that you have made a mistake. For this reason, many people are afraid to work with the registry. If you follow the rule of backing up the registry before you make any change, you can feel confident that even if you happen to make a mistake, you can restore the registry to its original condition. In this lab you will backup, change and restore the registry.

Estimated completion time: **45 minutes**

ACTIVITY

Follow these directions to back up the registry:

1. Click **Start** on the taskbar, click **Run**, type **scanreg** and then click **OK**.

2. The **Windows Registry Checker** utility opens. (You may see an MS-DOS prompt briefly and a message indicating that the registry has already been backed up. This is because, once a day by default, the registry is backed up the first time Windows successfully starts.)

3. Click **yes** to back up the registry again.

4. When the backup is complete, click **OK** to close the Windows Registry Checker. Windows, by default, stores the last five copies of the registry in the windows\backup folder. The backups are compressed in cabinet files, named rb001.cab or similar.

5. Open **Windows Explorer**, locate the **windows\sysbackup** folder and determine, by checking the date and time that the file was created, the name of the backup you just created. Record the name, date, and time of this file below:

_____

As you know, it's possible to modify many features of Windows by using the appropriate tools included in Windows. But in some cases, the only way to make a modification is to edit the registry. In these steps, you will see examples of one feature that you can modify using a Windows shortcut menu and one that you can only modify via the registry. Follow these steps:

1. Right-click the **My Computer** icon on your desktop. Note that the shortcut menu gives you the option of renaming this icon.

2. Right-click the **Recycle Bin** icon. Note that the shortcut menu does not give you the option of renaming this icon. In order to rename it, you would have to install and use a special Microsoft utility, called **TweekUI**, which allows you to make some special changes to Windows. Alternately, you can change the name of the recycle bin via the registry.

3. Click **Start** on the taskbar, click **Run**, type **regedit** and then click **OK**. The **Registry Editor** opens, displaying the system registry hierarchy in the left pane and any entries for the selected registry item in the right pane.

The registry is very large, and searching through it manually (that is, by scrolling down through all the entries) can be tedious even if you have a good idea of where to look. To save time, you can use the Registry Editor's search feature. You'll use this feature now to find the section governing the Recycle Bin.

1. To ensure you are searching the entire registry, if necessary, collapse the Registry Keys and then click **Edit** on the menu bar and then click **Find**.

2. Type **Recycle Bin** in the search field. Notice that you can further narrow your search by limiting which items to search. What four ways can you further define your search?

_____

3. Click **Find Next** to begin searching the registry. What is the first instance of Recycle Bin shown in the right pane?

_____

4. Press **F3** to find the next instance. At this point, the right pane of your Registry Editor should display the two items shown in Figure 5-2.

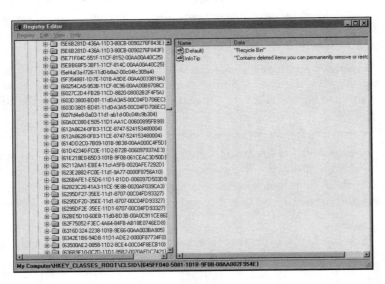

Figure 5-2   The Windows registry

5. Double-click the **Default** entry. The Edit String dialog box opens.

6. In the Value data field, replace "Recycle Bin" with **Trash** and then click **OK**.

7. Notice that "Trash" has replaced "Recycle Bin" in the right pane.

Next, you will edit the Info Tip for the Recycle Bin. (The Info Tip is the popup text that appears when your mouse pointer hovers over a Windows item.)

1. Double-click the **Info Tip** entry, type **This used to be named Recycle Bin** and then click **OK**.

2. Note the change in the right pane. Next, you will close the Registry Editor.

3. Click **Registry** on the menu bar and then click **Exit**. Note that you were not prompted to save your changes to the registry—your changes were saved the instant you made them. This is why editing the registry is so unforgiving. There are no safeguards. You can't undo your work by choosing to exit without saving changes, as you can, for instance, in Microsoft Word.

4. Right-click the desktop and then click **Refresh** in the shortcut menu. Note that the Recycle Bin icon is now named "Trash."

5. Move the mouse pointer over the Trash icon. The new Info Tip appears.

Finally, you need to undo your changes to the Recycle Bin by restoring the previous version of the registry. Follow these steps to use the Registry Checker to restore the previous version:

1. Restart Windows. Hold down the **Ctrl** key during the boot process to activate the Startup Menu.

2. In the Startup Menu, select **Command Prompt Only**. A command prompt appears.

3. Type **scanreg** and then press **Enter**. The Microsoft Registry Checker starts.

4. Press **Enter** to start a registry scan that will check for a corrupted registry. The Microsoft Registry Checker will not usually find errors if the registry has been correctly modified via the Registry Editor. Thus, assuming you performed the steps in this lab correctly, the Microsoft Registry Checker will not find any errors. However, if the Microsoft Registry Checker detects any corruption in the registry it will offer to repair it.

5. After the scan is complete, select **View Backups** and use your knowledge about the registry to restore the most current saved state.

Review Questions

1. How often does Windows automatically save the registry?

_____

2. Where are registry backups usually stored?

_____

3. What type of safeguards does the Registry Editor provide to keep you from making mistakes?

_____

4. What files constitute the registry? As what type of file are they saved during backup?

_____

_____

_____

5. In the example above, how did you check to make sure that your registry was restored?

_____

_____

LAB 5.6 CRITICAL THINKING: SABOTAGE AND REPAIR WINDOWS 98

Objectives

The goal of this lab is to give you practice troubleshooting Windows 98 by repairing a sabotaged system.

Materials Required

This lab will require the following:

➤ Windows 98 operating system installed on a PC designated for sabotage

➤ Access to the Windows installation CD or the setup files stored in another location

➤ Workgroup of 2-4 students

Activity Background

You have learned about tools and methods you can use to recover Windows 98 when it fails. In this lab you can use these skills in a troubleshooting situation. Your group will work with another group to sabotage a system and then recover the failed system.

Estimated completion time: **60 minutes**

ACTIVITY

1. If the hard drive contains important data, back up that data to another media. Is there anything else you should back up before the system is sabotaged by another group? Note that item here and then back it up.

_____

2. Trade systems with another group and sabotage the other group's system while they sabotage your system. Do one thing that will cause the system to fail to boot or to generate errors after booting. The following list offers some sabotage suggestions. You can choose one of these options, or do something else. Do *not*, however, alter the hardware.

   ■ Rename a system file (in the root directory) that is required to boot the system (for example, IO.SYS or MSDOS.SYS). Alternately, you could move one of these files to a different directory. Note that you should *not* delete any system files.

   ■ Using the Registry Editor, delete several important keys (or values) in the registry.

   ■ Rename important system files in the \Windows directory or move one of these files to another directory.

   ■ Put a corrupted program file in the folder that will cause the program to automatically launch at startup. Record the name of that folder here:

   _____

   ■ Use display settings that are not readable, such as black text on a black background.

3. What did you do to sabotage the system?

   _____

   _____

4. Return to your system and troubleshoot it.

5. Describe the problem as the user would describe it to you if you were working at a help desk.

   _____

   _____

6. What is your first guess as to the source of the problem?

   _____

7. List the steps you took in the troubleshooting process.

   _____

   _____

   _____

_____

_____

_____

8. What did you do that finally solved the problem and returned the system to good working order?

_____

_____

Review Questions

1. Now that you have been through the troubleshooting experience above, what would you do differently the next time you encounter the same symptoms?

_____

2. What Windows utilities did you use or could you have used to solve the problem?

_____

3. What third-party software utility might have been useful in solving this problem?

_____

4. In a real-life situation, what might actually cause this problem to happen? List three possible causes.

_____

_____

_____

UNDERSTANDING AND SUPPORTING WINDOWS NT WORKSTATION

Labs included in this chapter

➤ Lab 6.1 Manage User Accounts in Windows NT

➤ Lab 6.2 Create Windows NT Setup and Repair Disks

➤ Lab 6.3 Repair Windows NT Workstation

➤ Lab 6.4 Observe and Repair Video Problems

 ➤ Lab 6.5 Critical Thinking: Sabotage and Repair Windows NT

LAB 6.1 MANAGE USER ACCOUNTS IN WINDOWS NT

Objectives

The goal of this lab is to give you experience adding and modifying user accounts via User Manager. After completing this lab, you will be able to:

➤ Add users

➤ Reset passwords

➤ Control password policies

➤ Unlock user accounts

Materials Required

➤ Windows NT Workstation installed on a FAT partition system (with additional NTFS partitions for data if necessary)

➤ Administrator account and password

Activity Background

Creating user accounts in Windows NT is easy. NT just needs a few things to get a user set: a unique username; user's full name; a description of the user (typically their title and department); and a password. Managing users can take quite a bit of administration time. Much of this time is taken up by helping users who have forgotten their passwords or who entered their passwords incorrectly multiple times, causing Windows NT to lock their accounts. In this lab you will practice managing user accounts and passwords via User Manager.

Estimated completion time: **30 minutes**

ACTIVITY

Your first task is to start User Manager. Follow these steps:

1. Log on as an administrator.

2. Using Windows Explorer, create a folder named **Users** in the root directory of drive **C:**.

3. Click **Start** on the taskbar, point to **Programs**, point to **Administrative Tools (Common)** and then click **User Manager**. The User Manager window

appears, as shown in Figure 6-1. Examine the User Manager window and answer the following questions:

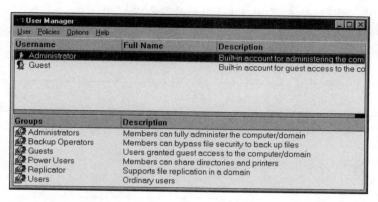

Figure 6-1   The Windows NT User Manager window

- Based on your knowledge of Windows NT, what two User accounts are included on a Windows NT system by default?

  _____

  _____

- Does your system contain any personal user accounts? If so, list them here:

  _____

  _____

- What user groups are included on your Windows NT system?

  _____

  _____

  _____

In User Manager you can add and configure users on a local computer. To learn how, follow these steps:

1. From the User Manager menu, click **User** and then click **New User**. The New User window opens.

2. Type a username—that is, the name that will be used to log on to Windows NT. Keep in mind that each username in your system must be unique. For user names, you can use alphanumeric characters, and some symbols (such as "!" and "." but not "\"). Also, note that user names in Windows NT are not case sensitive.

3. Type a full name and description for the account.

4. Enter and confirm a password, then make sure that the **User Must Change Password at Next Logon** check box is selected.

5. Note that User Manager provides other options concerning password setup. Do not select these options now, but record them here:

_____

_____

_____

What other check box could you select?

_____

_____

To add the new user to a user group, do the following:

1. Click on the **Groups** button at the bottom of the New User window. The Group Membership window opens.

   What group is the New User a member of by default?

   _____

   How does membership in this group differ from membership in the Administrators group?

   _____

   _____

   _____

2. In the **Not Member of** list box, click **Power Users** and then click **Add**. This makes the New User a member of both Users and Power Users groups.

3. Click **OK**. The Group Membership window closes.

4. Click the **Profiles** button next to the Groups button. The User Environment Profile window opens. Note that, in the User Profiles section, you can configure the profile and logon script location. (You will not do that now, however.)

Now you will set up the user's home directory under the C:\Users directory. With the User Environment Profile window still open, do the following:

1. In the Home Directory section of the User Environment Profile window, click **Local Path** and then type **C:\Users\%username%**. The entry "%username%" tells User Manager to use the account's logon name as the folder

name for the user's home directory. The "C:\Users\" part of the entry tells User Manager to place the home directory under C:\Users. (If you wanted to place the Home Directory on a remote system somewhere on the network, you would select Connect, specify a drive letter, and then specify a path in the To section.)

2. Click **OK**. The User Environment Profile window closes and you return to the User Properties window.

   NOTE: That if you wanted a user to be able to access this computer via a dial-up connection, you would click Dialing and then grant permission and configure this user account for dial-up access using Remote Access Service (RAS). You will not do that at this time, however.

3. Click **OK** to add this user to the system.

4. You have now finished adding a user to the system. Repeat this process to set up accounts for each user in your lab group.

Follow these steps to examine the settings created for new accounts and discover what you can and cannot do with the newly created accounts:

1. Log off as an administrator and log back in using one of your new user accounts.

   What did you have to do when you logged on with your user account?

   _____

2. Open a **command prompt** window. Judging by the command prompt, what folder are you currently working in?

   _____

   _____

3. Open **User Manager** and add a new user account called **Test**. Do not adjust group memberships or profiles. When might you not be able to create this account?

   _____

4. Log out and then log in as **Test**.

5. Open a **command prompt** window. What folder are you currently working in?

   _____

6. Open **User Manager**, add an account called **Test1** without adjusting profiles or group membership, and then attempt to delete the **Guest** account. Why could you not create an account?

_____

_____

Why could you not delete the Guest account?

_____

_____

When attempting to gain unauthorized access to a system, hackers sometimes try to enter multiple combinations of usernames and passwords until they happen to find a combination that works, giving them access to a user account. To prevent this type of unauthorized access, you can configure a system to lock an account after a user makes several unsuccessful attempts to log on to it. Once an account is locked, an administrator must intervene to make the account accessible again. Follow these steps to configure the lockout feature:

1. Log off as **Test** and log on as an administrator.

2. Open **User Manager**, click **Policies** on the menu bar, and then click **Accounts**. The Account Policy window opens. The Password restrictions provide four ways to customize a password policy. Record and explain these options here:

_____

_____

_____

_____

3. In the section below the Password Restrictions of the Account Policy window, click **Account Lockout**.

4. Set the Lockout after field to **3 bad logon attempts**.

5. In the **Lockout Duration** section, select **Forever**. This option tells Windows NT to keep the account locked until the administrator unlocks it.

6. Click **OK** to close the Account Policy dialog box.

To lock and unlock an account, follow these steps:

1. Log off as an administrator and then attempt to log on as **Test** several times, using an incorrect password. What message appears at the fourth logon attempt?

   _____

   _____

2. Log on as an administrator and open **User Manager**.

3. Double-click the **Test** account, deselect the **Account Locked-out** check box and then click **OK**.

4. Log off as an administrator and then log back on as **Test**. Explain what happens.

   _____

Review Questions

1. Besides adding and deleting users, what other tasks can you perform with User Manager? List five.

   _____

   _____

   _____

   _____

   _____

2. Besides the Administrators group, what other group has permission to add and delete users? What group does not?

   _____

   _____

   _____

3. List the steps required to change the group to which an account belongs.

_____

_____

_____

_____

4. What setting determines the current directory when the command prompt window opens?

_____

_____

5. How would you implement a policy dictating that all passwords be at least eight characters long?

_____

_____

_____

_____

LAB 6.2 CREATE WINDOWS NT SETUP AND REPAIR DISKS

Objectives

The goal of this lab is to show you how to create special floppy disks to use when setting up and repairing Windows NT workstations. After completing this lab, you will be able to:

➤ Create Windows NT setup floppy disks

➤ Create a Windows NT Emergency Repair Disk (ERD)

➤ Identify files used on the setup disks and the ERD

Materials Required

This lab will require the following:

➤ Windows NT Workstation Version 4 installed on a FAT partition (with additional NTFS partitions for data if necessary)

➤ Four blank floppy disks

➤ Access to a copy of Windows NT setup files or installation CD

➤ User account with administrative privileges

Activity Background

Windows NT relies heavily on floppy disks for installation and repair. For example, the setup disks are used to boot the PC if the hard drive becomes corrupted. Another important tool, the Emergency Repair Disk (ERD), is used along with the startup disks to recover from errors. You can make the Emergency Repair Disk while installing Windows NT. If necessary, you can also create one after Windows NT is installed. The Windows NT setup disks can be created on any computer and used on any computer, but the Emergency Repair Disk must be created on the same computer it will be used on. Also, note that the Windows NT setup disks can be created on a computer running an operating system other than Windows NT, as long as you have access to the Windows NT setup files. In this lab, you will learn to create these setup disks and an ERD.

6

Estimated completion time: **30 minutes**

ACTIVITY

To create the Windows NT setup disks, you need to open a command prompt window and switch to the directory containing the Windows NT setup files. Then you need to type the correct command. When creating the disks from a command prompt in real mode, you would use the following command: **winnt /ox**. When creating the setup disks from a command prompt using a 32-bit operating system (such as Windows 9x or Windows NT), you would use this command: **winnt32 /ox**. Because you're working on a Windows NT system, you'll use the latter command. Follow these steps:

1. Log in as an administrator.

2. Open a command prompt window, and make the directory containing the Windows NT setup files the current directory. (In most cases, you'll find the files for systems with Intel compatible processors in the \i386 directory on the Windows NT installation CD.)

3. At the command prompt, type **winnt32 /ox** and then press **Enter**.

4. The Windows NT 4.00 Upgrade/Installation utility window opens. What does the message say about copying files?

_____

_____

_____

5. Specify the path to the Windows NT setup files (typically the i386 directory on the installation CD), and click **Continue**.

6. The three setup disks are created in reverse order (3, 2, 1). When prompted, label the disk **Setup Disk 3**, insert the disk, and then click **OK**. Setup files are written to each disk. Repeat the procedure for Disks 2 and 1.

7. When the last disk is finished, the utility closes and you return to the command prompt window. Remove Disk 1.

You are now ready to create the Emergency Repair Disk. Follow these steps:

1. Open a command prompt window.

2. At the command prompt, type **Rdisk / S** and then press **Enter**.

3. The Repair Disk Utility opens and begins by notifying you that it is saving the configuration which should only be used to recover a bootable system in case of failure. What options are included in this utility?

_____

_____

4. Label a floppy disk "ERD" and insert it in the drive. Click **Create Repair Disk** to create an Emergency Repair Disk. Windows formats the floppy, examines the system's configuration, and creates an ERD that matches the system's current configuration. (Note that each time you change your system's configuration you need to make a new ERD.)

5. Remove the ERD, click **Exit** and then close the command prompt window.

Now you can examine the contents of the disks you've created. Use Windows Explorer to display the contents of each disk and answer the following questions:

1. On Setup Disk 1, what files with .exe extensions are included?

_____

_____

2. On Setup Disks 2 and 3, what file extensions are used?

_____

_____

3. Name five files that are included on the ERD. What types of information do you think these files contain?

_____

_____

_____

_____

_____

_____

Review Questions

1. What command do you use to create Windows NT setup disks when using DOS?

_____

2. Why might it be convenient to copy the files on the Windows NT installation CD to a hard drive shared over the local network?

_____

_____

_____

3. In what directory are Windows NT setup files for Intel-based computers stored?

_____

4. When should you create a new ERD?

_____

_____

5. Why should you safeguard your ERD?

_____

_____

_____

LAB 6.3 REPAIR WINDOWS NT WORKSTATION

Objectives

The goal of this lab is to help you use setup disks and an ERD to repair a Windows NT installation. After completing this lab, you will be able to:

➤ Generate a Windows NT boot error

➤ Boot with the Windows NT setup disks

➤ Use the ERD to repair Windows NT

Materials Required

This lab will require the following:

➤ Computer designated for sabotage, with Windows NT Workstation installed

➤ The three setup disks for Windows NT that you created in Lab 6.2

➤ Windows NT Workstation installation CD or access to the installation files

➤ A current version of the Emergency Repair Disk created for the PC you'll be working on

➤ Access to the Internet

NOTE: Some educational institutions have polices applied to their Internet firewalls that prevent you from downloading Microsoft updates. If you cannot download the updates from your institution's lab PC, you might have to perform this lab at home or skip the part of the lab to update Windows.

Activity Background

Unlike Windows 9x or Windows 2000, Windows NT lacks Safe Mode or a related recovery process. To repair Windows NT, you only have a few options. If Windows NT is damaged to the point that it will not boot, you must boot with the setup disks and then use the ERD to repair Windows NT. By using these disks, you can restore the system to a bootable state. However, they will not restore the software configuration that existed before the problem. To do that, you will need to reinstall software applications, service packs, and so on. In this lab, you will remove system files to make Windows NT unbootable, boot with a startup disk, and then repair the files with the ERD.

Estimated completion time: **30 minutes**

ACTIVITY

In the following steps you will sabotage your Windows NT computer so that it will no longer boot. You'll do this by removing the Windows NT system files required to boot the system. You'll begin by displaying hidden files, because system files are not displayed by default. Follow these steps:

1. Log on as an administrator.

2. Open Windows Explorer, in the left pane highlight the root directory of drive C, click **View** on the menu bar, and then click **Options**. The Options dialog box opens.

3. Click the **View** tab, select the **Show All Files** option button, deselect the **Hide file extensions for known file types** check box, and then click the **OK** button. Your changes are applied and the Options window closes. Hidden files are now visible in Windows Explorer.

4. In the right pane, right-click **boot.ini** and then click **Properties**. The Boot.ini Properties dialog box opens.

5. Deselect the **Hidden** and **Read-only** check boxes, so that the files will appear and so that you can make changes to them.

6. Click **OK**. The Boot.ini Properties dialog box closes and you return to Windows Explorer.

7. Right-click **boot.ini** and then click **Open**. Boot.ini opens in Notepad.

8. Delete the line that begins "Default=".

9. Click **File** on the Notepad menu bar and then click **Save**. The boot.ini Default= line specifies where to find system files, so removing this line renders the system unbootable.

10. Windows NT is now damaged. To verify this, attempt to boot your system and record the process. What do you see?

_____

_____

_____

_____

_____

_____

Next, you will boot from the ERD:

1. Insert the ERD and boot the system.

2. Describe what happens:

_____

_____

To repair the system, do the following:

1. Insert the Windows NT Workstation installation CD in the CD-ROM drive.

2. Insert setup Disk 1 and reboot the PC.

3. Insert Disk 2 when prompted.

4. At the Windows NT setup menu, press **R** to repair the installation.

5. Setup displays a list of tests that it will perform in order to find the problem. If you had a very good idea of what was wrong, you could deselect some of these options in order to save time. With Continue highlighted, press **Enter** to proceed as though you have no idea what the problem is.

6. To allow setup to detect disk controllers, press **Enter**.

7. When prompted, insert disk 3 and press **Enter**.

8. Setup detects your hard disk controller and loads the drivers needed for this controller as well as other drivers needed to access critical devices. Do not be tempted to choose the S option (to skip this step) because Setup needs to load drivers for disk controllers so that it can detect the CD-ROM drive.

9. After Setup detects other drives, press **Enter** to allow Setup to load drivers. If Setup fails to detect a necessary drive, press **S**, follow instructions provided by your instructor to enable your device, and then return to this step in the lab.

10. If Setup notifies you that it has discovered large hard drives, press **Enter** to continue.

11. Setup asks if you have the ERD. What will Setup attempt if you do not have the ERD?

_____

_____

12. Press **Enter** to indicate that you have the ERD.

13. Insert the ERD when prompted and press **Enter**.

14. Press **Enter** to let Setup examine the hard drives.

15. Setup examines the hard drive and then displays a warning about restoring the registry. What might occur when you restore the registry?

_____

_____

16. Setup displays a list of registry components and system files it can repair and also lists those that appear to be corrupt or missing. To repair Windows NT, Setup will overwrite these selected files with good copies. Because Setup detects no problems with boot.ini, it is not listed as either missing or corrupt. Therefore, no repair options will be automatically selected. Using the up and down arrow keys and the Enter key, select all components except Security and SAM, highlight **Continue** and then press **Enter**. If you overwrite the SAM (which contains username and account information for all users), only default user accounts will be restored to the system.

17. If you are informed that the files do not match the original files, press **A** to continue replacing all files anyway.

18. When the repair process is finished, remove the ERD and the CD.

19. Press **Enter** to reboot the PC, then log on to Windows NT with your user name and password.

CRITICAL THINKING (additional 30 minutes)

After Windows NT is restored, access the Internet, check for the latest service packs for this workstation and then install them. What service packs did you install?

Review Questions

1. Recall that the Windows 9x ERD is bootable. Is the Windows NT ERD bootable?

_____

_____

2. In theory, is there any hope of successfully completing the repair process if you do not have an ERD? Explain.

_____

_____

_____

3. In the repair process, what steps must not be skipped so that the CD–ROM drive is detected?

_____

_____

4. What happens to user accounts you created after installing Windows NT if you restore the security and SAM files during the repair process?

_____

5. What should you do immediately after you restore the system to a bootable state?

_____

Lab 6.4 Observe and Repair Video Problems

Objectives

The goal of this lab is to help you use the Last Known Good Configuration option and VGA Mode Only option to recover from startup problems. After completing this lab, you will be able to:

➤ Install and correct video drivers

➤ Observe the effect of incorrect display drivers

➤ Use the Last Known Good Configuration to recover from an improper driver

➤ Use VGA Only mode

Materials Required

This lab will require the following:

➤ Windows NT Workstation installed on a FAT partition (with additional NTFS partitions for data if necessary)

➤ Incorrect video drivers designated by your instructor

Activity Background

Windows NT provides minimal recovery options. One of the few options at your disposal is the Last Known Good Configuration, which boots the system to the last configuration used to run Windows NT successfully. You can use another option, VGA Only mode, to boot the system with generic display drivers; this is useful in situations when the display is unreadable, allowing you to correct the problem. In this lab, you will install incorrect display drivers, try to recover with the Last Known Good Configuration option, and boot using the VGA Only mode to correct problems with the display drivers.

Estimated completion time: **30 minutes**

ACTIVITY

If you have not reinstalled the correct video adapter after the repair process in the last lab, follow these steps to install the correct adapter:

1. Boot Windows NT and log on as an administrator.

2. Right-click the desktop and then click **Properties**.

3. Click the **Settings** tab and then click **Display Type**.

4. Click **Change**. Select the proper adapter from the lists or click **Have Disk** and browse to the location of the setup files provided by your instructor. If necessary insert the Windows NT Workstation installation CD or point to its location. Also, if necessary, select the correct adapter and then click **OK**.

5. Click **OK** when the drivers have been set up successfully.

6. Click **Close** to exit the Display Type dialog box. You return to the Display Properties dialog box.

7. Click **Apply**. The Display Properties dialog box closes, and you are asked if you want to restart the system.

8. Click **Yes** to restart the system. Windows boots and a message appears indicating that a new display has been adjusted.

9. Click **OK**. The Display Properties dialog box opens, where you can adjust the color and resolution to suit your preference.

10. Click **Test** to test the settings and then click **OK** on the Testing Mode warning message. You see a test bitmap, which is a series of colored and shaded boxes on a green background.

11. The test pattern disappears after five seconds. If you could read the test bitmap display, click **Yes** to keep the settings. Otherwise repeat the test using different display settings until you can read the test bitmap, and then click **Apply** on the Display Properties window. The settings are applied to your desktop.

12. Click **OK** to close Display Properties.

Now that you are sure the correct display adapter is installed, follow these steps to make the display unreadable. (Or follow the directions supplied by your instructor to modify the contents of \Winnt\system32\drivers.):

1. Boot Windows NT and log on as an administrator.

2. Right-click on the desktop and then click **Properties** in the shortcut menu. The Display Properties dialog box opens.

3. Select the **Settings** tab and then click **Display Type**. The Display Type dialog box opens.

4. Record your current display adapter and click **Change**. The Change Display dialog box opens.

_____

_____

5. Select the Manufacturer and Display adapter specified by your instructor (drivers that your instructor knows will not work with your display adapter) and then click **OK**.

6. The Third-party Drivers warning appears. Click **Yes** to continue.

7. Next, you need to specify the location of the installation files for this adapter. If necessary insert the Windows NT Workstation installation CD or point to the location of the Windows NT setup files using the Browse button, select the file and then click **OK**.

8. Click **OK** when the drivers have been installed successfully.

9. Click **Close** to exit the Display Type dialog box. You return to the Display Properties dialog box.

10. Click **Close**. The Display Properties dialog box closes and you are asked if you want to restart the system.

11. Click **Yes** to restart the computer.

Now that you have configured the display improperly, follow these steps to observe the results:

1. Observe the boot process and record the point at which the display became unreadable.

_____

_____

2. Even though the display is unreadable, press **Ctrl+Alt+Del** to access the Logon dialog box. Next, press the **Tab** key four times (five times if you log onto a domain controller) and then press **Enter** twice. This should shut the system down.

In order to restore video on a failed system, new technicians often try the following steps. As you will see, these steps will not in fact solve the problem:

1. Restart the computer.

2. When the Windows NT Start Up menu appears, press the spacebar to invoke the **Last Known Good** option.

3. Select **Original Configuration** and then press **Enter**. Did this solve the display problem? Explain why or why not.

_____

_____

4. Again, restart your computer.

Complete the following steps to correct the display problem:

1. Boot the PC and at the Windows NT Start Up menu, highlight **Windows NT Workstation (VGA Only)** and then press **Enter**.

2. Log in to Windows NT as an administrator.

3. Now that you know how to change display adapters, change your adapter back to the one recorded in step 4, above, where you configured the incorrect adapter.

4. Reboot, and then select **Windows NT Workstation** at the Start Up menu.

5. Verify that you can read the display.

Review Questions

1. Why can you not just start in Safe Mode to troubleshoot a video problem?

_____

2. Suppose your Windows NT display is unreadable and that you need to shut down the system. What keystrokes can you use to shut down the system?

_____

_____

3. For each of the keystrokes that you listed in Question 2, list the corresponding task performed in Windows NT.

_____

_____

_____

_____

_____

4. What key can you press to invoke the Last Known Good Configuration?

_____

5. When changing display properties, what is the advantage of using the Test option before you apply settings?

_____

_____

_____

LAB 6.5 CRITICAL THINKING: SABOTAGE AND REPAIR WINDOWS NT

Objectives

The goal of this lab is to learn to troubleshoot Windows NT by repairing a sabotaged system.

Materials Required

This lab will require the following:

➤ Windows NT Workstation installed on a PC designated for sabotage

➤ Access to the Windows NT installation CD or the Windows NT setup files stored in another location

➤ Workgroup of 2–4 students

Activity Background

You have learned about several tools and methods that you can use to repair Windows NT when it fails. This lab gives you the opportunity to use these skills in a troubleshooting situation. Your group will sabotage another group's system while that group sabotages your system. Then your group will repair its own system.

Estimated completion time: **45 minutes**

ACTIVITY

1. If your system's hard drive contains important data, back up that data to another media. Is there anything else you would like to back up before the system is sabotaged by another group?

_____

_____

2. Trade systems with another group and sabotage the other group's system while they sabotage your system. Do one thing that will cause the system to fail to boot or give errors after booting. The following list offers some sabotage suggestions. Do something included in this list, or think of another option. (Do *not* alter the hardware.)

- Find a system file in the root directory that is required to boot the computer, and either rename it or move it to a different directory. (Don't delete the file.)

- Using the Registry Editor, regedit.exe, delete several important keys or values in the registry.

- Locate important system files in the \Winnt directory and either rename them or move them to another directory.

- Put a corrupted program file in the folder that will cause the program to automatically launch at startup. Note the name of that folder here:

_____

- Use display settings that are not readable, such as black text on a black background.

3. What did you do to sabotage the other team's system?

_____

_____

_____

4. Return to your system and troubleshoot it.

5. Describe the problem as the user would describe it to you if you were working at a help desk.

_____

_____

_____

6. What is your first guess as to the source of the problem?

_____

_____

7. List the steps you took in the troubleshooting process.

_____

_____

_____

_____

_____

_____

_____

8. How did you finally solve the problem and return the system to good working order?

_____

_____

_____

Review Questions

1. What would you do differently the next time you encountered the same symptoms?

_____

2. What Windows utilities did you use or could you have used to solve the problem?

_____

3. What third-party software utility might have been useful in solving this problem?

_____

4. In a real-life situation, what might cause this problem to happen? List three possible causes.

_____

_____

_____

_____

INSTALLING AND USING WINDOWS 2000

Labs included in this chapter

➤ Lab 7.1 Install or Upgrade to Windows 2000

➤ Lab 7.2 Use Windows Help and Troubleshooters

➤ Lab 7.3 Install and Use Windows 2000 Support Tools

➤ Lab 7.4 Use the Windows 2000 Setup Manager Wizard

➤ Lab 7.5 Use Task Manager

Lab 7.1 Install or Upgrade to Windows 2000

Objectives

The goal of this lab is to help you to install, or upgrade to, Windows 2000 Professional. After completing this lab, you will be able to:

➤ Plan an upgrade or installation

➤ Identify the benefits of an upgrade or a new installation

➤ Install or upgrade to Windows 2000 Professional

Materials Required

This lab will require the following:

➤ Windows 98 operating system

➤ Access to drivers or Internet access for downloading drivers

➤ Windows 2000 Professional installation files or installation CD

➤ Key from installation CD

Activity Background

Many people are intimidated at the thought of installing or upgrading an operating system. The process doesn't need to be difficult. In fact, if you carefully plan your installation and are prepared to supply required information and device drivers, your main complaint might be that the process is time consuming. Even that annoyance can be minimized, using techniques designed to reduce the total installation time. In this lab, you will plan and prepare for an installation or an upgrade to Windows 2000 Professional and then perform the upgrade or installation.

Estimated completion time: **120 minutes**

Activity

Follow these steps to plan and prepare for a Windows 2000 Professional installation on your computer:

1. Obtain a list of devices in the system and detailed system specifications, like processor speed and drive capacity. If no list currently exists, you can use Device Manager or SANDRA to compile one.

2. Make another list of important applications and check to see if they are compatible with Windows 2000. If you find any that are not compatible, check to see if any patches or upgrades are available to make them compatible.

3. Check each system specification and device against both the Hardware Compatibility List and the system requirements list for Windows 2000 on the Microsoft Web site (*www.microsoft.com*). Your system will most likely be compatible with Windows 2000. However, in the future, when working on other systems, you might discover significant incompatibilities. In that case, you would have to decide whether or not upgrading to Windows 2000 was really an option. If you decided to go ahead with the upgrade, you would then have to decide which applications or hardware you needed to upgrade before upgrading the operating system. The Windows 2000 installation CD offers a Check Upgrade Only mode that you can use to check for incompatibility issues in your system before you actually install the OS; however, the information on the Microsoft Web site, which you are using in this step, is often more current and easier to access. Answer the following:

- Does your system qualify for Windows 2000?

  _____

- If not, what hardware or application does not qualify?

  _____

- Will you install using FAT32 or NTFS? Explain your decision.

  _____

  _____

4. Download, or otherwise obtain, all necessary drivers, service packs and application patches from the manufacturers or the Microsoft Web site for both installed applications and hardware. Record a summary of the components you were required to install to make your system compatible with Windows 2000.

  _____

  _____

  _____

  _____

5. Gather any network-specific information in preparation for the installation. If you are connected to a network, answer the following:

- If you are using a TCP/IP network, how is your IP address configured?

  _____

- For a static IP address, what is the IP address?

  _____

7

- What is the workgroup name or domain name of the network?

  _____

- What is your computer name?

  _____

6. Make sure you have the correct CD key for your installation CD. The CD key, which is provided with the Windows 2000 installation CD, usually consists of a set of alphanumeric characters. You must enter the CD key in order to complete the installation even if you are installing the operating system from setup files located somewhere other than on the installation CD.

7. Review the information you've collected so far, and then decide whether to do a fresh installation or an upgrade. For instance, if all the important applications on your system are compatible with Windows 2000, an upgrade will probably save time because it leaves compatible applications in working condition. On the other hand, if you know that you will have to install new applications anyway because of incompatibilities, you might choose to perform a fresh installation. In many ways a fresh installation is preferable because it ensures that no misconfigured system settings will be carried over to the new operating system.

   - Will you perform a clean install or an upgrade?

     _____

   - Give a brief explanation as to why you chose the option you chose.

     _____

     _____

     _____

8. Back up any critical data files (that is, any work you or others have stored on your computer that you cannot afford to lose during the installation process.)

   - If you have critical data files on the PC, where did you back them up to?

     _____

You are ready to begin installing Windows 2000 Professional. This lab assumes that you have Windows 98 installed and running. This is not the only situation in which you would install, or even upgrade to, Windows 2000 but it is very common. It is possible to install the operating system using files on the installation CD, on a network drive, or on a local hard disk. To speed up the installation process, consider copying the setup files from the installation CD (or from a network drive) to a local hard disk. This takes extra time initially, but is faster overall.

- Are you performing the installation from (a) the Windows 2000 CD, (b) files stored on your hard drive, or (c) a network drive?

The following steps are representative of a typical installation. Your installation process will probably vary in minor ways depending on the installation options you choose, your system's hardware configuration, and other considerations. The following steps are provided as a general guide to let you know what to expect during the process. Do not become alarmed if your experience differs slightly from the process outlined in these steps. Use your knowledge to solve any problems on your own. Ask your instructor for help if you get stuck. Use the blank lines after the installation steps to record any differences between the steps provided here and your own experience. Also, record any decisions you make during the installation process and any information you enter during the installation process.

1. Before you insert the installation CD or run the setup files from a location on your hard drive or network, use antivirus software to scan the computer's memory and hard drive for viruses. Once the scan is complete, make sure to disable any automatic scans and close the antivirus program before beginning installation.

2. The Setup program starts. This program will guide you through the actual installation. If the Setup program doesn't begin automatically, use the Run command on the Start menu to run WINNT32.exe from the \I386 folder.

   - Did Setup start automatically for you or did you have to use the Run command?

---

3. Setup informs you that you are running an older version of Windows and asks whether you want to upgrade to Windows 2000. Click **Yes** to continue and follow the instructions in the Setup program. Note that although Setup initially uses the word "upgrade" you will be given the option of doing an upgrade from Windows 98 or a fresh installation of Windows 2000.

4. Accept the EULA (end user license agreement) and click **Next**.

5. When prompted, enter the CD key and click **Next**.

6. Setup examines your system and reports any situations that could cause problems during installation. You are given the opportunity to print the report and exit Setup to correct the problems. Even if some problems are reported, you have done your homework during planning and likely have the solution, so continue the installation.

7. You are given the opportunity to review the Hardware Compatibility List. If you wish to review it again, do so and click **Next** to continue.

8. Specify your file system, either NTFS or FAT32. Windows 98 does not support NTFS, which will be required in a future activity. Instructions will be given on how to convert to NTFS once Windows 2000 is installed. For now, select FAT32 and click **Next**. The system begins to copy files for the installation. Then the text portion of the installation, which provides a DOS interface

rather than a Windows GUI, begins. This portion of the installation includes the following:

- Examining hardware
- Deleting old Windows files, if applicable
- Copying Windows 2000 operating system files
- Automatically rebooting your computer

After your computer reboots, the Windows 2000 Setup portion begins. This part of the installation includes the following:

- Verifying the file system
- Checking the file structure
- Converting the file system to NTFS, if applicable
- Automatically rebooting again

1. Choose **Windows 2000 Professional** on the startup menu. If you converted your file system to NTFS, you see a message indicating that the conversion was successful.

2. The system installs software for detected devices.

3. When prompted, provide the requested network information. After you have specified how your network is configured, Setup performs some final setup tasks, including the following:

   - Configuring the startup menu
   - Registering components
   - Upgrading programs and system settings
   - Saving settings
   - Removing temporary files

4. The computer reboots one more time. You are now able to log on as an administrator and install any new applications or devices.

5. Verify that the system is working correctly.

In the space below, record any differences you noted between the preceding installation steps and your own experience. Also record any decisions you made during the installation process and any information you entered during the installation process.

_____

_____

_____

_____

_____

_____

_____

Review Questions

1. Name five things you should do before you start the installation process.

_____

_____

_____

_____

_____

2. How can you find out if your video card will work with Windows 2000?

_____

3. What type of installation can save time because it usually retains system settings and leaves applications in working condition?

_____

_____

4. What step is critical to ensure that you do not lose important data during installation?

_____

_____

5. What step can you take to help speed up the actual installation process?

_____

_____

LAB 7.2 USE WINDOWS HELP AND TROUBLESHOOTERS

Objectives

The goal of this lab is to demonstrate how to use Windows Help tools to find information and how to use Windows Troubleshooters to correct common problems. After completing this lab, you will be able to:

➤ Find information on various topics in Windows Help

➤ Use a Windows Troubleshooter

Materials Required

This lab will require the following:

➤ Windows 2000 Professional operating system

Activity Background

You can use Windows 2000 Help to look up information on various topics related to the operating system. To access Windows 2000 Help, use the Start menu or, with the desktop active, press the F1 key. Help is useful when you need information. If you actually want help solving a problem, you can use the Windows Troubleshooters, which are interactive utilities that walk you through the problem of repairing a misconfigured system. Windows Troubleshooters are often launched automatically when Windows detects a problem. You can also start them manually from within Windows Help.

Estimated completion time: **30 minutes**

ACTIVITY

In the following steps, you will learn to use the main features of Windows 2000 Help. Note that pressing the F1 key starts Help for whatever application happens to be active at that time. To start Windows Help, you need to close or minimize any open applications, thereby making the desktop active. Once the desktop is active, you can press F1 to start Windows Help. To learn more, follow these steps:

1. Log on to your computer as an administrator.

2. Close or minimize any applications that start automatically so that the desktop is active.

3. Press **F1**. (Note that to avoid having to make the desktop active, you could choose to click Start on the taskbar and then click Help.) Windows 2000 Help launches. As you can see, the Windows Help interface is similar to a Web browser.

- What four tabs are available in Windows Help?

  Contents   index   search   Favorites

- What are the five menu bar items?

  hide   Back   forward   options   webhelp.

4. If no one has used Windows Help on your computer before, the Contents tab will be visible. If Help has been opened previously, the most recently used tab will be visible. Click the Contents tab if it is not already visible.

5. Move the mouse pointer over the Introducing Windows 2000 Professional topic in the left pane, and note that the pointer becomes a hand, as it does in Internet Explorer when you move it over a link. Notice that when you point to the topic, the topic becomes underlined, like a hyperlink.

6. Click **Introducing Windows 2000 Professional** in the left pane. The topic Introducing Windows 2000 Professional expands in the left pane, displaying subtopics. Notice that the right pane has not changed yet.

7. Click **Tips for new users**. Subtopics are displayed in the right pane.

8. Scroll the right pane to get a sense of the information provided there, and then click **locate lost files** in the right pane. The topic expands to show a description of what it contains as well as a link to more information under Overview for locating lost files.

9. Click **Overview for locating lost files**. The right pane displays a list of locations where lost files might be found, along with steps for looking for files in each of these locations. Note that the list begins with the most likely locations for lost files, with less likely possibilities at the bottom of the list. Record the possible locations for lost files here:

   The my Documents folder on the desktop.

   the list of recently used documents

   Perform Search.

   RBDC9-VTRC8-07972-J97JY-PRVMG

10. The Windows Help toolbar contains buttons similar to those found in a Web browser, including a Back button (a left-facing arrow) which you can use to display a previous topic. Click the **Back** button in Windows Help. The Tips for new users topic is again displayed in the right pane.

You can also look for topics in Windows Help using the Index and Search tabs, both of which allow you to type in keywords to locate the information you need. These features are useful when you are familiar with Windows Help but don't know where to look for a specific topic in the Contents list. Follow these steps to use the Index and Search features.

1. Click the **Index** tab. If this is the first time the Index has been used, Help will display a small box with a flashlight icon and the message "Preparing index for first use." At the top of the Index tab is a text box where you can type keywords you want to search on. Below the textbox is a list of all possible Help topics.

2. Type **los** in the text box.

   ■ As you type, what happens to the list of topics?

   _____

   _____

3. Finish typing "lost files" (without the quotation marks) into the text box. The list of topics below the text box should now include lost files. Highlight the topic **lost files**, if necessary, in the list of topics. Click the **Display** button at the bottom of the pane to display the topic.

   ■ What does Windows prompt you to do?

   _____

4. In the list of topics, click **locating** and then click the **Display** button. The Topics Found dialog box appears, displaying two topics. These topics should look familiar to you.

5. In the Topics Found dialog box, click **Locating lost files** (if necessary to select it), and then click the **Display** button. The Topics Found window closes and information on locating lost files is displayed in the Help window's right pane. How does the information currently displayed compare to the information recorded earlier?

   _____

6. Now click the **Search** tab. Note that the Search tab looks similar to the Index tab except that it does not automatically display topics. Search for Help is an alternative to browsing the Index for a topic. You simply type a topic into the Search box and click the List Topics button. Keep search topic strings as short as possible to better focus your search.

7. Type **lost files** in the textbox at the top of the tab and then click the **List Topics** button. A list of topics is displayed below the text box. Did the Search tab return more topics than the Index tab or fewer?

_____

8. Click **Tips for new users** and then click the **Display** button. How does the display in the right pane change?

_____

On the Favorites tab, you can record a list of topics that you want to refer to again without having to search for them. Follow these steps:

1. Click the **Favorites** tab.

2. The topic "Tips for new users" is listed at the bottom of the tab, below a blank pane. Click the **Add** button to add this item to your list of favorite topics.

The Windows Help feature enables you to search for information on specific topics related to using Windows. The Troubleshooters provide information on how to fix problems with Windows and its applications. You can access Troubleshooters from within Windows Help. In the following steps you will use a Troubleshooter to troubleshoot non-functioning DOS applications:

1. Click the **Contents** tab in the Help window.

2. In the left pane, locate and click **Troubleshooting and Maintenance**. A list of subtopics appears below "Troubleshooting and Maintenance" in the left pane.

3. In the list of subtopics, click **Windows 2000 troubleshooters**.

4. A table appears in the right pane, with a list and description of Windows troubleshooting tools. In the chart, click **MS-DOS programs**.

5. The Windows Troubleshooter for MS-DOS programs starts in the right pane of Windows Help. The Troubleshooter asks you for details about the problem you are troubleshooting so that it can provide a solution tailored to that problem. For this portion of the activity, assume the following:

   ■ You have only one DOS application that is not working.

   ■ The NTVDM subsystem is working.

   ■ The program works when it is the only program running.

6. To troubleshoot the problem, click the appropriate option buttons for the specified scenario. Use the Next button to advance through the Troubleshooter screens. Notice that the Troubleshooter also provides buttons that you can use to go back to a previous screen and to start over at the beginning of the process. What solution does the Troubleshooter offer for your problem?

_____

_____

7. Click the **Start Over** button to troubleshoot a slightly different problem. This time, assume the following:

- No DOS applications work.
- The NTVDM does work.
- The program does not run by itself.
- The program does run in Safe Mode.

Answer the following questions.

- What conclusion does the Troubleshooter reach?

_____

_____

- What two options are offered to temporarily correct the problem?

_____

_____

Review Questions

1. What type of program is Windows Help similar to?

_____

2. What two Help search tabs operate in similar ways? What are the differences between them?

_____

_____

3. What are two ways to launch Windows Help?

_____

_____

4. What tool, accessible from Windows Help, will take you step-by-step through the process of diagnosing and perhaps repairing common problems?

_____

_____

5. Are Troubleshooters ever launched automatically? Explain.

_____

_____

_____

LAB 7.3 INSTALL AND USE WINDOWS 2000 SUPPORT TOOLS

Objectives

The goal of this lab is to help you install and become familiar with Windows 2000 Support Tools. After completing this lab, you will be able to:

> ➤ Install Support Tools

> ➤ Access Support Tools

> ➤ Use Error and Event Message Help to investigate Event Viewer events

> ➤ Use the Windows 2000 Support Tools Help feature to find out about other tools

> ➤ Use the Windows 2000 System Information tool to access software information

Materials Required

This lab will require the following:

> ➤ Windows 2000 Professional operating system

> ➤ Windows 2000 Professional installation files or installation CD

Activity Background

Windows 2000 provides support tools that you can use to prepare to install Windows 2000, to customize and configure Windows 2000, and to find information on Windows 2000. In this lab you will install these tools and then practice using some of them.

Estimated completion time: **30 minutes**

ACTIVITY

Follow these steps to install Windows 2000 Support Tools.

1. Log on as an administrator.

2. Open Explorer, navigate to the Support\Tools directory in the Windows 2000 installation files on your hard drive or click **Browse This CD** on the Windows 2000 setup CD. Then double-click **Setup.exe**. The Setup Wizard launches and welcomes you.

3. Click **Next** to continue.

4. In the User Information window, enter your name and organization in the appropriate fields and click **Next** to continue.

5. In the Select an Installation Type window, select **Typical Installation** and click **Next** to continue.

6. The Begin Installation window appears to let you know that the wizard is ready to begin copying files. Click **Next** to continue.

7. The Installation Progress window appears and displays a progress bar informing you of the progress of the installation. When the installation is complete and the Start menu is set up, the wizard indicates that the installation was successful. Click **Finish** to exit the wizard.

From a student's point of view, one of the most useful support tools is the Error and Event Messages Help tool. This tool gives information on error messages and tells you what steps to take in order to correct the problems that caused the error messages. Another very useful tool is the Event Viewer, which you will learn more about in Lab 8.2. In Event Viewer, individual events are assigned Event ID numbers. These same Event ID numbers are used in another Windows 2000 Support Tool, the Error and Event Message tool, which allows you to search by Event ID number for further information on the event. The Error and Message tool can explain the situation that caused the error and recommend what to do if the event happens again. To familiarize yourself with the Error and Event Message Help tool, follow these steps:

1. In the Control Panel, double-click the **Administrative Tools** icon. The Administrative Tools window opens.

2. Double-click the **Event Viewer** icon to launch the Event Viewer.

3. In the left pane of Event Viewer, click **System Log** and view the event entries in the right pane.

4. If you see any warning or error events, double-click one of them. Otherwise, double-click an information event. When you double-click on any event, the Event Details window opens. Read the information in this window, and record below the Event ID number and description.

6005

The event log service was started.

5. Click **Start** on the taskbar, point to **Programs**, point to **Windows 2000 Support Tools** and then click **Error and Event Messages.** The Error and Event Messages Help window opens.

6. Click the **Search** tab.

7. Click the **Type in word(s) to search for** field, and then type the Event ID number recorded in Step 4. (Type the number only; do not type the number sign or the words "ID number".) Then click the **List Topics** button. The Select Topic field displays all Help topics that refer to this Event ID number.

8. In the Select Topic field, highlight the item whose title matches the event description recorded in Step 4.

9. Click the **Display** button. Information about the highlighted item is displayed in the right pane. Record the explanation of the event and the relevant user action, if that information is provided:

Contact your tech support group.

fatal error   5 51

You already know how to use Windows Help to locate information about the operating system. When you need information specifically about the Windows 2000 Support Tools, you can use Tools Help. Follow these steps to find and print information about a particular support tool:

1. Click **Start** on the task bar, point to **Programs**, point to **Windows 2000 Support Tools** and then click **Tools Help**. Tools Help opens in a familiar Help window.

2. Now you will use the Search tab to find information about the executable file for the Windows 2000 System Information tool, which provides information on the hardware resources and software environment for your system. The name of this file is "msinfo32.exe." Click the **Search** tab (if necessary), type **msinfo32.exe** in the box labeled **Type in the word(s) to search for** and then click **List Topics**. Topics related to msinfo32.exe are displayed in the Select topic pane.

3. Double-click the topic ranked second. Information on msinfo32.exe is displayed in the right pane.

4. Click **Options** on the Tools Help menu bar and then click **Print**. The Print dialog box opens. If necessary, select a printer and change any settings as necessary.

5. Click **Print** to print the information on msinfo32.exe. Keep the printed information handy so you can refer to it in the next part of this lab.

In the following steps you will actually use the System Information tool (msinfo32.exe). Follow these steps to record information about your system's software environment:

1. Launch System Information, following the directions in the Help information you printed in Step 5 above.

2. In the left pane, double-click the **Software Environment** category to display a list of subcategories. Record the subcategories below.

Drivers

environment variables

Jobs

Net connections

Running tasks

3. In the left pane, click **Program Groups**. The program groups for Windows are displayed, showing the software that is installed on the system. What five program groups are always added for each user?

Startup.

accessories

"   "   accessibility

"   "   Entertainment

"   "   System tools.

4. In the left pane, click **Startup Programs**. Are the programs listed associated with your Start Menu or are they the programs that launch automatically when you log on to the system? Explain.

auto launch.   its an exe.

Review Questions

1. What directory contains the files necessary to set up Windows 2000 Support Tools?

support/tools/setup.

2. What support tool allows you to search for information based on the Event ID numbers used in Event Viewer?

error and event messages.

3. What Windows 2000 Support Tool offers information about all other support tools?

ns info 32   system info tool

4. What is the executable file for the System Information tool?

msinfo32.exe

5. Can you run all of the Support Tools by selecting them from the Start menu?

no

LAB 7.4 USE THE WINDOWS 2000 SETUP MANAGER WIZARD

Objectives

The goal of this lab is to help you use the Windows Setup Manager Wizard to create an answer file and distribution folder for unattended Windows 2000 installations. After completing this lab, you will be able to:

➤ Install Windows 2000 Setup Manager

➤ Use the Windows 2000 Setup Manager Wizard to create an answer file and distribution folder

Materials Required

This lab will require the following:

➤ Windows 2000 Professional operating system

➤ Windows 2000 installation files or installation CD

➤ WinZip or similar file compression utility

Activity Background

Windows 2000 Professional (and other versions of Windows) allows you to perform an unattended installation. This type of installation can be a time-saver, especially if you have a number of machines on which you want to install Windows 2000. As you know, several pieces of information must be provided during the installation process in order to correctly configure the operating system. During an unattended installation, this information is supplied by an answer file. In the past, creating an answer file meant typing or editing a text file saved in a specific text format. To speed up the process of setting up an unattended installation and creating an answer file, Windows 2000 offers a support wizard designed to guide you through the process. In this lab you will install and use this wizard, which is called the Windows 2000 Setup Manager Wizard.

Estimated completion time: **30 minutes**

ACTIVITY

Follow these steps to install the Windows 2000 Setup Manager:

1. Open Explorer and select the **C:** drive. Create a new folder named **Deploy**.

2. Using Explorer, navigate to the Support\Tools directory in the Windows 2000 installation files on your hard drive or on the Windows 2000 setup CD.

3. Double-click **Deploy.cab** and follow directions on screen to copy **contents of Deploy.cab** to the Deploy directory on drive C:.

Now that you have installed the Windows 2000 Setup Manager, you can use Windows 2000 Setup Manager Wizard to create an unattended installation answer file. Follow these steps:

1. Verify that the C:\Deploy directory is still open in Windows Explorer, and then double-click **setupmgr.exe**. The Windows 2000 Setup Manager Wizard starts and displays a welcome message.

2. Click **Next** to continue.

3. In the New or Existing Answer File section, select **Create a new answer File** and then click **Next**.

4. In the Product to Install section, select **Windows 2000 Unattended Installation**. What other types of products does this wizard support?

   Pro or server

5. Click **Next** to continue.

6. In the Platform Type section, select **Windows 2000 Professional** and then click **Next** to continue.

7. In the User Interaction Level section of the wizard, select **Fully Automated** and then click **Next** to continue.

8. In the License Agreement section, accept the EULA and then click **Next** to continue.

9. In the Customize the Software section, specify the user name and the organization name and then click **Next** to continue.

10. In the Computer Names section, type the computer name and then click **Add**. Note that you could use the answer file you are creating to install Windows 2000 on several computers as long as the computers' hardware configurations are identical.

11. Click **Next** to continue.

12. In the Administrator Password section, specify the Administrator password for this computer, confirm the password, and then click **Next** to continue.

13. In the Display Settings section of the wizard, specify **Preferred Video Settings**. These settings include color, screen area, and refresh rate and will depend on the settings supported by the video cards in the computers on which the unattended installation will be performed.

14. Click **Next** to continue.

15. In the Network Settings section, select the correct Network Type and Settings for your network and then click **Next**.

16. In the Workgroup or Domain section, specify whether the computer is part of a workgroup or domain. If the computer is a part of a domain, specify the Administrator user name and password account.

17. Click **Next** to continue.

18. In the Time Zone section, specify your time zone and then click **Next**.

19. In the Additional Settings section, you could select additional settings that are required for other devices. These settings include telephone information, regional settings such as country and currency, the preferred language for menus and other operating system features, and printers that you might want to install automatically. For this exercise, click the **No, do not edit the additional settings** option button and then click **Next** to continue.

20. In the Distribution Folder section, you can specify whether you want to install the operating system from a CD or to create a distribution folder, typically on a network location. When you use a distribution folder, all necessary source files are copied to that location. For this exercise, however, you will choose to install from a CD. Click the option button indicating installation from a CD and then click **Next** to continue.

21. In the Answer File Name section, specify the name (sysprep.inf) and location for the answer file you are creating (the Sysprep folder at the root level of the drive on which Windows will be installed). Click **Next** to continue.

22. Click **Finish** to exit the wizard and close Windows 2000 Setup Manager. The wizard creates the answer file in the specified location.

CRITICAL THINKING: USING THE ANSWER FILE (additional 120 minutes)

Install Windows 2000 using the answer file you just created and then answer these questions:

➤ Where were the installation files located?

root

➤ How did you launch the installation process?

Double clicked sysprep . Bat

➤ How did you tell Setup to use your answer file?

Double clicked sysprep .

➤ What, if anything, did you have to do while the installation was in progress?

CD key

➤ What error messages, if any, did you see? What did you do about them?

none

Review Questions

1. What type of file does the Windows 2000 Setup Manager Wizard create, and what is this file used for?

2. Before the wizard was developed, how was this type of file created?

3. What other operations does this wizard support?

4. Could you use the Setup Manager Wizard to create a file to assist an unattended installation that automatically creates an account on a Windows domain? Explain.

_____

5. If you choose to create a distribution folder, why won't the Windows 2000 Professional installation CD be necessary during the unattended installation?

_____

_____

7

LAB 7.5 USE TASK MANAGER

Objectives

The goal of this lab is to help you use Task Manager to examine your system. After completing this lab, you will be able to:

➤ Identify applications that are currently running

➤ Launch an application

➤ Display general system performance and process information in Task Manager

Materials Required

This lab will require the following:

➤ Windows 2000 Professional operating system

➤ Installed CD drive, installed sound card, and audio CD

Activity Background

Task Manager is a useful tool that allows you to switch between tasks, end tasks, and observe system use and performance. In this lab, you will use Task Manager to manage applications and to observe system performance.

Estimated completion time: **30 minutes**

ACTIVITY

Follow these steps to use Task Manager:

1. Log on as an administrator.

2. Press **Ctrl+Alt+Shift** to open the **Task Manager**, or right-click any unoccupied area on the Windows 2000 taskbar and select **Task Manger** from the

menu. The Task Manager window opens. This window consists of tabs providing information about applications, processes, and programs running on the computer, as well as information about system performance.

3. If necessary, click the **Applications** tab. What information is currently listed in the Tasks list?

_____

_____

_____

4. Use the Start menu to open Windows Help and then observe the change to the Tasks list in the Applications tab of Task Manager. What change occurred in the Task list?

_____

5. In the Application tab of Task Manager, click the **New Task** button. The Create New Task window opens. This window is almost identical to the one that opens when you use the Run command on the Start menu.

6. In the Open text box, type **command.com** and then click **OK**. A command prompt window opens. Examine the Application tab in Task Manager and note that \Winnt\System32\command.com now appears in the Task list.

7. Click the command prompt window. The command prompt window is now the active window, but notice that the Task Manager window remains on top of all other open windows. This ensures that you can keep track of changes in the system while opening and closing applications.

You can customize Task Manager to suit your preferences. Among other things, you can change the setting that keeps the Task Manager window on top of all other open windows. You can also change the way information is displayed within the Task Manager window. To learn more about changing Task Manager settings, follow these steps:

1. In Task Manager, click **Options** on the menu bar. A menu with a list of options opens. List the available options on the lines below. Note that the check marks indicate which of these options are currently applied. The Always On Top option is currently selected. This is the option that keeps the Task Manager window on top of all other open windows.

2. Click **Always On Top** to remove the check mark and then click the command prompt window. What happens?

_____

_____

_____

3. Click **Options** on the Task Manager menu bar and then click **Always On Top** to select it again.

4. In the Task Manager menu bar, click **View**. You can use the options on this menu to change the way information is displayed within the Task Manager window. Selected settings are indicated by a dot. List the available settings and the current settings here:

_____

_____

_____

5. Click **Large Icons** to select this setting. Note how this affects the way information is displayed in Task Manager.

6. Return the view to the **Detailed** setting.

Follow these steps to use Task Manager to end a task and observe system usage information:

1. Notice that three types of information are listed at the bottom of the Task Manager window. What three types of information do you see and what are their values?

_____

_____

_____

2. While observing these values, move your mouse around the screen for several seconds and then stop. Which of the three values changed?

_____

3. In the Tasks list, click **Windows 2000 Help** and then click **End Task**.

4. Compare the current processes, CPU time, and memory to the information recorded in Step 1. How much memory was Windows 2000 Help using?

_____

Follow these steps to use Task Manager to observe process and performance information.

1. In Task Manager, click the **Processes** tab. This tab lists current processes under Image Name and displays four pieces of information about each process: Process ID (PID), CPU Percent Used By (CPU), a running total of CPU time (CPU Time), and Memory Usage (MEM Usage).

7

2. Scroll down and examine each process. What process is currently using the highest percentage of CPU resources?

_____

3. Use the Start menu to start Windows 2000 Help.

4. Drag the Windows 2000 Help window to position it as shown in Figure 7-1, so that the left pane is visible on the left side of the Task Manager window.

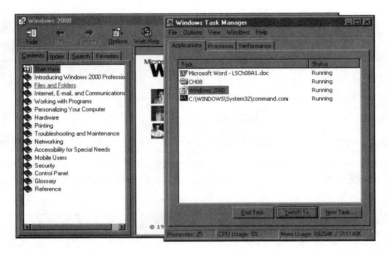

Figure 7-1   Position the Windows 2000 Help window to the left of the Task Manager window

5. Verify that the Windows 2000 Help window is the active window, then observe the process information in Task Manager as you move the mouse pointer up and down over the topics in the left pane of Windows 2000 Help. Which process or processes begin to use more CPU resources as the mouse moves from topic to topic?

_____

6. In the Processes tab of Task Manager, click **hh.exe** (the Windows 2000 Help program file) and then click **End Process**. What message is displayed?

_____

_____

_____

7. In addition to processes for optional user applications, the Processes tab displays and allows you to end core Windows processes. Thus, this warning serves to

warn you of the consequences of ending a potentially essential task. Because Windows 2000 Help is not critical to core Windows functions, it is safe to end this task. Click **Yes** to end.

8. Click the Performance tab and notice that this tab displays CPU usage and memory in bar graphs. This tab also contains a running history graph for both CPU usage and memory. What other four categories of information are displayed on the Performance tab?

_____

_____

9. Insert an audio CD. Configure it to begin playing if necessary. Observe the CPU and memory usage values and record them below.

_____

10. Stop the CD from playing and again observe the CPU and memory usage. Compare the usage to the values from Step 9. Which value changed the most?

_____

Review Questions

1. Explain one way to launch Task Manager.

_____

_____

_____

2. What Task Manager tab allows you to switch between applications and end a task?

_____

3. Why could it be dangerous to end a process with Task Manager?

_____

_____

4. How could you tell if the processor recently completed a period of intensive use but is now idle?

_____

_____

5. Did the playback of an audio CD use more system resources than moving the mouse? Explain.

_____

_____

SUPPORTING AND TROUBLESHOOTING WINDOWS 2000

LAB 8.1 USE THE MICROSOFT MANAGEMENT CONSOLE

Objectives

The goal of this lab is to help you add snap-ins and save settings to create a customized console using the Microsoft Management Console (MMC). After completing this lab, you will be able to:

➤ Use the MMC to add snap-ins

➤ Save a customized console

➤ Identify how to launch a console from the Start menu

Materials Required

This lab will require the following:

➤ Windows 2000 Professional operating system

Activity Background

The Microsoft Management Console (MMC) is a standard management tool that you can use to create a customized console by adding administrative tools called snap-ins. You can use snap-ins provided by Microsoft or other vendors. Many of the administrative tools you have already used (such as Device Manager) can be added to a console as a snap-in. The console itself serves as a convenient interface that helps you organize and manage the administrative tools you use most often. In this lab you will use MMC to create a customized console.

Estimated completion time: **30 minutes**

ACTIVITY

Follow these steps to build a customized console:

1. Log on as an administrator.

2. Click **Start** on the task bar and then click **Run**. The Run dialog box opens.

3. In the Open text box, type **mmc** and then click **OK**. An MMC window named "Console 1" opens. Inside the Console 1 window is another window named "Console Root," which is used to display the contents of the console. In the Console 1 menu bar, click **Console** and then click **Add/Remove Snap-in**.

4. The Add/Remove Snap-in window opens. Console 1 is currently empty—that is, it doesn't yet contain any snap-ins. As you can see in the "Snap-ins added to" text box, any new snap-ins will be added to the Console Root folder.

5. Click **Add**. The Add Standalone Snap-in window opens, displaying a list of available snap-ins. Note that this list includes some of the administrative tools you have used so far (such as Device Manager and Event Viewer).

6. Click **Device Manager** and then click **Add**.

7. A Device Manager dialog box opens. Here you need to specify which computer you want this Device Manager snap-in to manage. You want it to manage the computer you are currently working on, so you need to select the Local Computer option. (See Figure 8-1.) Verify that the **Local Computer** option button is selected and then click **Finish**. The Device Manager on the local computer is added to the Add/Remove Snap-in window. The Add Standalone Snap-in window remains open.

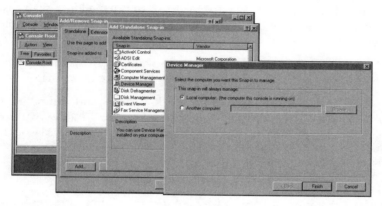

Figure 8-1   Steps to add a new snap-in to a customized console include selecting the computer you want the snap-in to manage

8. Next, you'll add Event Viewer as a snap-in. Click **Event Viewer** in the Standalone Snap-in window and then click **Add**. The Select Computer window opens.

9. Verify that the **Local Computer** option button is selected and then click **Finish**. The Select Computer window closes, and Event Viewer (Local) is added in the Add/Remove Snap-in window. The Add Standalone Snap-in window remains open.

You are finished adding snap-ins for the local computer to your console. Next, you will add another Event Viewer snap-in to be used on a network computer. If your computer is not connected to a network, you can read the following set of steps, but do not attempt to perform them. If your computer is connected to a network, follow these steps:

1. Add another Event Viewer snap-in, and then, in the Select Computer window, click the **Another computer** option button. Now you need to specify the name of the computer you want this Event Viewer snap-in to apply to. You could type the name of the computer, but it's easier to select the computer using the Browse button.

2. Click the **Browse** button. A different Select Computer Window opens and begins searching the network for eligible computers. Eventually, it displays a list of eligible computers.

3. In the new Select Computer window, click the name of the computer you want to apply this Event Viewer Snap-in to, and then click **OK**. The second Select Computer dialog box closes, and you return to the first Select Computer dialog box.

4. Click **Finish.** The Select Computer dialog box closes, and a second Event Viewer snap-in is added to the Add/Remove Snap-in window. The new Event Viewer listing is followed by the name of the remote computer in parentheses.

At this point, whether or not your computer is connected to a network, the Add Standalone Snap-in window should be active. You are finished adding snap-ins and are ready to return to the Console1 window and save your new, customized console so that you can use it whenever you need it. Perform the following steps:

1. Click **Close** in the Add Standalone Snap-in window. The Add Standalone Snap-in window closes and you return to the Add/Remove Snap-in window.

2. Click **OK.** The Add/Remove Snap-in window closes, and you return to the Console1 window. The left pane of the Console Root window (within the Console1 window) now contains the following items: Device Manager (local), Event Viewer (local), and Event Viewer (remote computer name).

3. In the Console1 window, click **Console** on the menu bar and then click **Save As**. The Save As window opens with the default location set to C:\Documents and Settings\Administrator\Start Menu\Programs\Administrative Tools. If you save your customized console in this location, Administrative Tools will also be added directly to the Start menu. Instead, choose C:\Documents and Settings\Administrator\Start Menu\Programs for the save location. Be sure to double-click Programs so that the file goes inside the Programs folder.

4. Name the console **Custom.msc** and then click **Save**. The Save As dialog box closes.

5. Close the Console1 window.

Follow these steps to open and use your customized console.

1. Click **Start** on the taskbar, point to **Programs**, and then click **Custom**. Your customized console opens in a window named "Custom – [Console Root]."

2. Maximize the console window if necessary.

3. In the left pane, click **Device Manager on local computer** and observe the options in the right pane.

4. In the left pane, click the plus sign next to **Event Viewer (Local)**. Subcategories are displayed below "Event Viewer (Local)." List the subcategories you see here:

_____

_____

_____

5. Click **Event Viewer (*remote computer name*)** and observe that the events displayed are events occurring on the remote computer.

6. In the Custom – [Console Root] menu bar, click **Console** and then click **Exit**. A message appears asking if you want to save the current settings.

7. Click **Yes**. The console closes.

8. Launch the customized console from the Start menu again and record the type of information displayed in the right pane when the console opens.

_____

Review Questions

1. What term is used to refer to the specialized tools that you can add to a console using MMC? What are they used for?

_____

2. Suppose you have not yet created a customized MMC. How would you start MMC?

_____

_____

3. How can a customized console be used to manage many computers from a single machine?

_____

_____

4. What information do you see when you open a customized console?

_____

_____

5. How do you add a customized console to the Start menu?

_____

_____

Lab 8.2 Analyze a System with Windows NT/2000/XP Event Viewer

Objectives

The goal of this lab is to help you learn to work with Windows NT/2000/XP Event Viewer. After completing this lab, you will be able to use Event Viewer to:

➤ View normal start up events

➤ View failed events

➤ Record event logs

➤ Compare recent events to logged events

Materials Required

This lab will require the following:

➤ Windows 2000 Professional installed on a FAT partition (with additional NTFS partitions for data if necessary)

➤ Network access using the TCP/IP protocol suite

➤ Administrator account and password

Activity Background

Most of the things that happen to your computer while running Windows 2000 are recorded in a log. Windows lets you look at these events with a tool called Event Viewer. Event Viewer is an application included with Windows 2000 that provides information on various operations and tasks (known as events) within Windows. Event Viewer notes the occurrence of various events, lists them chronologically and gives you the option of saving the list so that you can compare it to a future list. You can use Event Viewer to find out how healthy your system is and to diagnose nonfatal boot-up problems. Fatal boot-up problems don't allow you into Windows far enough to use the Event Viewer. What you learn about Windows 2000 Event Viewer in this lab works the same as it does using Windows NT or Windows XP.

Estimated completion time: **30 minutes**

ACTIVITY

Follow these steps to begin using Event Viewer:

1. Boot the system and log on as an administrator.

2. Click **Start** on the taskbar, point to Settings and click **Control Panel**. The Control Panel opens.

3. Double-click the **Administrative Tools** icon. The Administrative Tools applet opens.

4. Double-click **Event Viewer**. This opens Event Viewer, with the latest events displayed in chronological order from most recent to oldest. See Figure 8-2. The symbols to the left of each event provide important information about the event. For example, the red X indicates a failed event, a lower case "i" indicates an event that provides information about the system, and an exclamation mark in a triangle indicates a warning, such as a note that a disk is near its capacity. The listing for each event also includes a brief description, along with the time and date the event occurred.

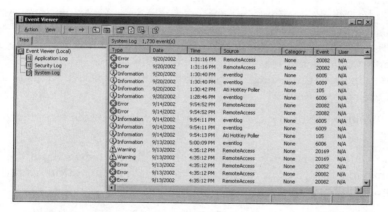

Figure 8-2   The Event Viewer tracks failed events and many successful ones

5. Locate the listings for the four most recent events on your system. For each of those four events, list the source (what triggered the event), the time, and the date:

_____

_____

_____

6. Double-click the top (most recent) event. The Event Properties dialog box opens. What additional information does this dialog box provide? Note that you can also see an event's properties by selecting an event and then clicking Action on the menu bar. Then select Properties.

_____

_____

_____

7. Close the Event Properties box.

You can save the list of events shown in Event Viewer as a special file called a log file. When naming a log file, it's helpful to use the following format: EV*mm-dd-yy*.evt (where *mm*= month, *dd*= day and *yy*= year). For example, you would name a log file saved on January 13, 2004 as EV01-13-04.evt. After you create a log file, you can delete the current list of events from Event Viewer, allowing the utility to begin creating an entirely new list of events. Follow these steps to save the currently displayed events as a log file and then clear the current events:

1. Using Windows Explorer, create a folder called **Logs** in the root directory of drive C.

2. Open Event Viewer (if it is not already open), click somewhere on the Event Viewer window so no one event is selected. Then click **Action** on the menu bar and click **Save Log File As...**.

3. Select the **Logs** folder (which you created in Step 1), name the file **EV*mm-dd-yy*.evt** (where *mm*= month, *dd*= day and *yy*= year) and then click **Save**. Now you are ready to clear the current list of events from Event Viewer.

4. Click **Action** on the menu bar, and then click **Clear all Events**.

5. When asked if you want to save system log, click **No**. The Event Viewer window no longer displays any events.

6. Close Event Viewer.

Now you will attempt to create an intentional problem by attempting to remove a system file. Recall that Windows 2000 File Protection feature will not allow you to delete or rename a system file. If you attempt to do that, the event will be recorded in Event Viewer. To attempt to delete a system file, do the following:

1. Open Windows Explorer and locate the file named **tcpip.sys** in the **\winnt\system32\drivers** folder.

2. Click **tcpip.sys** and press the **Delete** key. The message displays, "Are you sure you want to send "tcpip.sys" to the Recycle Bin?" Click **Yes**. It appears as though tcpip.sys is deleted. Tcpip.sys makes it possible for the computer to communicate over the network. It's a protected system file, so Windows immediately replaces the file. (You will learn more about TCP/IP in later chapters.)

3. Close Windows Explorer and open Event Viewer. Double-click the event labeled **Windows File Protection**. What is the description of the event?

_____

_____

_____

4. What is the Type assigned to this event? _____

5. Close the Event Properties box.

6. Open Windows Explorer. Is tcpip.sys in the \winnt\system32\drivers folder?

_____

You will now create an intentional problem by disconnecting the network cable from your PC, and then see how the resulting errors are recorded in Event Viewer. Do the following:

1. Carefully disconnect the network cable from the network port on the back of your PC.

2. Restart the computer and log in as an administrator. Record any messages you receive, if any.

_____

_____

_____

3. Open My Network Places. Are you able to browse the network?

_____

4. Close My Network Places and then open Event Viewer. How many events are displayed?

_____

_____

5. List the source, date, and time for any error events (indicated by red X signs) that you see:

_____

_____

_____

_____

_____

6. Click each of the error or warning events and read the details on that event. For each event, write a summary of the information in the Description field. (Within the Event Properties box, click **Close** to exit after you have read the description for each event, or use the arrow buttons on the Event Properties box to scroll through and locate the next error.)

_____

_____

_____

_____

_____

_____

_____

When troubleshooting a system, it's often helpful to compare current events with a list of events that you previously stored in a log file. This can help you spot the point in time when a particular problem occurred. Follow these steps to compare the current list of events to the log you saved earlier:

1. Open another instance of Event Viewer (that is, open a second Event Viewer window without closing the first one).

2. In the new Event Viewer window, click somewhere off the list of events so no one event is selected. Then click **Action** on the menu bar and click **Open Log File**.

3. Open the **Logs** folder, click the log file you created earlier. Under Log Type, select **System** and then click **Open**. If a dialog box appears asking you to confirm opening the file, click **OK**.

4. To position the two instances of Event Viewer on your desktop so you can compare them, right-click a blank spot on the taskbar, and a pop-up menu appears, giving you a selection of how to arrange all the open windows—to cascade the windows or tile them horizontally or vertically. Click **Tile Vertically** to position the two open windows side-by-side. You may notice that the current list of events contains one more successful event than the log of previous events. One of these successful events may in fact be the cause of a failed event. For instance, a service starting and allocating resources that another component was previously using would be listed as a successful event. But the allocation of resources currently in use would in turn cause the component that had been using the resources to fail, thereby resulting in a failed event. Judging by the log file you created earlier, how many events occur in a normal startup?

_____

_____

To restore the network connection and verify that the connection is working properly, follow these steps:

1. Reconnect the network cable to the network port on the back of your computer, restart your computer, and log in. Did you receive any messages after you started Windows 2000 this time?

_____

_____

2. Open Event Viewer and verify that no errors occurred during startup.

3. Open another instance of Event Viewer, open the log you saved earlier (in the Logs folder) and verify that the same events occurred in both cases.

4. Close both Event Viewer windows.

Review Questions

1. Judging by the path to Event Viewer using the Start menu, what type of tool is Event Viewer?

   _____

2. Based on what you learned in this lab, what might be your first indication that a problem occurred after startup?

   _____

   _____

3. How can you examine events after you have cleared them from Event Viewer?

   _____

   _____

4. Explain how to compare a log file with the current set of listed events.

   _____

   _____

5. Why might you like to keep a log file of events that was made when your computer booted correctly? List the steps to create this log of a successful boot.

   _____

   _____

   _____

   _____

   _____

CRITICAL THINKING (additional 30 minutes)

Using the Internet for research, find answers to the following questions. Be sure to list the Web site URLs that support your answers.

1. Which version of Windows introduced Windows File Protection? Explain what Windows File Protection does.

   _____

2. Does Windows 2000 need DOS to run? Explain your answer.

   _____

3. Name two benefits to upgrading to Windows 2000 and explain your answers.

   _____

8

LAB 8.3 USE DISK MANAGEMENT

Objectives

The goal of this lab is to help you use Disk Management to work with local hard drives. After completing this lab, you will be able to:

➤ Create a partition from unused disk space

➤ Specify a file system

➤ Format a partition

➤ Delete a partition

Materials Required

This lab will require the following:

➤ Windows 2000 Professional operating system

➤ Unallocated disk space

Activity Background

Disk Management is a Microsoft Management Console snap-in and an administrative tool installed in the Computer Management console by default. To start Disk Management, you first need to start Computer Management. Unlike Fdisk, Disk Management allows you to partition and format disk space from within Windows. In this lab, you will create and delete two different partitions using unallocated disk space.

Estimated completion time: **30 minutes**

ACTIVITY

To work with your local hard drive using Disk Management, follow these steps:

1. Open the Control Panel, and then double-click the **Administrative Tools** icon. The Administrative Tools window opens.

2. Double-click **Computer Management**. In the left pane, click **Disk Management**. The Disk Management interface opens in the right pane. See Figure 8-3.

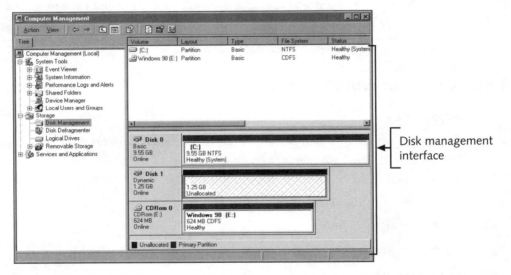

Figure 8-3   Use Windows 2000 Disk Management to manage hard drives

3. Use the information in the top of the right pane to complete the following table for your computer:

Volume	Layout	Type	File System	Status	Capacity

4. In the bottom section of the right pane, information about each physical drive is displayed. In addition, a graphic illustrates each drive's space distribution. Note that drives are labeled with numbers (0, 1, and so forth) in a gray space and that logical drives or volumes are labeled with letters (C:, D:, E: and so forth) in white space. If a hard drive has just been installed and not yet partitioned, the graphic will show

all unallocated (unpartitioned) space, as in Figure 8-3. What drive letters are used on your system?

_____

5. Right-click the right side (white space) of the C: drive space in the bottom right part of the window. A Shortcut menu opens with the following options:

- **Open:** Displays the contents of the drive in a window similar to a My Computer window
- **Explore:** Displays contents of the drive in a window similar to a Windows Explorer window
- **Change Drive Letter and Path:** Allows you to select a new letter for the drive. For instance, you might change the drive letter from C: to F:.
- **Format:** Allows you to format a partition and make partition-related choices, including specifying the file system and sector size
- **Delete Partition:** Allows you to delete an entire partition and all contents
- **Properties:** Displays information about the partition, such as how it is formatted
- **View Help:** Provides information about Disk Management

6. Right-click the unpartitioned area of the disk drive, which is labeled Unallocated. List the differences between the options provided in this Shortcut menu and the menu you examined in Step 5.

_____

_____

In the next set of steps you will create a new partition from unpartitioned space. Note that the partition you are creating should *only use currently unpartitioned* space. Follow these steps:

1. Using *only unpartitioned space*, create a new partition, format the partition using the FAT32 file system and drive letter S:. List the steps required to perform this task:

_____

_____

_____

_____

8

2. Print a screen shot of the Disk Management window showing the FAT32 drive S:.

3. Delete the partition you just created. List the steps required to perform this task here:

_____

_____

4. Using *only unpartitioned space*, create and format a new NTFS partition using the drive letter H:. List the steps required to perform this task here:

_____

_____

_____

5. Print a screen shot of the Disk Management window showing the NTFS drive H:.

6. Close the Computer Management window.

CRITICAL THINKING: MANAGING PARTITIONS FROM THE RECOVERY CONSOLE (additional 60 minutes)

Do the following to practice managing partitions from the Recovery Console:

1. Access the Windows 2000 Recovery Console. List the steps required to perform this task here:

_____

_____

_____

2. Open Help and print information about the Diskpart command, including possible command line options. List the steps required to perform this task here:

_____

_____

_____

3. Delete the partition created earlier using Disk Management. List the steps required to perform this task here:

_____

_____

_____

4. Create and format a new NTFS partition, using the drive letter R:. List the steps required to perform this task here:

_____

_____

_____

5. Delete the newly created partition. List the steps required to perform this task here:

_____

_____

_____

Review Questions

1. Name an advantage that Disk Management has over Fdisk.

_____

2. What happens to all the information in a partition if you delete the partition?

_____

_____

3. What feature opens if you choose Explore from a shortcut menu in Disk Management?

_____

4. Is it possible to create two partitions, using different file systems, out of one area of unallocated disk space? Explain.

_____

_____

_____

5. List the steps involved in removing two empty partitions and creating one single NTFS partition that is assigned the drive letter T:

_____

_____

_____

_____

_____

_____

_____

_____

LAB 8.4 USE DR. WATSON

Objectives

The goal of this lab is to help you troubleshoot program errors that occur when you are running Windows. After completing this lab you will be able to:

➤ Use Dr. Watson to collect detailed information about the state of your operating system

➤ Use Dr. Watson to troubleshoot program errors

➤ Customize Dr. Watson

Materials Required

➤ Windows 2000 Professional

➤ Access to the Internet

Activity Background

Dr. Watson for Windows is a program error debugger. Dr. Watson is designed to detect problems caused by applications and stop them before the problems affect other applications. The information collected and logged by Dr. Watson can be used by technical support personnel to diagnose a program error for a computer running Windows. If an error occurs, Dr. Watson will start automatically. A text file (Drwatson.log) is created whenever an error is detected, and can be delivered to support personnel by various methods.

Estimated completion time: 30 minutes

ACTIVITY

Dr. Watson cannot prevent errors from occurring, but the information recorded in the log file can be used to diagnose the problem. Dr. Watson (drwtsn32.exe) is installed in your system folder when you set up Windows. The default options are set the first time Dr. Watson runs, which can be either when a program error occurs or when you start Dr. Watson yourself.

There are three ways to start Dr. Watson:

➤ Enter the program name (drwtsn32) in the Run dialog box

➤ Enter the program name (drwtsn32) at a command prompt using a Command Prompt window

➤ Use the Tools menu of the System Information window. (To access the System Information window, click Start, Programs, Accessories, and System Tools.)

In this lab, you will start Dr. Watson using the first method. Do the following:

1. Click **Start** and click **Run**. The Run dialog box opens. Type **drwtsn32** and then click **OK**. The Dr. Watson for Windows dialog box opens and an icon for Dr. Watson is displayed on the taskbar.

2. Click the **Browse** button to the right of the Log File Path. What is the path to the log file?

   _____

3. Using Windows Explorer, look in this folder. Is there a log file there? If so, what is the size of the file in bytes?

   _____

4. Double-click the log file. The file should open using Notepad. A sample log file is showing in Figure 8-4. Scroll through the file looking for dates that information was recorded to the file. What applications caused errors and on what dates did these errors occur?

_____

_____

_____

5. Close the log file.

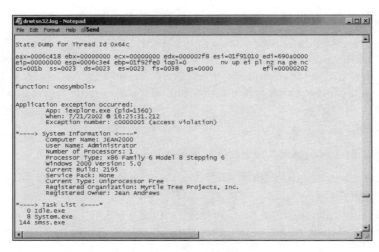

Figure 8-4   A sample Dr. Watson log file

Dr. Watson is available under Windows 98 and Windows NT/2000/XP, but the filename and path to the program file and log file are not the same in each OS. Research the information about these file names and paths, and fill out the following table. You can get your information by searching the hard drives of computers that have these Windows OSs installed, or you can search the Microsoft Web site (*support.microsoft.com*) for the information.

Operating System	Path and filename to the Dr. Watson program	Path and filename to the Dr. Watson log file
Windows 98		
Windows NT		
Windows 2000		
Windows XP		

Review Questions

1. Describe the purpose of the Dr. Watson utility.

   _____

   _____

2. Who might find the information recorded in the Dr. Watson log file or dump file useful?

   _____

3. What is the name of the Dr. Watson log file used by Windows 98?

   _____

4. What is the name of the Dr. Watson log file used by Windows XP?

   _____

5. What type of event causes Dr. Watson to automatically launch?

   _____

LAB 8.5 CRITICAL THINKING: SABOTAGE AND REPAIR WINDOWS 2000

Objectives

The goal of this lab is to give you practice troubleshooting Windows 2000 by repairing a sabotaged system. After completing this lab, you will be able to:

➤ Troubleshoot and repair a system that is not working correctly

Materials Required

This lab will require the following:

➤ Windows 2000 operating system installed on a PC designated for a sabotage

➤ Access to the Windows installation CD or the installation files stored in another location

➤ Workgroup of 2-4 students

Activity Background

You have learned about several tools and methods that you can use to recover Windows 2000 when it fails. This lab gives you the opportunity to use these skills in a troubleshooting situation. Your group will work with another group to first sabotage a system and then repair the failed system.

Estimated completion time: **60 minutes**

ACTIVITY

1. If the hard drive contains important data, back up that data to another media. Is there anything else you should back up before the system is sabotaged by another group? Note that item here and then go ahead and back it up.

   _____

2. Trade systems with another group and sabotage the other group's system while they sabotage your system. Do one thing that will cause the system to fail to boot or give errors after the boot. The following list offers some sabotage suggestions. You can choose one of these options, or do something else. Do not, however, alter the hardware.

   - Rename a system file (in the root directory) that is required to boot the system (for example, Ntldr or Ntdetect). Alternately, you could move one of these files to a different directory. Note that you should not delete any system files.

   - Using the Registry Editor, delete several important keys or values in the registry.

   - Rename important system files in the \Windows directory or move one of these files to another directory.

   - Put a corrupted program file in the folder that will cause the program to automatically launch at startup. Record the name of that folder here:

   - Use display settings that are not readable, such as black text on a black background.

3. Since Windows 2000 has features that are designed to prevent sabotage, reboot and make sure the system does indeed have an error.

4. How did you sabotage the system?

   _____

   _____

5. Retrieve your original system and troubleshoot it.

6. Describe the problem as the user would describe it to you if you were working at a help desk.

_____

_____

7. What is your first guess as to the source of the problem?

_____

8. List the steps you took in the troubleshooting process.

_____

_____

_____

_____

_____

_____

9. How did you finally solve the problem and return the system to good working order?

_____

_____

Review Questions

1. Now that you have been through the troubleshooting experience above, what would you do differently the next time you encounter the same symptoms?

_____

2. What Windows utilities did you use to solve the problem? What other Windows utilities might you have used?

_____

3. What third-party software utility might have been useful in solving this problem?

_____

4. In a real-life situation, what might actually cause this problem? List three possible causes.

_____

_____

_____

CHAPTER NINE

INSTALLING AND USING WINDOWS XP

Labs included in this chapter

- ➤ Lab 9.1 Install Windows XP
- ➤ Lab 9.2 Allow Two Users to Log on Simultaneously
- ➤ Lab 9.3 Navigate and Customize Windows XP
- ➤ Lab 9.4 Manage User Accounts in Windows XP
- ➤ Lab 9.5 Windows Media Player

LAB 9.1 INSTALL WINDOWS XP

Objectives

The goal of this lab is to help you install, or upgrade to, Windows XP Professional. After completing this lab, you will be able to:

➤ Plan an upgrade or installation

➤ Identify the benefits of an upgrade or new installation

➤ Install or upgrade to Windows XP Professional

Materials Required

This lab will require the following:

➤ Windows 98SE operating system

➤ Access to drivers or Internet access for downloading drivers

➤ Windows XP Professional operating system

➤ Key from installation CD

➤ Floppy disks (to store updated device drivers)

Activity Background

Windows XP is designed to be reliable and has a new user interface to give you a more personalized computing experience. The operating system's updated look uses more graphics to simplify the user interface. It has a task-oriented design which gives you options specifically associated with the task or file you are working on. You can upgrade your computer's operating system to Windows XP Professional from Microsoft Windows 98/98SE, Windows Me, Windows NT Workstation 4.0, Windows 2000, or Windows XP Home Edition. For this activity, you will upgrade from Windows 98SE. The process for installing or upgrading an operating system is not difficult. Careful planning will minimize or eliminate many of the headaches some users have experienced when upgrading to Windows XP.

Estimated completion time: **90 minutes**

ACTIVITY

Your lab system will most likely be compatible with Windows XP. However, in the future, when working on other systems, you might discover significant incompatibilities. In that case, you would have to decide whether or not upgrading to Windows XP Professional is really an option. Many users have experienced significant problems with device drivers when upgrading to Windows XP. For this reason, it is extremely important to do your research and download device drivers that will be compatible with Windows XP Professional before you install the upgrade. You may need to visit the Web sites of the manufacturers of all your devices, such as scanners, printers, modems, keyboards, mouse, camera, etc., to see if they are compatible with Windows XP Professional. If the manufacturer provides an updated device driver to support Windows XP Professional, you will need to download the files to a storage media. Also, when planning an upgrade, it is helpful to record information collected in a table, such as the one in Table 9-1. Follow these steps to create a plan and prepare for a Windows XP Professional upgrade on your computer:

1. Use Device Manager or SANDRA to compile the information in the first row of Table 9-1.

Table 9-1   Things to do and information to collect when planning a Windows upgrade

Things to Do	Further Information
Does the PC meet the minimum or recommended hardware requirement?	CPU: _____ RAM: _____ Hard drive size: _____ Free space on the hard drive: _____
Have you checked all your applications to verify that they qualify for Windows XP or need patches in order to qualify?	Applications that need to be upgraded: _____ _____ _____
Have you checked the Microsoft Web site to verify that all your hardware qualify?	Hardware that needs to be upgraded: _____ _____ _____
Have you decided how you will join a network?	Workgroup name: _____ Domain name: _____ Computer name: _____
Do you have the product key available?	Product key: _____
Have you backed up critical data?	Location of backup files: _____
Verify that your hard drive is ready.	Size of the hard drive partition: _____ Free space on the partition: _____ File system you plan to use: _____

2. Compare your information to the requirements for Windows XP listed in Table 9-2.

   ■ Does your system meet the minimum requirements?

   _____

   ■ Does your system meet the recommended requirements?

   _____

9

Table 9-2   Minimum and recommended requirements for Windows XP Professional

Component or Device	Minimum Requirement	Recommended Requirement
One or two CPUs	Pentium II 233 MHz or better	Pentium II 300 MHz or better
RAM	64 MB	128 MB up to 4 GB
Hard drive partition	2 GB	2 GB or more
Free space on the hard drive partition	640 MB (bare bones)	2 GB or more
CD-ROM drive	12x	12x or faster
Accessories	Keyboard and mouse or other pointing device	Keyboard and mouse or other pointing device

3. Make a list of important applications and verify if they are compatible with Windows XP Professional. If you find any applications that are not compatible, check to see if any patches or upgrades are available to make them compatible. List in Table 9-1 any applications that do not qualify, or need patches in order to qualify. List below any software upgrades or patches you downloaded in order to prepare your applications for Windows XP:

---

4. Install any application upgrades or patches that you have downloaded.

5. Check each hardware device against both the Hardware Compatibility List and the System Requirements list for Windows XP Professional on the Microsoft website (*www.microsoft.com*). List in Table 9-1 any hardware devices that need updated drivers.

6. Download, or otherwise obtain, all necessary drivers from the manufacturers or the Microsoft Web site for your hardware. List any drivers you were required to install to make your hardware compatible with Windows XP Professional:

---

7. Gather any network-specific information in preparation for the installation. If you are connected to a network, answer the following:

   ■ If you are using a TCP/IP network, how is your IP address configured?

- For a static IP address, what is the IP address?

  _____

- What is the workgroup name or domain name of the network?

  _____

- What is your computer name?

  _____

  Record the workgroup or domain name and the computer name in Table 9-1.

8. Based on the information you have collected in Table 9-1, answer the following:
   - Does your system qualify for Windows XP Professional?

     _____

   - If not, what hardware or application does not qualify?

     _____

9. Make sure you have the correct CD key for your installation CD and record it in Table 9-1. The CD key, which is provided with the Windows XP Professional installation CD, usually consists of a set of alphanumeric characters. You enter the CD key in order to complete the installation even if you are installing the operating system from setup files located somewhere other than on the installation CD.

10. Review the information you've collected so far, and then decide whether to do a fresh installation or an upgrade. For instance, if all the important applications on your system are compatible with Windows XP Professional, an upgrade will probably save time because it leaves compatible applications in working condition. On the other hand, if you know that you will have to install new applications because of incompatibilities, you might choose to perform a fresh installation. In many ways a fresh installation is preferable because it ensures that no misconfigured system settings will be carried over to the new operating system.

11. Backup critical data files (that is, any work you or others have stored on your computer that you cannot afford to lose during the installation process).

12. If you have critical files on the PC, where did you back them up? Record that information in Table 9-1.

13. The hard drive partition that is to be the active partition for Windows XP must be at least 2 GB in size and have at least 2 GB free. Record the size of the hard drive partition and the amount of free space on that partition in Table 9-1. Answer these questions:

   ■ What Windows utility (utilities) or command(s) did you use to determine the size of the active partition?

   _____

   ■ What Windows utility (utilities) or command(s) did you use to determine how much free space is on that partition?

   _____

   _____

14. When installing Windows XP, you have a choice of using the FAT or NTFS file systems. For this installation, use the FAT file system already installed. Record that in Table 9-1.

You are ready to begin installing Windows XP Professional. This lab assumes that you have Windows 98SE installed and running. This is not the only situation in which you would install or upgrade to Windows XP Professional, but it is very common. It is possible to install Windows XP using setup files stored on the installation CD, on a network drive, or on a local hard disk.

The following steps are representative of a typical upgrade. Your installation process will probably vary in minor ways depending on the installation options you choose, your system's hardware configurations, and other considerations. The following steps are provided as a guide to let you know what to expect during the process. Do not become alarmed if you experience differs slightly from the process outlined in these steps. Use your knowledge to solve any problems on your own. Ask your instructor for help if you get stuck. Use the blank lines after the installation steps to record any differences between the steps provided here and your own experience. Also, record any decisions you make during the installation process and any information you enter during the installation process.

1. Before you insert the installation CD or run the installation files from a location on your hard drive or network, use antivirus software to scan the computer's memory and hard drive for viruses. Once the scan is complete, make sure to disable any automatic scans and close the antivirus program before beginning installation.

2. Insert the Windows XP Professional CD. The Setup program starts. This program will guide you through the actual installation. If the Setup program doesn't begin automatically, use the Run command on the Start menu to browse for the Setup.exe file to begin the installation.

3. The Welcome to Microsoft Windows XP window appears with three options. What options do you see?

_____

_____

_____

4. Click **Install Windows XP**. The setup program begins collecting information. The Welcome to Windows Setup window opens with the Installation Type: Upgrade (Recommended) in the text box. Click **Next**.

5. Accept the EULA (End user license agreement) and click **Next**.

6. When prompted, enter the CD key and click **Next**.

7. The Windows Setup Upgrade Report window opens. If necessary, select the option, **"Show me hardware issues and a limited set of software issues (Recommended)"**, and click **Next**.

8. The Windows Setup Get Update Setup Files window opens. Because we can check for updates at a later time and we are focusing on upgrading for now, select **"No, skip this step and continue installing Windows"**, and click **Next**.

9. Windows is now preparing the installation of Windows XP Professional by analyzing your computer. The setup will complete in approximately 60 minutes. Read the informational screens as they appear. You can gain a lot of insight into Windows XP through this mini tutorial. Your computer will reboot several times during the installation and setup process.

10. When the installation is complete and Windows XP has rebooted for the last time, you will see the Welcome to Microsoft Windows screen. Click **Next** to continue.

11. At the "Ready to Register with Microsoft" screen, click **"No, not at this time"** and then click **Next**.

12. You are now ready to enter your user information. You can type the name of each person who will use this computer. Windows will create a separate user account for each person so you can personalize the way you want Windows to organize and display information, protect your files and computer settings, and customize the desktop. The user names you enter will appear at the Welcome screen in alphabetical order. When you start Windows, you will simply click on your name in the Welcome screen to begin working in Windows XP Professional. For now, enter only your first name and click **Next**.

13. You will receive a Thank You message. Click **Finish** to continue.

14. You can also set a password for all Windows XP accounts. Enter a password to be used for all of the listed accounts. If you want to change the passwords later, go to the User Accounts applet in Control Panel.

15. To begin using Windows XP, click your user name and enter your password. A Welcome screen will appear. Wait while Windows XP loads your personal settings. The first time you start Windows XP, the Start menu is displayed until you click something else. Thereafter, you will open the Start menu by clicking the Start button at the left end of the taskbar.

16. Remove the installation CD from the drive and return it to the instructor.

Review Questions

1. Was the Windows XP upgrade a success? If so, what did you find to be most challenging about the upgrade process?

   _____

   _____

2. Describe the Windows XP desktop.

   _____

   _____

3. By default, which icon appears on the Windows XP desktop?

   _____

   _____

4. At first glance, what is your impression of the user interface?

   _____

   _____

5. How does Windows XP offer to help you learn about the exciting new features in Windows XP?

   _____

   _____

LAB 9.2 ALLOW TWO USERS TO LOG ON SIMULTANEOUSLY

Objectives

The goal of this lab is to help you understand Windows XP's support for multiple logons. After completing this lab, you will be able to:

➤ Create a user account

➤ Log on as two different users simultaneously

➤ Customize desktop settings for both users

➤ Switch between two user accounts that are both logged on to the system

Materials Required

This lab will require the following:

➤ Windows XP Professional operating system (If you are using Windows XP Home Edition, some of the instructions in this lab might work differently.)

➤ User account with administrative privileges

Activity Background

Windows XP includes a new feature that allows more than one user to be logged on to the same computer at the same time, each with his or her own preferences set and programs open. This is useful when more than one person needs to use the same computer. In this lab, you will create a new user account, log onto that account, open a program, change desktop settings, switch back to your own account, and observe the effects of switching between the two user accounts.

Estimated completion time: **30 minutes**

ACTIVITY

Follow these steps to create a new user account and open an application using the new account:

1. Log on to your computer under your user account which should have administrative privileges.

2. In the Start menu, right-click **My Computer** and choose **Manage** from the shortcut menu.

3. The Computer Management console opens. Click the **plus sign (+)** next to **Local Users and Groups** to expand it.

4. Under Local Users and Groups, right-click the **Users** folder and choose **New User** from the shortcut menu. The New User dialog box opens.

5. In the New User dialog box, enter a user name, full name, description, and password for your new user. Deselect the **User must change password at next logon** check box, and then select the **User cannot change password** and **Password never expires** check boxes. (The remaining check box disables the account, which you do not need to do at this time.) Record the user name, full name and password here.

_____

_____

6. Click the **Create** button to create the new user account, and then click **Close** to close the New User Dialog box.

7. Double-click the **Users** folder so that the list of users on your computer appears in the right-hand pane of the Computer Management console, and verify that the new user is listed.

8. Open Microsoft Word, WordPad, or some other application.

Follow these steps to switch between users and make changes as the new user:

1. In the Start menu, click the **Log Off** icon and then answer these questions:

   ■ What options does the Log Off Windows dialog box provide?

   _____

   ■ Hold your mouse pointer over the **Switch User** icon. If balloon text is enabled on your system, some balloon text appears. If the balloon text appears, write down the keyboard shortcut for switching users.

   _____

2. Click the **Switch User** icon. The login screen appears, just as it does when you first turn the computer on and log on to your account. The new user you just created should be listed. Click the icon for that user's name and enter the password for the user when prompted.

3. Now that you are logged on as the new user, right-click an empty area of the desktop, and then click **Properties**. The **Display Properties** window opens. Click the **Desktop** tab and change the desktop background for this user. Next, open an application other than the one you opened earlier. For instance, you might open Microsoft Excel.

4. Choose **Log Off** on the Start menu again and click **Switch User** to display the logon screen.

   ■ What information is listed under your user name and under the new user's name?

   _____

   _____

5. Switch back to your user name, and then switch back to the new user again.

   ■ Does the desktop background change for each user? Do the users' programs remain open?

   _____

6. While logged on as the new user, choose **Turn Off Computer** from the Start Menu and then click the **Turn Off** button.

   ■ What message do you receive?

   _____

   _____

7. Click **No** in the dialog box that appeared when you tried to turn off the computer. You return to the new user's desktop.

8. Now you are ready to log off. To do that, click **Log Off** in the Start menu again. Then, in the Log Off Windows dialog box, click **Log Off** instead of **Switch User**. The logon window reappears.

   ■ What information appears under your user name now? What information appears under the new user's name?

   _____

   _____

Review Questions

1. How do you think the process of switching between users would have been different if you did not assign the user a password? How would it have been different if you had required the user to change the password at the next logon?

   _____

   _____

2. When multiple users are logged on to the same computer, does the logon screen show which programs each user has open? Why do you think this is so?

   _____

   _____

3. What are three advantages to multiple logons?

_____

_____

_____

4. List the steps required to render the new user's account inactive without deleting it. After the account has been rendered inactive, would the user still be listed on the logon screen? Explain.

_____

_____

_____

_____

5. In what situation might it be appropriate to disable a user account?

_____

_____

_____

Freddflinstone 2003 @ Yahoo.com.   @ barney

LAB 9.3 NAVIGATE AND CUSTOMIZE WINDOWS XP

Objectives

The goal of this lab is to help you become comfortable navigating and customizing the Windows XP user interface. After completing this lab, you will be able to:

➤ Customize the taskbar

➤ Work with a program shortcut

➤ Customize the Start menu

➤ Clean up the Windows XP desktop

➤ Locate essential system information

Materials Required

This lab will require the following:

➤ Windows XP Professional operating system

Activity Background

Becoming proficient at navigating a new operating system can be unnerving. Windows XP is the newest version of Windows. Upgrading from Windows 98SE to Windows XP Professional is a giant step to take, especially once you look at the differences in the user interface. From the redesigned Start menu to the new task links in folder windows, just about everything looks a bit different in Windows XP, and locating previously used utilities might prove a challenge. In this lab you will explore how Windows XP handles some of your routine tasks.

> Estimated completion time: **30 minutes**

ACTIVITY

To customize the taskbar, follow these steps:

1. Place the mouse pointer over an empty part of the taskbar. Press and hold the left mouse button and drag the taskbar to the right side of the screen.

   ■ Were you able to move the taskbar? If not, what do you think the problem might be?

   _____

2. Right-click an empty area of the taskbar. Deselect **Lock the Taskbar** by clicking on it. Now try to move the taskbar to the right side of the screen. Return the taskbar to its default position.

   ■ Were you able to move the taskbar?

   _____

You can create shortcuts and place them on the desktop to provide quick access to programs. You can also rename and delete a shortcut on your desktop. To create, rename, and delete a desktop shortcut, follow these steps:

1. Click **Start** and place the mouse pointer over **All Programs** and then **Accessories**.

2. Right-click **Calculator**. On the menu that opens, choose **Send To**, and then select **Desktop (create shortcut)**. Windows adds the shortcut to your desktop. (You might need to minimize any open windows to see it.)

3. Right-click the shortcut. In the menu that opens, click **Rename**.

4. Type a new name for the shortcut, and press **Enter**.

5. To delete a shortcut icon from the desktop, right-click it, and choose **Delete** on the menu that appears. In the Confirm File Delete dialog box, click **Yes** to delete the shortcut. The shortcut is deleted from the desktop.

The Start menu has been significantly redesigned in Windows XP to provide the user with easy access to programs. When it first opens, it looks something like Figure 9-1. When you install most programs, they are added automatically to the Start menu. If a program is not added during installation, you can add it yourself. Windows XP enables you to "pin" a program to your Start menu.

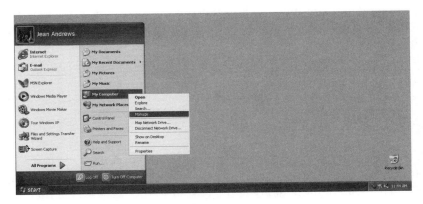

Figure 9-1 The Windows XP desktop and Start menu

To customize the Start menu, follow these steps:

1. First you will need to navigate your folder structure to locate a program to pin to the Start menu. Because performing a backup is an essential task in maintaining your PC, we will pin the backup utility to the Start menu. Click **Start** and place the mouse point over **All Programs**, then **Accessories**, and then **System Tools**. Right-click **Backup**.

2. Choose **Pin to Start Menu** on the menu that appears. The program is added to your Start menu.

   ■ Write the steps you would take to unpin the Backup program from the Start menu.

   _____

   _____

   _____

If you are accustomed to the Windows 98SE Start menu style, which is now called Classic menu, you might find the changes to the Start menu take some getting used to. It is recommended that you give the new Start menu a try because it was designed to increase efficiency. If you are unable to adjust, you have the option of changing to the Classic version.

To revert to the Classic version Start menu, follow these steps:

1. Right-click the **Start** button and select **Properties** on the menu that appears.

2. Click the **Classic Start menu** radio button and click **Apply**. Click **OK**.

3. Which Start menu version do you prefer, and why?

_____

_____

The Desktop Cleanup Wizard helps you clean up your desktop by moving rarely used shortcuts to a desktop folder called Unused Desktop Shortcuts. The Unused Desktop Shortcuts folder is a temporary holding area for shortcuts you are not using. You can restore shortcuts from this folder or delete the entire folder. In this exercise, you will use the Desktop Cleanup Wizard to clean up your desktop, and you will then delete some desktop shortcuts.

To use the Desktop Cleanup Wizard to remove rarely used shortcuts, follow these steps:

1. Right-click any open area of the desktop, point to **Arrange Icons By** on the shortcut menu, and then click **Run Desktop Cleanup Wizard**. The first page of the Desktop Cleanup Wizard appears.

2. Click **Next** to open the Shortcuts dialog box. A list of Shortcuts to Clean Up is displayed along with the Date Last Used.

3. To leave a shortcut on your desktop, clear its check box. Only those shortcuts with a check mark in the box will be moved to the Unused Desktop Shortcuts folder. Select a shortcut from your list and then click **Next**.

4. You will see a confirmation message indicating which shortcuts will be moved. Click **Finish**.

5. Click **Yes to All**. You will be returned to the Windows desktop. You should see a new folder called Unused Desktop Shortcuts.

6. Next you will move the entire folder to the Recycle Bin. Before you do, take notice of the Recycle Bin icon. Now, left-click and drag the new folder to the Recycle Bin.

   ■ Did the appearance of the Recycle Bin icon change? If so, explain the change.

_____

_____

You may have noticed by now that there are quite a few changes to the way you view and navigate Windows XP compared to Windows 98SE. In the next exercise, you will locate essential system information using My Computer and Control Panel. Remember, however, with the new interface, it may not be so easy to locate some of these items.

To locate essential system information using My Computer and Control panel, follow these steps:

1. Click the **Start** menu and then click **My Computer**.

   - How does the way Windows XP display the information in My Computer differ from that of Windows 98?

   _____

   _____

   - What happens when you click the drive C: icon?

   _____

   _____

2. Double-click the **drive C: icon**.

   - Describe how Windows XP displays information about your hard drive.

   _____

   _____

   - What happens when you click **Show the contents of this drive**?

   _____

   _____

3. Click the **Back** button on the Standard buttons bar; the bar below the menu bar. Close the My Computer window.

4. Click **Start**, and then click **Control Panel**.

   - What categories of information are displayed in the Control Panel?

   _____

   _____

   - List the steps you would take to view information or make changes to your mouse settings.

   _____

_____

_____

_____

5. Close the Control Panel and return to the Windows XP desktop.

Review Questions

1. What steps must you take to locate the Device Manager?

_____

_____

_____

2. Using the Help and Support feature in Windows XP, locate information on installing new or updated printer drivers. How did you find the information?

_____

_____

_____

3. What Windows XP utility can you use to transfer user files and preferences from one computer to another?

_____

4. Why does Windows XP allow you to change to a Classic Start menu?

_____

_____

5. What Windows XP tool can be used to remove unused shortcuts from the desktop?

_____

9

LAB 9.4 MANAGE USER ACCOUNTS IN WINDOWS XP

Objectives

The goal of this lab is to give you experience adding and modifying user accounts via Computer Management. After completing this lab, you will be able to:

➤ Add users

➤ Reset passwords

➤ Control password policies

Materials Required

➤ Windows XP Professional

➤ Administrator account and password

Activity Background

Creating user accounts in Windows XP is easy. XP just needs a few things to get a user set: a unique username; user's full name; a description of the user (typically their title and department); and a password. Managing users can take quite a bit of administration time. Much of this time is taken up by helping users who have forgotten their passwords, or who entered their passwords incorrectly multiple times, causing Windows XP to lock their accounts. In this lab you will practice managing user accounts and passwords via Computer Management.

Estimated completion time: **30 minutes**

ACTIVITY

Your first task is to start Computer Management. Follow these steps:

1. Log on as an administrator.

2. Click **Start** on the taskbar, click **Control Panel**, and then click **Performance and Maintenance**.

3. Click **Administrative Tools** and double-click **Computer Management**. The Computer Management window appears, similar to that shown in Figure 9-2. (Another way to get to the Computer Management window is to right-click My Computer and select Manage from the shortcut menu.)

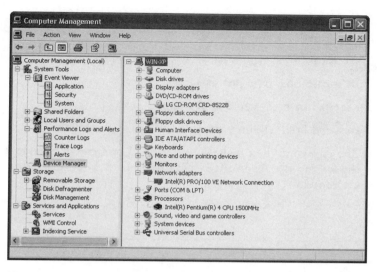

Figure 9-2   The Computer Management console

4. Click the plus sign next to **Local Users and Groups** to expand the category. Examine the Computer Management window and answer the following questions:

- Based on your knowledge of Windows XP, what two User accounts are included on a Windows XP system by default?

  _____

  _____

  _____

- Does your system contain any personal user accounts? If so, list them here:

  _____

  _____

  _____

- What user groups are included on your Windows XP system?

  _____

  _____

  _____

In Computer Management you can add and configure users on a local computer. To learn how, follow these steps:

1. From the left pane of the Local Users and Groups, click the **Users** folder to display a list of current user names.

2. Right-click **Users** and select **New User** from the shortcut window. The New User window opens.

3. In the **User name** box, type **James**.

4. In the **Full name** box, type **James Clark**.

5. In the **Description** box, type **Supervisor**.

6. In the **Password** box, type **newuser**.

7. Confirm the password, then make sure that the **User must change password at next logon** and the **Account is disabled** check boxes are cleared, and then click **Create**.

   ■ What other check box could you select?

   _____

   _____

8. Close all open windows.

When Windows XP creates a new user, that user is automatically added to the Limited group, which means the account cannot create, delete or change other accounts, make system-wide changes or install software. To give the account administrative privileges, do the following:

1. Open the Control Panel and double-click the **User Account** applet. The User Account window opens listing all accounts.

2. Click **Change an Account** and select the account for **James Clark**. The User Accounts window changes so that you can change the account.

   ■ What are the five things you can do to an account on this window?

   _____

   _____

   _____

   _____

   _____

3. Select **Change the account type**.

4. On the next window, select **Computer administrator** and click **Change Account Type**. Click **Back** on the menu bar to return to the opening window.

5. Log off your computer and log on as James Clark. List the steps you did in order to accomplish that.

_____

_____

_____

Review Questions

1. Besides adding and deleting users, what other tasks can you perform with Computer Management for Local Users and Groups?

_____

2. List the five types of Windows XP user groups created when Windows XP is first installed, and what each group can do.

_____

_____

_____

_____

_____

_____

_____

9

3. List the steps required to change the group to which an account belongs.

_____

_____

_____

4. List the steps to delete a user account.

_____

_____

_____

5. Why is it a good idea to have the user change his or her password the first time the user logs on?

_____

LAB 9.5 WINDOWS MEDIA PLAYER

Objectives

The goal of this lab is to give you experience managing Audio and Video using Windows Media Player. After completing this lab, you will be able to:

➤ Launch Windows Media Player

➤ Change Windows Media Player options

➤ Create and use a Music Playlist

Materials Required

➤ Windows XP Professional

➤ Internet Access

➤ Music CD that is not copyrighted

Activity Background

Many people enjoy playing music or videos on their computers. Windows Media Player gives you the possibility of having an entertainment center on your desktop. Windows XP Professional comes with Windows Media Player 8 which you can use to play, copy, and catalog audio and video files from your computer, CDs, DVDs, or the Internet. You can display Media Player in one of two modes: **full mode** or **skin mode**. By default, Media Player will open in skin mode.

Estimated completion time: **30 minutes**

ACTIVITY

To launch Windows Media Player, follow these steps:

1. If necessary, log on to Windows XP.

2. On the Start menu, point to **All Programs**, and then click **Windows Media Player**. The Windows Media Player opens. A sample playlist will probably open and start playing the first selection. The display area shows the default visualization.

3. On the taskbar, click **Now Playing**, if necessary, to display the current playlist. To play a song, double click on a song in the list.

Visualizations are shapes and colors that appear on the Windows Media Player window to enhance the audio while songs are playing. You can change the visualization options. Do the following:

1. Click the **Select visualization or album art button** (round button with * on it labeled in Figure 9-3), and then click **Spikes** on the drop-down list.

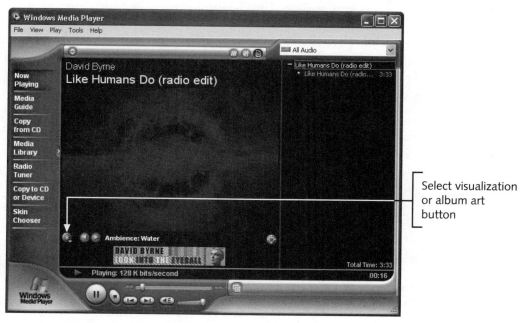

Figure 9-3   Windows Media Player window

2. Click the **Next visualization** button to move to the next Spikes options, **Spikes: Amoeba**.

3. Use the Select visualization or album art button and the Next visualization button to view other available options. List five of these options here:

_____

_____

_____

_____

Using Windows Media Player, you can browse the Internet for songs. Do the following:

1. On the taskbar, click **Media Guide**. If you are connected to the Internet, the Windows Media Web site opens.

2. Browse through the Web site to see what it has to offer.

3. On the taskbar, click **Radio Tuner**. The Radio Tuner opens with a list of featured stations displayed.

4. In the **Featured Stations** list, click through the radio stations until you find one that has a Play button.

5. Click the **Play** button to hear the station. The radio station's Web site opens in a new window in the background.

6. Describe how the Web site is set up so that you can choose what music you want to hear:

_____

_____

_____

7. Click **Close** to close the Windows Media Player window and then close the window displaying the radio station's Web site.

Those who have used Media Player and taken advantage of downloading files to their hard disk soon find out that they have accumulated hundreds of songs. Just as important as managing data files on your hard drives, you should also practice good file management of the music files you accumulate. Windows XP helps solve the problem of scrolling through endless lists of files searching for the next song you want to hear by creating playlists. A playlist is a list of digital media files, such as songs, video clips, and links to radio stations. You can create a playlist as a collection, which will allow you to play, copy, or burn it to a CD.

To create a Music Playlist and add a song to it, follow these steps:

1. Open the Windows Media Player window.

2. Click **Media Library**, and then click **New Playlist** in the upper-left part of the window. The New Playlist dialog box appears.

3. Type **MyBestSongs**, which will be a subgroup under MyPlaylists. Click **OK**. MyBestSongs is now listed under My Playlists. If you click MyBestSongs, no songs are listed.

Now you will copy two songs from a CD to your hard drive and then add one of these songs to your playlist, MyBestSongs. Do the following:

1. Insert a music CD that is not copyright protected in the CD-ROM drive; the music CD might start playing. Click **Copy from CD**. A list of songs on the CD displays in the right pane. All songs on the CD are selected for copying. Clear the check boxes next to all the songs except two songs.

2. Click **Copy Music** to copy the two selected songs to your hard drive.

3. A dialog box displays informing you that, if the CD is copy protected, you cannot proceed. Click **OK**.

4. The two selected songs are copied to your My Music folder and are also listed under Media Library. When the copying completes, click **Media Library**. The two songs are listed in the right pane.

5. Click and drag one of the songs to the **MyBestSongs** playlist under My Playlists. Your musical selection will appear in your custom playlist. Play the selection.

6. Stop the current selection from playing and close Windows Media Player.

There is a simple way to listen to songs you have put into your My Music folder. Do the following:

1. Click **Start**, **My Music**.

2. Locate the song in the folder or its subfolder and double-click the song.

   - What application launches to play the song?

Review Questions

1. Describe how visualizations are used by Windows Media Player.

2. Using Windows Media Player, is it possible to copy music files to a CD? If so, explain how you would accomplish that task.

_____

_____

3. When you first open Windows Media Player, a default mode (windows style) appears. How many other available modes are there? Explain how you change the mode in Media Player.

_____

_____

_____

4. Explain how you switch from skin mode to full mode and back again.

_____

_____

_____

SUPPORTING AND TROUBLESHOOTING WINDOWS XP

LAB 10.1 SET DISK QUOTAS

Objectives

The goal of this lab is to teach you how to set and monitor disk quotas. After completing this lab, you will be able to:

➤ Convert a logical drive from FAT to NTFS

➤ Set disk quotas for new users

➤ Monitor quota logs

➤ Identify when quotas have been exceeded

Materials Required

This lab will require the following:

➤ Windows XP Professional operating system

➤ An NTFS partition which might or might not be the partition where Windows XP is installed

Activity Background

When a system is used by more than one account or when server storage space is limited, it is often desirable to set storage limits for each user. No one account should monopolize storage space by filling up the server and preventing other users from storing data. Note, however, that you can only impose disk quotas on drives formatted with NTFS. In this lab, you will use disk quotas to limit user storage space.

Estimated completion time: **30 minutes**

ACTIVITY

In the following steps you will set very small disk quotas for all users. That way you can later easily exceed the disk quota limit and observe the results. Do the following to verify that you are using an NTFS file system:

1. Log on as an administrator.

2. Using Windows Explorer, right-click drive **C:** (or another logical drive designated by your instructor) and select **Properties** on the shortcut menu. The Local Disk (C:) Properties window appears. On the **General** tab, verify that the drive is using the NTFS file system.

If you currently have the FAT32 file system and need to convert to NTFS, follow the steps below, and then begin again with step 1 above. If you already have NTFS, skip the next three steps.

1. Open a command prompt window.

2. In the command prompt window, type: **convert C: /fs:ntfs**. (If necessary, substitute the drive letter for another logical drive in the command line as specified by your instructor.)

3. After the command executes, reboot your computer for the conversion to NTFS to complete.

To enable Disk Quotas, do the following:

1. In the Disk Properties window, click the **Quota** tab.

2. Select the **Enable quota management** check box. This option allows you to set and change quotas.

3. Select the **Deny disk space to users exceeding quota limit** check box. This option prevents a user from using more disk space after using up his or her quota.

4. Verify that the **Limit disk space to** option button is selected, and that **1** appears in the text box to the right. Then select **MB** in the drop-down list. This sets the disk quota to 1 MB of storage space.

5. Click the **Set warning level to** text box, type **500** and then verify that **KB** is displayed in the text box to the right. This ensures that users will receive warnings once they have used 500 KB of disk space.

6. Select **Log event when a user exceeds their quota limit**. This ensures that a record will be made when a user exceeds the quota limit.

7. Select **Log event when a user exceeds their warning level**. This ensures that a record will be made when a user reaches his warning limit. (You will be able to view the records from the Disk Properties window.)

8. Click **OK** to apply the new settings and close the Disk Properties window.

Follow these steps to exceed the quota limits you have just set:

1. Using what you learned in Lab 9.4, create a new restricted user called **Quota Test**.

2. Create a directory called **Quota** in the root of the NTFS drive.

3. Log out as an administrator, and log in as **Quota Test**.

4. Open the **Windows** or **WINNT** folder in Explorer and click **Show Files**. One at a time, copy (*do not cut*) all .gif and .bmp files in the Windows or WINNT folder and paste them into the Quota folder.

   - What happens when you exceed the warning level and then the storage quota? Record what happens here.

   _____

   _____

5. Log out as the Quota Test user.

Because of the options you checked when you created the disk quota, logs were created when you exceeded the warning level and the storage quota. To view these quota logs, follow these steps:

1. Log in as an administrator.

2. Open the NTFS Disk Properties window, click the **Quota** tab, and then click the **Quota Entries** button. The Quota Entries window opens, displaying the quota log of quota entries for certain events.

   - What types of information are displayed for each entry?

   _____

   _____

3. Double-click an entry for Quota Test. The Quota Settings window for that user opens. Note that in this window you can raise or lower the user's disk quotas.

4. Check the Quota Settings for each entry, and record any entry for which you were unable to adjust settings.

   _____

   _____

Review Questions

1. How would you set up disk quotas on a drive formatted with FAT32?

   _____

   _____

2. Why might you wish to impose disk quotas?

   _____

   _____

3. What option must be checked in order to specify a warning level?

   _____

   _____

4. What options must be selected in order to prevent a user from exceeding her quota?

_____

_____

5. Explain how to monitor and change disk quotas.

_____

_____

LAB 10.2 USE ENCRYPTION

Objectives

The goal of this lab is to help you work with encryption and observe the effects of trying to use an encrypted file without permission. After completing this lab, you will be able to:

➤ Encrypt a directory

➤ Save files to the encrypted directory

➤ Access the encrypted files as a different user

10

Materials Required

This lab will require the following:

➤ Windows XP Professional operating system

➤ An NTFS partition which might or might not be the partition where Windows XP is installed

➤ Blank floppy disk

Activity Background

Despite your best efforts, unauthorized users might sometimes gain access to sensitive files. To protect these files from such a security breach, you can use file encryption, which prevents unauthorized users from actually being able to view files, even if they do manage to gain access to them. You can encrypt individual files or entire directories. As with disk quotas, you can only use file encryption on NTFS drives. The FAT file systems do not support file encryption. In this lab, you will create and encrypt an entire directory and then create a test file in that encrypted directory.

Estimated completion time: **30 minutes**

ACTIVITY

Follow these steps to create an encrypted directory and a test file within that directory:

1. Log on as an administrator.

2. Create a directory in the NTFS root called **Encrypt**.

3. Right-click the **Encrypt** folder, and then click **Properties**. The Folder Properties dialog box opens.

4. Click the **Advanced** button to open the Advanced Attributes window.

5. In the Advanced Attributes window, check the **Encrypt contents to secure data** option to choose to encrypt the contents of the Encrypt folder.

6. Click **OK** to apply the settings and close the Advanced Attributes window. You return to the Encrypt Properties window.

7. Click **OK** to apply encryption.

8. Double-click the **Encrypt** folder to open it.

9. Select the **Encrypt** folder, point to **File** on the menu bar, point to **New**, and click **Text Document**. Double-click the **New Text Document** and type **This file is encrypted**. Close the file, saving it as **Secure.txt**.

Follow these steps to see the effects of encrypting a file in Windows:

1. Double-click **Secure.txt** in the Encrypt folder and record what happens.

_____

2. Log out as an administrator, and log back in as a different user.

3. Double-click **Secure.txt** in the Encrypt folder and record the results.

_____

_____

4. Copy **Secure.txt** to the **Quota** folder and record the results.

_____

5. Log out and then log back in as an administrator.

6. Copy **Secure.txt** to the **Quota** folder and record the results.

_____

7. Insert a blank formatted floppy disk and copy **Secure.txt** to drive A: and record the results.

8. Log out and then log back in as the previous user.

9. Double-click **Secure.txt** in the **Quota** folder and record the results.

_____

10. Double-click **Secure.txt** in drive A: and record the results.

_____

_____

11. Right-click the **Secure.txt** file located on drive A: and then click **Properties** on the shortcut menu. The file's Properties window opens. Is there an **Advanced** button?

_____

12. Right-click the **Secure.txt** file located in the Quota directory and then click **Properties** on the shortcut menu. The file's Properties window opens.

13. Click the **Advanced** button, deselect the **Encrypt contents to secure data** check box, and then click **OK**. Record the results.

_____

_____

Review Questions

1. Which file system must be used to enable encryption?

_____

2. How would you encrypt a single file?

_____

3. What happens when an unauthorized user tries to open an encrypted file?

_____

_____

4. What happens when an unauthorized user tries to unencrypt a file?

_____

_____

5. What happens to an encrypted file that is removed from a NTFS partition?

_____

_____

LAB 10.3 RESTORE THE SYSTEM STATE

Objectives

The goal of this lab is to help you restore the system state on a Windows XP computer. After completing this lab, you will be able to:

➤ Create a restore point using System Restore

➤ Change system settings

➤ Restore the system state using the restore point you created

Materials Required

This lab will require the following:

➤ Windows XP Professional operating system

Activity Background

The System Restore tool in Windows XP enables you to restore the system to the time a snapshot, called a restore point, was taken of the system state. The settings recorded in a restore point include system settings and configurations, and files necessary for a successful boot. When the system state is restored to a restore point, user data on the hard drive is not affected, but software and hardware might be affected. Restore points are useful if, for example, something goes wrong with a software or hardware installation. In this lab you will create a restore point, make changes to system settings, and then use the restore point to restore the system state.

Estimated completion time: **30 minutes**

ACTIVITY

To use the System Restore tool to create a restore point, follow these steps:

1. On the Start menu, point to **All Programs**, point to **Accessories**, point to **System Tools**, and then click **System Restore**.

2. The System Restore window appears, giving you two choices: Restore my computer to an earlier time and Create a restore point. The first option restores your computer to an existing restore point. Read the information on the left side of the window and answer these questions:

   - Can changes made by System Restore be undone? What type of data does System Restore leave unaffected?

   _____

   - What is the term for the restore points that the system creates automatically?

   _____

   - As you've read, it's helpful to create a restore point before you install software or hardware. In what other situations might you want to create a restore point?

   _____

   _____

3. Click the **Create a restore point** option button and click the **Next** button.

4. In the next window, type a description of the restore point. The description should be something that makes it easy to identify the restore point at a later time such as: Restore [*today's date*].

5. Click the **Create** button.

6. A message appears indicating that the restore point was created. The date, time, and name of the restore point are also shown. Click the **Close** button.

Next, you'll make two changes to the system: uninstalling a Windows component and changing display settings. First, you will uninstall the MSN (Microsoft Network) Explorer component. (If this is currently not installed, then ask your instructor which Windows component you should uninstall instead.)

1. From the Control Panel, double-click the **Add or Remove Programs** icon.

2. The Add or Remove Programs window appears. To see a list of Windows components, click the **Add/Remove Windows Components** icon.

10

3. The Add or Remove Programs window remains open, and the Windows Components Wizard launches. In the list box in the middle of the screen, components that are checked are currently installed. Scroll down until you see the **MSN Explorer** component and then click the check box next to its name.

4. A message appears asking whether you want to uninstall this component. Click **Yes** to continue.

5. The message disappears, and the MSN Explorer check box is deselected. Click **Next** to continue.

6. A progress window indicates the component the system is currently uninstalling. When the process is complete, a message appears indicating that you have completed the Windows Components Wizard. Click **Finish**.

7. Click **Close** in the Add or Remove Programs window.

Next, you will change some display settings:

1. From the Control Panel, switch to Classic View, and then double-click the **Display** icon.

2. The Display Properties window appears. Click the **Desktop** tab.

3. In the Background list, click a background and then click the **OK** button.

4. The Display Properties window closes. Close the Control Panel window. Notice that the background has changed to the one you selected.

Follow these steps to use the restore point you created to restore the system state:

1. Open the System Restore tool as specified earlier in this lab.

2. Click the **Restore my computer to an earlier time** option button and click **Next**.

3. A window appears showing a calendar of the current month, with the current date highlighted, and all dates on which restore points were made shown in bold. Answer these questions:

   ■ How many restore points were created in the current month?

   _____

   ■ Click each bold date and list the reasons why the restore points were made.

   _____

   _____

   _____

4. Click the current date. In the list on the right, click the name of the restore point you created earlier in the lab, and then click **Next**.

5. A confirmation screen appears. Click **Next** to continue.

   ■ Describe what happens when you click the Next button.

   _____

   _____

   _____

6. After the system restarts, click your login name to return to the Windows XP desktop. A message appears indicating that the restoration is complete. Click **OK**.

   ■ Did the display settings change back to their original settings?

   _____

7. Access the Windows Components Wizard as you did earlier in this lab.

   ■ Is MSN Explorer installed?

   _____

Review Questions

1. List three situations in which you might want to create a restore point.

   _____

   _____

2. What types of restore points are created by the system, and what types are created by the user?

   _____

   _____

3. How often does the system automatically create restore points?

   _____

   _____

4. Can more than one restore point be made on a specific date?

   _____

5. Which of your changes was reversed when you used the restore point to restore the system state, and which change was not reversed? Explain why you think this happened.

_____

_____

_____

Lab 10.4 Install Recovery Console as an Option on the Startup Menu

Objectives

The goal of this lab is to help you install the Recovery Console as a startup option. After completing this lab, you will be able to:

➤ Install the Recovery Console

➤ Open the Recovery Console from the Startup Menu

Materials Required

This lab will require the following:

➤ Windows XP Professional operating system

➤ Windows XP Professional installation CD or installation files at another location accessible by a drive letter, as specified by your instructor.

Activity Background

The Recovery Console tool in Windows XP allows you to start the computer when other startup and recovery options, such as System Restore, safe mode, and the ASR (Automated System Recovery) process, do not work. In the Recovery Console, you can use a limited group of DOS-like commands to format a hard drive, copy files from a floppy disk or CD to the hard drive, start and stop certain system processes, and perform other administrative tasks and troubleshooting tasks. If the Recovery Console is not installed on your computer, you'll have to run it from the Windows XP installation CD. This lab shows you how to install the Recovery Console on your Windows XP computer so that it appears as an option when the computer starts up.

Estimated completion time: **30 minutes**

ACTIVITY

Follow these steps to install the Recovery Console as a startup option:

1. Insert the Windows XP installation CD into your CD-ROM drive. If the Autorun feature launches, close it. If your instructor has given you an alternate location for the installation files, what is the drive letter required to access them?

---

2. Click the **Start** button on the taskbar, and then click **Run**. The Run dialog box opens.

3. Type **cmd** and then click **OK**. A command window opens.

4. To switch to your CD-ROM drive (or other drive holding the installation files), type the drive letter followed by a colon and then press **Enter**.

5. You will now execute the Windows XP setup program stored on this drive. The path to the program might vary depending on the release of Windows XP you are using. Here are three possibilities. Try each one until you locate and execute the program:

   - Type **\i386\winnt32.exe /cmdcons** and then press **Enter**.
   - Type **\english\winxp\pro\i386\winnt32.exe /cmdcons** and press **Enter**.
   - Type **\english\winxp\home\i386\winnt32.exe /cmdcons** and press **Enter**.
   - Which command launched the setup program?

---

6. A message appears asking if you want to install the Recovery Console. Click **Yes** to continue.

7. The Windows Setup window opens and shows that Setup is checking for updates. When the update check completes, a progress indicator appears. When the installation is complete, a message appears indicating that the Recovery Console was successfully installed. Click **OK** to continue.

8. Restart your computer.

10

9. When the startup menu appears, select **Microsoft Recovery Console** and press **Enter**. What do you see when the Recovery Console launches?

_____

_____

_____

_____

10. Type **1** (to choose to log on to your Windows installation) and then press **Enter**.

11. When prompted, type the administrator password for your computer and press **Enter**.

12. Type **help** and then press **Enter** to see a list of commands available in the Recovery Console.

13. Type **Exit** to close the Recovery Console and restart the computer.

Review Questions

1. What is the advantage of being able to access the Recovery Console from your hard drive instead of from the CD drive?

_____

_____

2. What is another way to exit the Recovery Console without logging on to your Windows installation?

_____

3. In the Recovery Console, what command deletes a directory? What command can you use to list services that are running?

_____

4. Name at least two tasks that you think you might not be able to complete from within the Recovery Console.

_____

_____

_____

5. Why is an administrator password needed for access to the Recovery Console?

_____

6. Why should you use the Recovery Console only after other tools have failed?

_____

_____

LAB 10.5 USE RECOVERY CONSOLE TO COPY FILES

Objectives

The goal of this lab is to help you learn how to copy files using the Recovery Console. After completing this lab, you will be able to:

➤ Copy files from a floppy disk to your hard drive using the Recovery Console

Materials Required

This lab will require the following:

➤ Windows XP operating system

➤ Floppy disk

Activity Background

The Windows XP Recovery Console is useful when you need to restore system files after they have been corrupted (perhaps by a virus) or accidentally deleted from the hard drive. In this lab, you will use the Recovery Console (which you installed in Lab 10.4) to restore a system file, System.ini, from a floppy disk. (Windows XP does not need this file to boot; it is included in Windows XP to allow for backward compatibility with older Windows software.)

Estimated completion time: **30 minutes**

ACTIVITY

Follow these steps to copy the file System.ini to a floppy disk and then copy it from the floppy to the hard drive using the Recovery Console:

1. Insert the floppy disk in the floppy drive.

2. Using Windows Explorer, locate the file **System.ini** (which is usually found in the C:\Windows folder).

10

3. Copy the file **System.ini** to the floppy disk and then eject the floppy disk from the drive.

4. Locate **System.ini** on your hard drive again and rename it as **System.old**. When prompted, click **Yes** to confirm that you want to rename the file.

5. Restart the computer again, this time choosing the **Recovery Console**.

6. Insert the floppy disk in the floppy disk drive. In the Recovery Console, log on using the Administrator password and type this command: **copy a:\ system.ini c:\windows\system.ini**. This command will copy System.ini from the floppy disk to its original location (C:\Windows).

7. Press **Enter**. What message does Recovery Console display?

_____

8. If C:\Windows is not the active directory, change to that directory and then use the **dir** command to view the contents of the directory. Verify that System.ini was copied to this directory. You might have to use the spacebar to scroll down.

9. Exit the Recovery Console and restart the computer again.

Review Questions

1. You could have used the Recovery Console to rename the System.old file instead of copying the original version from the floppy disk. What command would you have used to perform this task?

_____

_____

2. Assume you moved the System file to the My Documents folder. What command would you use in the Recovery Console to move it back to the C:\Windows folder?

_____

_____

3. When might it be useful to be able to copy files from a CD to the hard drive using the Recovery Console?

_____

_____

4. Why does Windows XP include the System.ini file?

_____

_____

5. When might you want to use Recovery Console to copy files from the hard drive to a floppy disk?

_____

_____

LAB 10.6 MONITOR THE MEMORY COUNTER

Objectives

The goal of this lab is to help you monitor the memory counter to investigate a possible memory shortage. After completing this lab, you will be able to:

➤ Add memory counters to System Monitor

➤ Defragment your hard drive

➤ Analyze memory usage during defragmentation

Materials Required

This lab will require the following:

➤ Windows XP Professional operating system

Activity Background

In Windows XP, you can use the System Monitor utility to observe system performance. You can add counters to Windows XP in order to collect data about the system. In this activity, you will add and monitor counters that measure available memory, memory paging, and the read and write times for disk access. These counters can help you determine how much of the total system resources a particular process (such as defragmenting the hard drive) is using.

> Estimated completion time: **30 minutes**

ACTIVITY

Follow these steps to add counters to System Monitor:

1. Click **Start** on the task bar, point to **All Programs**, point to **Administrative Tools** and then click **Performance**. (If Administrative Tools does not appear on your All Programs menu, you need to add it. To do this, right-click the Start menu, click Properties, click the Start menu tab on the Properties window, click Customize, click the Advanced tab in the Customize window, scroll down to System Administrative tools, click Display on the All Programs menu,

and then click OK in both windows. After adding Administrative Tools to the All Programs menu, begin again with Step 1.)

2. The Performance console opens. Make sure that System Monitor is selected in the left pane. In the right pane, right-click in the blank area, and then click **Add Counters** in the shortcut menu.

3. The Add Counters window opens. In the Performance object drop-down list, click the **Memory** object. Scroll down the **Select counters from list** scroll box, click the **Available Bytes** counter and then click the **Add** button. This adds the selected counter (Available Bytes) to the Performance console.

4. Click the **Explain** button and record the explanation of the selected counter (Available Bytes) here:

5. Repeat step 3 to add the **Pages/sec** counter for the Memory object, the **Processor Time** counter for the Processor object, and the **Disk Read Time** and **Disk Write Time** counters for the Physical Disk object. Record the explanations of each of these counters here:

6. Click the **Close** button in the Add Counters window. You return to the Performance Console, where the counters you added are listed in the right pane. Look in the Color column and make sure each counter is monitored using a different color. (If you find any of the colors difficult to read, you can change them. To change the color of the line indicating a particular counter, left-click the counter once to select it, then right-click it, select **Properties** from the shortcut menu, click a color in the Color drop-down list on the Properties window, and then click **OK**.)

Follow these steps to monitor the counters for two different applications:

1. With the Performance window still open, open the **Notepad** application. Wait a few seconds, and then close it again.

2. In the Performance window, click the **Freeze Display** button (a red circle with a white x) and then click the highlight button (a light bulb). Use the up and down arrows to move between counters in the list below the performance display.

- How did the display change when you highlighted a particular counter?

  _____

  _____

- Which resources did Notepad use primarily? What other resources did it use?

  _____

  _____

3. Click **Start** on the taskbar, point to **All Programs**, point to **Administrative Tools**, and then click **Computer Management**.

4. The Computer Management console opens. Under "Storage" in the left pane, click **Disk Defragmenter** and then click **Analyze** in the right pane. What message appears when the analysis is complete?

  _____

  _____

5. Click **Close** to close the message window.

6. Close the Computer Management console and return to the Performance window. Click the **Freeze Display** button and the highlight button as you did for Notepad. Which resources did Disk Defragmenter use primarily? Which other resources did it use?

  _____

  _____

Review Questions

1. Did Notepad and Disk Defragmenter use the same resources? Why do you think this is?

  _____

  _____

2. How do you think the performance display might have changed if both applications had been open at once?

  _____

  _____

3. What are some other counters that could be useful for monitoring system performance?

_____

_____

4. What system resources that you were monitoring might have been used if you had actually proceeded to defragment your hard drive?

_____

_____

5. If you were considering whether to upgrade your system's memory or processor, which counters would you choose to monitor and why? How would you decide whether you needed to make the upgrade or not?

_____

_____

_____

_____

LAB 10.7 CRITICAL THINKING: SABOTAGE AND REPAIR WINDOWS XP

Objectives

The goal of this lab is to learn to troubleshoot Windows XP by repairing a sabotaged system.

Materials Required

This lab will require the following:

➤ Windows XP Professional on a PC designated for a sabotage

➤ Access to the Windows XP Professional Installation CD or the Windows XP Professional setup files stored in another location

➤ Workgroup of 2-4 students

Activity Background

You have learned about several tools and methods that you can use to recover Windows XP when it fails. This lab gives you the opportunity to use these skills in a troubleshooting situation. Your group will sabotage another group's system, while that group sabotages your system. Then your group will repair its own system.

Estimated completion time: **45 minutes**

ACTIVITY

1. If your system's hard drive contains important data, back up that data to another media. Is there anything else you would like to back up before the system is sabotaged by another group?

2. Trade systems with another group and sabotage the other group's system while they sabotage your system. Do one thing that will cause the system to fail to boot, give errors after the boot, or prevent a device or application from working. The following list offers some sabotage suggestions. Windows XP has several features that are designed to prevent sabotage, so you might find it a little challenging to actually prevent it from booting by deleting or renaming system files. Do something included in this list, or think of another option. (Do *not* alter the hardware.)

   ■ Find a system file in the root directory that is required to boot the computer, and either rename it or move it to a different directory. (Don't delete the file.)

   ■ Using the Registry Editor, regedit.exe, delete several important keys or values in the registry.

   ■ Locate important system files in the \Windows directory and either rename them or move them to another directory.

   ■ Put a corrupted program file in the folder that will cause the program to automatically launch at startup. Note the name of that program file and folder here:

   ■ Use display settings that are not readable, such as black text on a black background.

   ■ Disable a critical device driver.

3. Reboot the system and verify that a problem exists.

4. How did you sabotage the other team's system?

5. Return to your system and troubleshoot it.

6. Describe the problem as the user would describe it to you if you were working at a Help desk.

_____

_____

7. What is your first guess as to the source of the problem?

_____

8. List the steps you took in the troubleshooting process.

_____

_____

_____

_____

_____

_____

9. How did you finally solve the problem and return the system to good working order?

_____

_____

Review Questions

1. What would you do differently the next time you encountered the same symptoms?

_____

2. What Windows utilities did you use or could you have used to solve the problem?

_____

3. In a real-life situation, what might cause this problem to happen? List three possible causes.

_____

_____

_____

4. If you were the PC support technician responsible for this computer in an office environment, what could you do to prevent this problem from happening in the future, or limit its impact on users if it did happen?

_____

10

SUPPORTING HARD DRIVES

Lab 11.1 Perform Hard Drive Routine Maintenance

Objectives

The goal of this lab is to help you perform routine maintenance on a hard drive. After completing this lab, you will be able to:

➤ Delete unneeded files on a hard drive

➤ Defragment a hard drive

➤ Scan a hard drive for errors

Materials Required

This lab will require the following:

➤ Windows 98 operating system

Activity Background

To ensure that your hard drive operates in peak condition, you should regularly perform some routine maintenance tasks. For starters, you need to ensure that your hard drive includes enough unused space (which it requires in order to operate efficiently). In other words, you should regularly remove unnecessary files from the drive.

In addition, files on a hard drive sometimes become fragmented over time; defragmenting the drive can improve performance. Other routine maintenance tasks include scanning the hard drive for errors and repairing them. In this lab you will learn about three tools that you can use to perform important disk maintenance tasks. You should use these tools regularly, in the order given in this lab, to keep your hard drive error-free and performing well.

Estimated completion time: **30 minutes**

Follow these steps to delete unnecessary files on your hard drive:

1. Close all open applications.

2. Click **Start** on the taskbar, point to **Programs**, point to **Accessories**, point to **System Tools**, and then click **Disk Cleanup**.

3. The Select Drive dialog box appears. Select the drive that you want to clean up on the drop-down menu and click **OK**. The Select Drive dialog box closes.

4. The Disk Cleanup dialog box opens. Here you need to select the types of files you want Disk Cleanup to delete. Select all of the possible options. Depending on your system, these options might include Downloaded Program Files, Recycle Bin, Temporary files and Temporary Internet file.

- How much disk space does each group of files take up?

_____

_____

- Based on information given on the Disk Cleanup dialog box, what is the purpose of each group of files?

_____

_____

_____

_____

- What is the total amount of disk space you would gain by deleting these files?

_____

5. Click **OK** to delete the selected groups of files.

6. When asked to confirm the deletion, click **Yes**. The Disk Cleanup dialog box closes, and a progress indicator appears while the cleanup is underway. The progress indicator closes when cleanup is complete, returning you to the desktop.

The next step in routine maintenance is to use ScanDisk to examine the hard drive and repair errors. Follow these steps:

1. Close all open applications.

2. Click **Start** on the taskbar, point to **Programs**, point to **Accessories**, point to **System Tools**, and then click **ScanDisk**. The ScanDisk window opens.

3. ScanDisk offers two options, Standard and Thorough. The Standard option checks for errors in files and repairs them. The Thorough option does the same, and in addition, scans the hard drive surface for problems that might cause future errors. If segments of the disk surface appear to be damaged in some way, ScanDisk marks that segment so it won't be used in the future. The Thorough option takes longer, but you should use it in order to get the best benefit from ScanDisk. Select **Thorough** and click **Start**.

4. If ScanDisk finds an error, it asks if you want to repair it. Click **OK** to repair any errors.

5. When the process is completed, ScanDisk reports what it found and corrected. Click **Close** in the report window. What errors, if any, did ScanDisk find?

_____

_____

_____

The last step in routine hard drive maintenance is to use the Disk Defragmenter tool to locate fragmented files and rewrite them to the hard drive in contiguous segments. Follow these steps:

1. Close all open applications.

2. Click **Start**, point to **Programs**, point to **Accessories**, point to **System Tools**, and then click **Disk Defragmenter**. The Disk Defragmenter window opens.

3. Select the drive you want to defragment and click **OK**.

4. Disk Defragmenter begins defragmenting the drive, displaying a progress indicator as it works. Click **Show Details** to expand Disk Defragmenter to a full screen. The Details view of Disk Defragmenter allows you to observe a graphical representation of the defragmentation process.

5. Open Microsoft Word or another program, use the space below to describe what happens, and then close the program and allow Disk Defragmenter to continue.

_____

_____

_____

_____

6. When defragmentation is complete, you are asked if you want to exit Disk Defragmenter. Click **Yes**.

Note that fully defragmenting your hard drive can take half an hour or more, depending on how fragmented your drive is. If you do not have time to wait, you can stop the process by clicking Stop and then clicking Exit on the confirmation dialog box.

Additional Activity (additional 30 minutes)

Using Windows 2000 or Windows XP, perform the following hard drive routine maintenance tasks, which are all accomplished using the Properties window of drive C:

■ Use Disk Cleanup on the General tab of the drive Properties window to delete unnecessary files on your hard drive.

- Use the Error-checking pane under the Tools tab of the drive Properties window to check the volume for errors.
- Use the Defragmentation pane under the Tools tab of the drive Properties window to defragment files on the volume.

To access the drive Properties window, using Windows Explorer, right-click the drive and select Properties from the shortcut menu.

Review Questions

1. Why do you think you need to begin your hard disk maintenance chores with Disk Cleanup?

   _____

2. Why do you think you should finish with Disk Defragmenter?

   _____

3. What type of information does the Details view of Disk Defragmenter display?

   _____

   _____

4. What happened when you tried to run another program while Disk Defragmenter was running? Why do you think this happened?

   _____

   _____

   _____

5. What is the disadvantage of deleting temporary Internet files?

   _____

   _____

11

LAB 11.2 BACK UP AND RESTORE FILES IN WINDOWS 2000/XP

Objectives

The goal of this lab is to help you use the Windows 2000 Backup and Recovery Tools to backup and recover lost files. After completing this lab, you will be able to:

➤ Back up files

➤ Delete files

➤ Recover deleted files

Materials Required

This lab will require the following:

➤ Windows 2000 or Windows XP operating system

Activity Background

Windows 2000/XP provides the Windows 2000/XP Backup and Recovery Tools to help you safeguard data in Windows system files. Using these tools, you can back up a single file or even an entire drive from either the local or remote computer. Backups, compressed into a single file, can be saved to a location of your choice, without the need for a dedicated backup device such as a tape drive. In this lab, you will back up, delete, and restore data files using the Windows 2000/XP Backup and Recovery Tools.

Estimated completion time: **45 minutes**

ACTIVITY

Follow these steps to select the files or folders that you wish to back up:

1. Log on to an account that is part of the Power Users group.

2. Create the folders **C:\Backups** and **C:\BackMeUp** and then create several text files in the C:\BackMeUp folder.

3. Click **Start** on the taskbar, point to **Programs** (for Windows XP, **All Programs**), point to **Accessories**, point to **System Tools**, and then click **Backup**. For Windows XP, click **Advanced Mode**. The Windows 2000/XP Backup and Recovery Tools utility opens. What three options are available on the Welcome tab?

_____

_____

_____

4. Click the **Backup** tab and then in the left pane, click the plus sign next to drive C:. The right pane displays all the items that you can back up.

5. First, you will back up an entire folder. Click the box beside the **BackMeUp** folder in the right pane. This indicates that you want to back up the entire contents of that folder.

6. Instruct the system to back up the entire contents of the Documents and Settings folder. Explain how you performed this task.

_____

_____

_____

7. In addition to the folders you just selected for backup, you will select a single file, DSKProbe.exe, for backup. Double-click the **Program Files** folder in the right pane. The Program Files folder is highlighted in the left pane and its contents are displayed in the right pane.

8. Double-click the **Support Tools** folder in either pane. The contents of the Support Tools folder are displayed in the right pane.

9. Check the box next to **DSKProbe.exe**. This indicates that you want to back up this file. (If Support Tools has not been installed on your PC, in this lab you can substitute Notepad.exe in the C:\Windows folder in place of DSKProbe.exe.)

10. In the **Backup media or file name** field, type **C:\Backups\Lab11.bkf**. This specifies the name and location of the backup file you will create.

Follow these steps to start the backup process:

1. Click **Start Backup** on the Backup tab. The Backup Job Information dialog box opens. Notice that the Backup description text box displays date and time information about this backup. This information will appear later to help you identify the backup during a recovery process. If you are ever in a situation where you need to perform many backup operations (and therefore have to keep track of multiple backup sets), you should always use this field to describe the files contained in this set. Alternately, you might wish to keep a backup log book and refer to an entry number in the log book that describes in detail what is contained in this backup set. Because this is your initial backup, you can ignore the other sections of the dialog box and click **Start Backup**.

2. The Backup Schedule dialog box briefly opens and then closes. Next, the Backup Progress dialog box opens. Quickly click **Cancel** in this dialog box.

3. The Backup dialog box opens and displays a message asking if you wish to complete the backup. Click the title bar of the Backup dialog box and drag it

11

aside so that you can view the Backup Progress dialog box. Answer these questions about the Backup Progress dialog box:

- What three things are provided to give you an idea of how the backup is progressing?

  _____

  _____

  _____

- Can you tell how many files must be backed up?

  _____

- Can you tell which files have already been completed or are currently being processed?

  _____

- What information continues to change even when the backup process is paused?

  _____

4. Click **Yes** in the Backup dialog box to indicate that you wish to continue the backup and watch as the backup process completes.

5. When the backup is complete, click **Report** on the Backup Progress dialog box to open the Backup Log in Notepad.

6. Print and examine the report. What errors and causes are reported?

   _____

   _____

Follow these steps to delete files and observe the effects:

1. Log off and log on as a different user and then right-click the **Recycle Bin** on the desktop. Select **Empty Recycle Bin** from the shortcut menu. Click **Yes** to confirm that you want to empty the Recycle Bin.

2. Open a command window. At the command prompt, type **DEL C:\BackMeUp*.***, and then press **Enter** to delete all files in the C:\BackMeUp directory. Confirm the deletion when prompted. Close the command window.

3. Delete **DSKProbe.exe** in the \Programs Files\Support Tools folder using Windows Explorer.

4. Double-click the **Recycle Bin** and note which files are displayed.

   - Of the files that you deleted, which ones are not displayed in the Recycle Bin?

     _____

     _____

   - Why do you think these files are missing?

     _____

     _____

   - Of the files that you deleted, which files can you restore without using your backups and why?

     _____

     _____

5. Empty the Recycle Bin again and then, using Windows Explorer, look for your text files in C:\BackMeUp to confirm that they are gone.

6. Click **Start** on the taskbar, point to **Programs**, point to **Windows 2000 Support Tools**, point to **Tools**, and then click **DSKProbe.exe**. Record the results below and then click **Cancel** to close the dialog box.

   _____

   _____

Follow these steps to restore the deleted files:

1. Log off and log on as an administrator. (Power Users do not have permission to restore files.)

2. Click **Start** on the taskbar, point to **Programs**, point to **Accessories**, point to **System Tools**, and then click **Backup**. The Backup window opens.

3. Click the **Restore** tab. In the left pane, click the plus sign to expand the file symbol and then expand the **Media Created *Date and Time*** symbol. Now attempt to expand the "**?**" folder on drive C:. This opens the Backup File Name dialog box.

4. In the Backup File Name dialog box, click **Browse**.

5. Select **Lab11.bkf** from the **C:\Backups** folder and then click **Open**. The Select File to Catalog dialog box closes and the Backup Filename dialog box opens with the Operations Status dialog box beneath it.

11

6. Click **OK** on the Backup Filename dialog box. The Operations Status dialog box, which appeared previously, closes when the cataloging process is completed. Your backup will appear in the left pane of the Restore tab.

7. To restore files and folders, select the necessary check boxes and then click **Start Restore**. Do you think you could choose to restore only part of the information? If so how?

_____

_____

8. The Confirm Restore dialog box opens. Click **OK** to continue.

9. The Enter Backup Filename dialog box opens and displays your backup file. Click **OK** to continue.

10. The Restore Progress dialog box opens. When the restore operation is complete, click **Close** to exit the Restore Progress dialog box.

11. To confirm that the restore operation is complete, look for your text files and launch **DSKProbe.exe** from the Start menu.

CRITICAL THINKING ACTIVITY (additional 15 minutes)

Assign a Power User to a specific group (not the Administrators group), that will result in a reduction in the errors you encountered during the backup. Log in as this user and perform a backup called **Lab11b.bkf**, and then view and print the backup file. Are the members of the group to which you assigned the Power User allowed to restore files? How could you tell?

_____

_____

_____

Review Questions

1. Is it more important to back up Windows 2000/XP system files or data files? Why?

_____

_____

2. What is the Start menu shortcut for launching Windows 2000/XP Backup and Restore Tools?

_____

3. What feature (or features) do the Windows 2000/XP Backup and Restore Tools provide to help you if you are unfamiliar with the backup/restore process?

_____

_____

4. What will the Backup Job Information dialog box allow you to define? Why is this useful?

_____

_____

_____

5. If time were a factor when restoring critical data files, what could you specify (or decline to specify) in the left pane of the Restore tab to speed up the restoration?

_____

_____

LAB 11.3 RESEARCH DATA RECOVERY SERVICES

Objectives

The goal of this lab is to help you research data recovery services. After completing this lab, you will be able to:

➤ Find tips on how to make recovery services less necessary

➤ Explain how to minimize data loss

➤ Describe some recovery options

Materials Required

This lab will require the following:

➤ Internet access

Activity Background

You've probably experienced the feeling that comes with accidentally deleting or over-writing an important file. To make matters worse, you probably couldn't replace the file unless you had backed it up previously. Now imagine if the lost file consisted of financial information that could affect the success or failure of a business employing one hundred employees, or if the lost file contained a creative work that took months to produce. You would certainly try to recover the data yourself, but if you were unable to, you might decide to seek the help of a professional data recovery service. In this lab, you will research sites offering such services.

Estimated completion time: **45 minutes**

ACTIVITY

Use your favorite search engine to research data recovery services. Alternately, search these Web sites and answer the following questions:

➤ *www.datarecoveryclinic.com*

➤ *www.savemyfiles.com*

➤ *www.drivesavers.com*

➤ *www.adv-data.com*

➤ *www.atl-datarecovery.com*

1. Name two Web sites that offer do-it-yourself data recovery options in addition to professional recovery services.

   atL-datarecovery

2. Give an example of a service that offers recovery of data in a Linux operating environment.

   cherry systems.

3. Give two examples of services that recover data from striped sets or volume sets.

   Data recovery clinic

4. From what type or types of media can files be recovered? Circle the correct answer(s):

   a. Tape
   b. CD-ROM
   c. Zip disk
   d. Floppy disk
   e. Hard disk

5. Give two examples of companies that will not charge you if they are unable to recover your important data.

   Adv

   Data recovery.

6. List two general levels of turn-around time for data recovery.

   Save my files 3days.

   1-2 days drive saver.

7. What measures are taken when recovering ultra-sensitive (secure) data?

   Limited access

   confidentiality statements.

   stored in GSA safe.

8. Besides natural disaster and mechanical failure, what are four other common causes of data loss?

   human error

   software corruption

   Viruses

   Power loss

9. If you learn that you have lost data on drive D:, what things should you absolutely not do? Circle the correct answer(s):

   a. Install recovery software on Drive C:
   b. Defragment Drive D:
   c. Restore objects in the Recycle Bin
   d. Install recovery software on Drive D:

11

10. Give two examples of services designed to proactively prevent data loss.

offsite data storage.

virus ~~safe~~ protection services.

11. List some reasons why it might be impossible to recover some data.

Physical damage.

too cheap.

12. Will you always be able to recover all the data that you lose? Why or why not?

no, if the harddrive is physically damaged you may get the
data back you may not.

13. Why is it important to perform hard drive data recovery in a clean room?

FOD

14. What class of clean room should be used for data recovery?

class 100 or better

15. In what ways can your recovered data be returned to you?

any type of of media.

16. Give one example of a company that specializes in recovery from optical media.

total recall

17. What site (or sites) include a "museum" of interesting recovery projects they have undertaken?

Drivesavers

18. What circumstances might require that the data recovery service perform a recovery attempt at your site?

exceptional security concerns.

19. List two companies that recover data from Flash cards or memory sticks.

Save my files.

Data recovery services

20. Pick two of the companies you researched and list some of the other services and products they offer.

Review Questions

1. Based on your research, what impression do you get about how expensive data recovery services are? Explain your answer.

very

2. Based on your research, do you think individuals or companies would be more interested in using data recovery services? Why?

3. In general, do companies specialize in recovery from specific types of media or do they tend to provide data recovery for all types of media?

4. Based on your research, what three factors would affect the amount you might pay for recovery services from a specific provider?

_____

_____

_____

LAB 11.4 USE DO-IT-YOURSELF DATA RECOVERY SOFTWARE

Objectives

The goal of this lab is to help you explore options for recovering data from a malfunctioning hard drive. After completing this lab, you will be able to:

➤ Search the Internet for recovery services

➤ Search *www.ontrack.com* to learn about data recovery

➤ Use EasyRecovery to locate files for possible recovery

Materials Required

This lab will require the following:

➤ Windows 98, Windows 2000, or Windows XP operating system

➤ Internet access

Activity Background

Probably nothing makes a computer user panic more than the prospect of losing important data. As a technician, you have to be prepared to recover data from a variety of storage media; most often, however, you will be asked to recover it from a hard drive. Data on a hard drive may be lost for a variety of reasons ranging from human error to a natural disaster that renders the drive inoperable. In this lab you will investigate various data recovery options and learn to use one of them.

Estimated completion time: **60 minutes**

Note that if you are using a modem and phone line to connect to the Internet, the time required to download software might increase the time required for this lab.

ACTIVITY

When you need to find information on the Internet, it's often helpful to start with a broad search via a search engine such as Google (*www.google.com*) or Alta Vista (*www.altavista.com*). To learn more, follow these steps:

1. Open your browser and go to your favorite search site on the Internet.

2. Search for information on data recovery services.

3. Explore as many links as you have time for. Then list five Web sites that offer data recovery services:

data recovery clinic

drive saver

save my files

Adv - data

atl - data recovery

One major data recovery company is called Ontrack. You'll explore the Ontrack Web site in the following steps:

1. Open your Internet browser and go to *www.ontrack.com*.

2. Answer the following questions, using the links on the Ontrack site. If you cannot obtain all the answers from this site, supplement it with information from one or more of the sites you found in your earlier search process. Print pages supporting all of your answers.

- According to the information you printed, what are the two top causes of data loss?

  hardware or system malfunction

  human error

- What data recovery options are available?

  Server recovery   Laptop Data recovery

  RAID Data recovery   tape Data recovery

  Desktop Data recovery

- What solutions will work with your operating system?

  do it yourself   Remote recovery

11

- What should you do if a hardware malfunction is detected?

  try to isolate it.

  _____

- Is Internet access necessary for this recovery option?

  _no_

- Will this option work if you cannot boot from the hard drive?

  _no_

3. Return to the Ontrack home page.

4. Locate and follow the link that leads to information about EasyRecovery DataRecovery software.

5. Using information on the EasyRecovery DataRecovery page, answer the following questions.

   - Does this software need to be installed prior to the data loss?

     yes

   - Does this software require that your system be healthy enough to boot from the hard drive?

     _no_

   - Can this product recover data from a deleted partition? Print the Web page supporting your answer.

     yes

   - Can this product recover data from removable media? If so, what types?

     yes floppy, zip, jaz

Now you will download and use the EasyRecovery Professional Trial edition software, but be aware that Web sites change often, so the links might not read exactly as described below. Do the following:

1. Create a folder on your hard drive named **C:\Downloads**. Under this folder, create a folder named **C:\Downloads\EasyRecovery**. If you put all downloaded files into folders under C:\Downloads, it is easy to find downloaded files and to know their purposes.

2. On the EasyRecovery DataRecovery Web page, under the description of EasyRecovery Professional Trial edition, click the link **Download Trial edition**. The Ontrack Login page appears.

3. Click the link to **Create My Profile**. The New User page appears.

4. Enter your information to create your profile and click **Continue**. The Download page and the File Download dialog box appears.

5. Download the file **Er.exe**, saving it to C:\Downloads\EasyRecovery.

6. Close all open windows and open Windows Explorer. Double-click the **Er.exe** icon. The EasyRecovery window opens.

7. To continue installing EasyRecovery, select English as the language. The InstallShield Wizard launches to complete the installation process.

8. Accept the End-User License Agreement (EULA).

   Note that installing the EasyRecovery software on the partition containing the data you want to recover may in fact overwrite the lost data. To avoid this problem, you should install EasyRecovery on a separate partition or PC and then create an EasyRecovery Emergency Boot Disk. For the purpose of this lab, however, it's okay to install on your current PC.

9. Click **Next** several times to continue through each window of the installation process using the default settings.

10. When prompted, select **Yes, I want to restart my computer now** and click **Finish** to complete the EasyRecovery installation. Your PC will restart.

The EasyRecovery Professional shortcut now appears on your desktop. Follow these steps to use the software:

1. Double-click the **EasyRecovery Professional** shortcut on your desktop. An EasyRecovery notice opens and informs you that the edition can identify recoverable files but that you must purchase the full version to recover files. Click **OK** to close the notice. The Ontrack EasyRecovery Professional application launches.

2. Select the **Data Recovery** button and then the **Advanced Recovery Option**. A warning message displays suggesting that you copy recovered data to a different media such as a Zip drive or floppy disk if you suspect all partitions on your hard drive might be damaged. Click **OK** to close the notice. The Data Recovery window appears. See Figure 11-1.

11

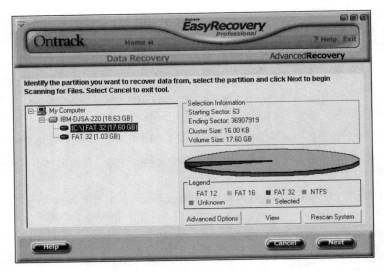

Figure 11-1   Easy Data Recovery window shows drives that can be scanned for missing or corrupt files

3. A list of drives on your system is displayed in the window. Notice that EasyRecovery graphically displays partition information along with a legend defining partition information and use. Select drive C: and answer the following questions:

   ■ What is the starting sector for drive C:?

   _____

   ■ What is the ending sector for drive C:?

   _____

   ■ What is the cluster size for drive C:?

   _____

   ■ What file system does drive C: use?

   _____

4. Click **Next** to begin scanning for files that the software might recover. The process might take some time as the software searches the entire drive C:. You can cancel the process at any time by clicking **Cancel** on the Scanning for Files dialog box. If you cancel the process, a question appears asking, "Would you like to save the state of your recovery to resume at a later time?" Click **No**.

5. A warning message appears stating that the version cannot recover files. Click **OK** to close the notice.

6. A list of files displays that the software can recover. A Condition status displays for each file. Status options are G, D, X, S, B and N. Click the **Filter Options** button and interpret each of these statuses:

   - The status G means: _____
   - The status D means: _____
   - The status X means: _____
   - The status S means: _____
   - The status B means: _____
   - The status N means: _____

7. Click **OK** to close the Filter Options window.

8. On the Data Recovery window, in the left pane, a hierarchical list of folders is displayed. The right pane shows recoverable files within those folders. You can select folders in order to search for a corrupted or lost file you are trying to recover. Open a folder on drive C and select a file in that folder. Click **View File** to view the contents of the file. Viewing the contents of a file can often help in locating just the right file.

9. If you were using the purchased version of the software, once you had located the files to recover, you would click Next and then specify a destination for the files. These files would then be copied from their current location to the specified destination. Notice that Next is grayed out because you are using the trial version of the software.

10. Click **Cancel** to return to the main window. A message appears asking if you would like to save the state of your recovery. Click **No**.

11. Besides the AdvancedRecovery option on the main window, there are five other options under Data Recovery, which are listed below. Give a brief explanation of each option:

   - DeletedRecovery

     _____

     _____

   - FormatRecovery

     _____

     _____

   - RawRecovery

     _____

     _____

- ResumeRecovery

  _____

  _____

- EmergencyDiskette

  _____

  _____

12. Using procedures listed in earlier labs, print a screen shot of this EasyRecovery window.

13. Close the EasyRecovery window.

14. Your instructor might tell you to uninstall the EasyRecovery software. If so, uninstall the software using the the Add/Remove Programs applet in Control Panel.

Review Questions

1. What are three causes of data loss?

   _____

   _____

2. Which of these causes would Remote Data Recovery and EasyRecovery fail to overcome?

   _____

3. Is it normally possible to recover lost data that has been overwritten by other data? Explain.

   _____

   _____

4. What are some symptoms of a hardware malfunction that would result in data loss?

   _____

   _____

5. List some steps to prevent mechanical drive failure.

   _____

   _____

Lab 11.5 Critical Thinking: Use Debug to Examine Disk Information

Objectives

The goal of this lab is to help you use the Debug utility to examine the beginning of a floppy drive. After completing this lab, you will be able to:

➤ Use Debug commands

➤ Explain how Debug displays information

➤ Examine and replace the boot record on a floppy disk

Materials Required

This lab will require the following:

➤ Windows 98 operating system

➤ Two Windows 98 startup disks

Activity Background

In this lab, you will use the Debug tool to examine and repair the boot record of a damaged floppy disk (specifically, a floppy disk that is configured as a startup disk). The file system on a floppy disk is similar to that of a hard drive, so what you learn here about floppy disks can be applied to hard drives.

It's important to know how to use Debug, because it's available on every computer that runs DOS or Windows 9x. Using Debug, you can see, at the "grass roots level," the contents of a disk. This will help you gain the strong technical insight that you need to take advantage of more user-friendly data recovery software, and to be confident that you understand how such products work. The better you understand how data is constructed on the disk and exactly what problems can arise, the better your chances of recovering lost or damaged data.

In this lab, you will introduce an error to the boot record of a startup disk so that the disk will not boot. Next, you will restore the boot record using a second startup disk, copying the good boot record on the second startup disk to the bad disk.

Estimated completion time: **45 minutes**

Activity

Follow these steps to damage the boot record of a startup disk.

1. Test both your startup disks to verify that you can boot from each disk. Label one disk Startup Disk 1 and the other disk Startup Disk 2. You will corrupt the first disk and restore it using the second disk.

2. Boot the PC using the first startup disk. At the Startup menu, select the **Start Without CD Support** option.

3. The system boots and a RAM drive is created. After the system has booted, examine the text above the command prompt to determine the drive letter of the RAM drive. (A RAM drive provides a place to write files into memory and allow that memory to behave like a logical drive. The Windows 98 Startup disk compresses various useful utilities that would not fit on the floppy disk in an uncompressed state. To be useful, these files must be uncompressed. Normally, compressed files are expanded and written to a hard drive. Because the Windows 98 Startup disk is often used to troubleshoot a malfunctioning system, its designers assumed that the hard drive might not be available for this purpose. Therefore, they designed the startup disk to expand these files to a RAM drive instead.)

4. Change to the RAM drive, type **Debug** and press **Enter**. The Debug utility runs and the prompt changes to a dash (-).

Next you will use the D command (which stands for "dump") to view memory contents expressed in hex values, and then you will learn to read the results of this Debug command. Follow these steps:

1. To view information starting at memory address 0000:0C00, type **D0000:0C00** and press **Enter**.

2. Observe the output of the D command, which shows the contents of memory beginning with memory address 0000:0C00. (See Figure 11-2.) Note that this command displays memory 128 bytes at a time. The information is presented in lines of 16 bytes each, with the start address on the left side of the window, the hex value of each byte in the middle of the window, and the ASCI interpretation (if any) of each byte at the right side of the window.

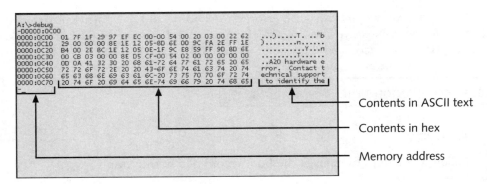

Figure 11-2   Results of the Debug D command showing contents of 128 bytes of memory

3. If the contents of memory is not ASCII text, then the attempt to display the ASCII interpretation of the contents will appear as gibberish in that ASCI section. Some of the code at these particular memory addresses should be readable in ASCI. What does the code at these memory addresses pertain to?

———————————————————————————————————

———————————————————————————————————

The Debug utility can be used as an editor to change the contents of memory, a floppy disk or some other drive. In order to corrupt the startup disk, you will write the contents of memory to the startup disk. Do the following:

1. Type **W0000:0C00 0 0 1** and press **Enter**. In this command, "W" indicates that you want to write, while "0000:0C00" indicates the location to begin writing. The first 0 in "0 0 1" indicates the drive (0=A, 1=B, 2=C...). The second 0 in "0 0 1" indicates the start sector to write to (0 being the first sector, 1 being the second sector, etc.). The 1 in "0 0 1" indicates that only one sector of information will be written. The information from memory is now written to the first (boot) sector of the floppy disk overwriting the existing boot sector.

2. To exit Debug, type **Q** and press **Enter**. You return to the prompt for your RAM drive.

3. Reboot your computer to test your corrupted startup disk. What error message do you see?

———————————————————————————————————

———————————————————————————————————

11

Now you will boot from the second startup disk and use it to repair the first disk. You will first find an unused area of memory in which you can work. Then you will copy the boot sector to this area of memory, switch disks, and copy the good boot sector from memory to the corrupted disk to repair it. Follow these steps:

1. You need 512 bytes of unused memory. Because the Debug command loads 128 bytes at a time, you will actually look for three consecutive 128 bytes of unused memory. You'll first try memory address 5000:0000. Type **D5000:0000** and press **Enter**. Is the area clear (as indicated by all zeroes)?

———————————————————————————————————

2. If the area is not clear, keep trying new memory addresses until you find a clear area. What memory address will you use as your first clear memory address?

———————————————————————————————————

3. Now check two more consecutive memory dumps, keeping in mind that you must have three consecutive memory dumps to work with. (A memory dump displays or "dumps" the contents of memory onto the screen.) Each time you dump memory, the pointer in memory moves to the next group of 128 bytes. By using successive dump commands, you can move through memory consecutively dumping 128 bytes of memory to screen. Type **D** and press **Enter** two times to verify that two more successive groups of 128 bytes of memory is empty, making a total of 512 bytes of unused memory addresses.

4. Once you have verified that these 512 consecutive bytes of memory are unused, the next step is to copy, or load, the good boot record into this memory. Type **L5000:0000 0 0 1** and press **Enter**. (If you are using some other memory address than 5000:0000, substitute that address in the command line.) You should hear the floppy drive run. Answer these questions to decipher the command.

   ■ What does "L" stand for?

   _____

   ■ What does "5000:0000" indicate?

   _____

   ■ What does the first 0 in "0 0 1" indicate?

   _____

   ■ What does the second 0 in "0 0 1" indicate?

   _____

   ■ What does the 1 in "0 0 1" indicate?

   _____

5. The information from this sector of the floppy disk is now loaded in system memory. To view this information, type **D5000:0000** and press **Enter**. Can you see any indication of what file system the floppy is formatted with? Explain.

   _____

   _____

6. Figure 11-3 shows a result of this Dump command for a startup disk formatted using DOS. Compare it to your dump and note the differences. What differences do you see? Table 11-1 lists the items in a boot record to help you with your comparisons.

_____

_____

_____

_____

7. To copy the good boot sector to the damaged disk, insert the damaged Windows 98 startup disk, type **W5000:0000 0 0 1** and press **Enter**.

8. To exit Debug, type **Q** and press **Enter**. You return to the prompt for your RAM drive.

9. Reboot your computer, test your repair and record your results below.

_____

_____

_____

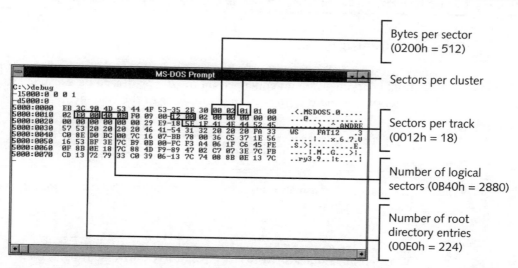

Figure 11-3   The first 128 bytes of the boot record of a 3½-inch floppy disk formatted with DOS

Table 11-1 Layout of the boot record of a floppy disk or hard drive

Description	Number of bytes
Machine code	11
Bytes per sector	2
Sectors per cluster	1
Reserved	2
Number of FATs	1
Number of root directory entries	2
Number of logical sectors	2
Medium descriptor byte	1
Sectors per FAT	2
Sectors per track	2
Heads	2
Number of hidden sectors	2
Total sectors in logical volume	4
Physical drive number	1
Reserved	1
Extended boot signature record	1
32-bit binary volume ID	4
Volume label	11
Type of file system (FAT12, FAT16, or FAT32)	8
Program to load operating system (bootstrap loader)	Remainder of the sector

Review Questions

1. What special feature, created by the Windows 98 Startup disk, allows compressed troubleshooting utilities contained on the floppy disk to be expanded to a useful state, even if there is no working hard drive in the system?

2. What Debug command dumps data contained at the very beginning of the memory address space?

3. What command loads two sectors from the C: drive, starting at the sixth sector?

4. Debug displays data _____ bytes at a time.

5. What term is used to refer to the information that was written to repair the damaged Windows 98 startup disk?

_____

6. Why do you think it is important to be very responsible and careful when tinkering with the Debug command?

_____

_____

11

WINDOWS ON A NETWORK

Labs included in this chapter

➤ Lab 12.1 Share Resources on a Network

➤ Lab 12.2 Use NetBEUI Instead of TCP/IP

➤ Lab 12.3 Use a Parallel Port for Direct Cable Connection

➤ Lab 12.4 Install a Network Printer

➤ Lab 12.5 Configure and Use Dial-Up Server

LAB 12.1 SHARE RESOURCES ON A NETWORK

Objectives

The goal of this lab is to demonstrate the process of sharing resources and using these shared resources on a remote computer on the network. After completing this lab, you will be able to:

> ➤ Share resources
> ➤ Control access to shared resources
> ➤ Connect to shared resources

Materials Required

This lab will require the following:

> ➤ Two or more Windows 98 or Windows 2000/XP computers on a network
> ➤ Windows 98 or Windows 2000/XP installation CD or installation files stored in another location
> ➤ Workgroup of 2–4 students

Activity Background

The primary reason to network computers is to make it possible to share files, printers, Internet connections and other resources. To share resources in a Windows workgroup, you need to make sure each computer has two Windows components installed: Client for Microsoft Networks, and File and Print Sharing. Those components are installed by default in Windows 2000/XP, and client for Microsoft Networks is installed by default in Windows 98. In this lab, you will install them on a Windows 98 computer (if they are not already installed or have been uninstalled). Then you will share resources and connect to these shared resources. Instructions are written for Windows 98, although they work about the same for Windows 2000/XP if you substitute My Network Places for Network Neighborhood in the instructions. Other differences between Windows 98 and Windows 2000/XP are noted.

Estimated completion time: **30 minutes**

ACTIVITY

To share resources on a Windows peer-to-peer network, computers must belong to the same workgroup. Do the following to verify that all computers in your group belong to the same Windows workgroup:

1. To determine the name of the workgroup, right-click **Network Neighborhood**, click **Properties** on the shortcut menu, and then click the **Identification** tab. For Windows 2000/XP, right-click **My Computer**, click **Properties** on the

shortcut menu, and then for Windows 2000, click the **Network Identification** tab. For Windows XP, click the **Computer Name** tab.

What is the workgroup name for this computer?

_____

2. Change the workgroup name if necessary so that all the computers in your group belong to the same workgroup. If you are asked to reboot the PC, wait to do that until after you have installed the components in the next group of steps.

For each Windows 98 computer, follow these steps to check to see if Client for Microsoft Networks and File and Print Sharing are installed on your computer, and, if necessary, install these components:

1. Right-click the **Network Neighborhood** icon on the desktop and then click **Properties** on the shortcut menu. The Network dialog box opens.

2. If Client for Microsoft Networks is not listed as an installed component, you need to install it. To do that, click **Add**. The Add Network Component Type dialog box opens.

3. Click **Client**, and then click **Add**. The Select Network Client dialog box opens.

4. In the left pane of the Select Network Client dialog box, click **Microsoft**, and then click **Client for Microsoft Networks** in the right pane. Click **OK** to continue. The Add Network Component Type dialog box and the Select Network Client dialog box close. You return to the Network dialog box.

5. If File and Printer Sharing for Microsoft networks is not listed as an installed component in the Network dialog box, you need to install it. To do that, click **Add**. The Add Network Component Type dialog box opens again.

6. Click **Service**, and then click **Add**. The Select Network Service dialog box opens.

7. Select **File and printer sharing for Microsoft Networks** and click **OK**. Insert the Windows installation CD or point to the location of the installation files as instructed in the dialog box that appears. When the service is installed, you return to the Network dialog box.

8. To enable File and Print Sharing, click **File and Print Sharing** in the Network dialog box. The File and Print Sharing dialog box opens.

9. Select the **I want to be able to give others access to my files** checkbox and the **I want to be able to allow others to print to my printers** checkbox. Selecting these two options makes it possible for other computers on the network to access this computer's files and printers. Click **OK** to close the File and Print Sharing dialog box. You return to the Network dialog box.

10. Click **OK** to close the Network dialog box and save your new settings. The Systems Settings Change dialog box appears and notifies you that before the settings will take effect the system must be restarted. Click **Yes** to reboot.

12

Now that you have enabled file and printer sharing, you are ready to set up folders or printers on your PC to be shared by others on the network. Follow these steps to share folders and control access to their contents:

1. Using Windows Explorer, create three folders at the root of drive C:. Name the folders **Read**, **Full** and **Depends**. Create a text file called **readtest.txt** in the Read folder, a text file called **fulltest.txt** in the Full folder, and a text file called **deptest.txt** in the Depends folder. Type a short sentence in each text file, save your changes, and close the files. If you need a refresher about how to create text files using Windows Explorer, see Lab 3.1.

2. In the right pane of Windows Explorer, right-click the **Read** folder and then click **Sharing** on the shortcut menu. The Read Properties dialog box opens, with the Sharing tab selected.

3. In the Access Type section, select **Read**. This setting gives users on the network read-only access to all the files in the Read folder.

4. In the Password section, click the **Read only Password** text box and then type **read**. Click **OK** in the Read Properties dialog box. The Password Confirmation dialog box opens. Click the **Shared As** option button.

5. In the Password Confirmation dialog box, re-enter **read** in the Read Only Password textbox and then click **OK**. Both the Confirm Password dialog box and the Read Properties dialog box close.

6. Repeat Steps 2-5 for the other two folders you just created, selecting the access types associated with their names. For the Full folder, use "full" as the Full Access Password. For the Depends folder, supply both Read Only and Full Access passwords. Use the password associated with the access type.

So far you have: verified that all computers that will share resources are in the same workgroup; installed Windows components to share resources; and set up the folders that will be shared. You are now ready to use shared resources over the network. Follow these steps to access the shared folders:

1. In Windows Explorer, click the **Network Neighborhood** icon. The right pane of Windows Explorer displays a list of computers on the network.

2. In the right pane of Windows Explorer, double-click your partner's computer icon to display the shared resources available on that computer.

3. In the right pane of Windows Explorer, double-click the **Read** folder. The Enter Network Password dialog box opens. Here you need to enter the password for this folder.

4. Type **Read** and click **OK**. The contents of the Read folder are displayed in Windows Explorer.

5. Double click **readtest.txt**. The file opens in Notepad. Attempt to save the file and record your results below.

_____

_____

6. Now attempt to save the file in the My Documents folder on your computer. Record the results below. Why did your results in Step 5 differ from your results here?

_____

_____

_____

7. Close Notepad, click the **Network Neighborhood** icon in the left pane of Windows Explorer, and double-click the icon for your partner's computer in the right pane.

8. Double-click the **Full** folder in the right pane and, when prompted, enter the password and click **OK**. The contents of the Full folder are displayed in Explorer.

9. Double-click **fulltest.txt**. The file opens in Notepad. Attempt to save the file and record your results below.

_____

_____

10. Attempt to save the file in the My Documents folder on your computer and record the results below. Did you note any difference between the results of Step 9 and Step 10? If so, explain the difference.

_____

11. Close Notepad, return to the desktop and open your **My Documents** folder.

12. Rename the file fulltest.txt using a new name of your choice. Attempt to copy, or drag and drop, this file into the Full folder on your partner's PC. Were you successful? Why or why not?

_____

You have just seen how you can use Network Neighborhood to access shared folders on the network. You can make these shared folders appear to be a local drive on your PC, thereby making it more convenient to access these folders. When a shared folder on the network is made to appear to be a local drive on your PC, the folder is called a network drive. Follow these steps to map a network drive and configure it to connect at logon:

1. In the left pane of Windows Explorer, click the **Network Neighborhood** icon. A list of computers on your network appears in the right pane.

2. Double-click the icon for your partner's computer. A list of shared resources appears.

3. Right-click the **Full** folder and then click **Map Network Drive** in the shortcut menu. The Map Network Drive dialog box opens.

4. In the Map Network Drive dialog box, click the **Drive** drop-down menu and then select the drive letter you wish to assign to this folder.

5. In the Map Network Drive dialog box, select the **Reconnect at Logon** checkbox and then click **OK**.

6. When prompted, enter the correct password and click **OK**. The drive is connected and a window opens displaying the contents of the Full folder. The title of the window includes the drive letter you assigned.

7. Check Windows Explorer and verify that the drive letter is now listed under My Computer.

8. Log off and then log back on to test that the drive will reconnect. What did you have to do in order to reconnect when you logged back on?

_____

_____

ALTERNATE ACTIVITY

To map a drive using a Windows 2000/XP computer, open Windows Explorer, right-click the **My Network Places** icon and then click **Map Network Drive** on the shortcut menu. The Map Network Drive dialog box opens. Click **Browse** and locate the folder on the network that you want to map to the network drive. Then begin with Step 3 above.

Review Questions

1. What is the main advantage of connecting computers into networks?

_____

_____

2. What term refers to the process of allowing others to use resources on your computer?

_____

3. What two Windows network components must be installed before you can grant others access to resources on your computer and use their resources?

_____

4. How can you provide full access to some of your files while giving read-only access to other files shared on the network?

_____

_____

5. Explain how to allow some people to make changes to files in shared folders while only allowing others to view and read the contents of the same folder.

_____

_____

_____

_____

LAB 12.2 USE NETBEUI INSTEAD OF TCP/IP

12

Objectives

Most networks use the TCP/IP network protocol suite. The goal of this lab is to demonstrate how to replace TCP/IP with NetBEUI. After completing this lab, you will be able to:

➤ Install NetBEUI

➤ Remove TCP/IP

➤ Observe the results of using NetBEUI

Materials Required

This lab will require the following:

➤ Windows 2000/XP operating system

➤ NIC configured to use only TCP/IP

➤ IP information or a DHCP server on the network

➤ Internet access

➤ Windows 2000/XP Professional installation CD or installation files stored in another location

➤ Network workgroup consisting of two computers

➤ Workgroup of 2–4 students

Activity Background

TCP/IP is probably the network protocol you are most familiar with. But it is not the only network protocol, nor is it the best for all situations. NetBEUI (NetBIOS Enhanced User Interface) was originally developed by IBM in order to make it possible to use NetBIOS names as official network addresses. NetBEUI is faster than TCP/IP and much easier to configure. Its main disadvantage is that it is non-routable (that is, it is only able to communicate with computers on its network.) In this lab you will configure one computer in your workgroup to use NetBEUI, and then observe the effect of this change on both computers in the workgroup. Then you will use NetBEUI as the only network protocol in your workgroup.

Estimated completion time: **30 minutes**

ACTIVITY

First you need to determine what the network looks like before you install NetBEUI and remove TCP/IP. Follow these steps:

1. On one of the two computers in the workgroup, open **My Network Places**. For Windows 2000, double-click **Computers Near Me**. For Windows XP, click **View workgroup computers**. A list of computers on your network appears. Take and print a screen-shot of this list. If you need a refresher of how to print a screen shot, see Lab 1.2.

2. Repeat Step 1 for the other computer on your network.

Now you are ready to follow these steps to install NetBEUI as the network protocol on one of the computers in your workgroup:

1. Right-click the **My Network Places** icon and click **Properties** on the short-cut menu. The Network and Dial-Up Connections window opens.

2. Right-click the **Local Area Connection** icon and select **Properties** on the shortcut menu. The Local Area Connection Properties dialog box opens.

3. In the Local Area Connection Properties dialog box, click **Install**. The Select Network Component Type dialog box opens.

4. Click **Protocol** and then click **Add**. The Select Network Protocol dialog box opens.

5. Click **NetBEUI Protocol** and then click **OK**. The Select Network Protocol and Select Network Component Type dialog boxes close.

Your next job is to uninstall TCP/IP on the computer on which you installed NetBEUI. You'll begin by recording the TCP/IP configuration information for that computer. Then you will uninstall TCP/IP. (You'll need configuration information when you reinstall TCP/IP at the end of this lab.) Follow these steps:

1. Right-click **My Network Places** and select **Properties** on the shortcut menu. The Network and Dial-Up Connections window opens.

2. Right-click the **Local Area Connection** icon and select **Properties** on the shortcut menu. The Local Area Connection Properties window opens.

3. Select **Internet Protocol (TCP/IP)** from the list of components and click **Properties**. The TCP/IP Properties window opens.

4. Record all the configuration information available in this window:

   _____

   _____

   _____

   _____

5. Click **Cancel** to close the TCP/IP Properties window.

6. In the Local Area Connection Properties dialog box, click **Internet Protocol (TCP/IP)** and then click **Uninstall**. A message appears informing you that you are about to remove the protocol from all connections.

7. Click **Yes** to continue. The Internet Protocol (TCP/IP) is removed from the Local Area Connection Properties dialog box.

8. The Local Network dialog box opens and informs you that you must restart the computer before the changes can take effect.

9. Click **Yes** to restart the computer.

Follow these steps to observe the effects of using NetBEUI:

1. Go to the computer that you did not alter (that is, to the computer that is still running TCP/IP).

2. If it is not already open, open the **My Network Places** window and double click **Computers Near Me**. If Computers Near Me was already open, then press **F5** to refresh the display. (For Windows XP, **View workgroup computers**.) Answer these questions:

   - What computers are displayed?

     _____

     _____

     _____

     _____

12

- Compare the current screen to the screen-shot you created earlier. What computers are missing?

  _____

  _____

  _____

  _____

- Why are they missing?

  _____

  _____

3. Go to the computer on which you installed NetBEUI.

4. Open My Network Places, and then open Computers Near Me or View workgroup computers. Answer the following questions:

   - What computers are displayed?

     _____

     _____

     _____

     _____

   - Compare the current screen to the screen-shot you created earlier. What computers are missing?

     _____

     _____

     _____

   - Why are they missing?

     _____

     _____

5. Press **F5** to refresh the list of computers on the network. Did any new ones appear? Why or why not?

_____

_____

_____

_____

6. On the computer on which you installed NetBEUI, attempt to connect to the Internet and then answer these questions:

- What message did you receive?

_____

_____

_____

_____

- Why do you think you were unable to connect to the Internet?

_____

_____

12

Next, you will use some network utilities to test your network connections. You'll start by running a loopback ping test. This test uses the IP address 127.0.0.1 with the Ping command to test the local computer. Follow these steps:

1. On the computer that's running TCP/IP (the one you didn't change), open a command prompt window, type **Ping 127.0.0.1** and then press **Enter**. Record the results of the loopback test:

_____

_____

_____

2. Another TCP/IP utility that you can use to test the network configuration and connectivity is Ipconfig. Type **Ipconfig /all** and then press **Enter**. Record the results of the command:

_____

_____

_____

3. On the computer on which you installed NetBEUI, open a command prompt window and then repeat Steps 1 and 2. Record the results below. Why did you receive the results you did?

_____

_____

_____

_____

Follow these steps to re-install TCP/IP:

1. On the computer on which you installed NetBEUI, right-click the **My Network Places** icon and select **Properties** on the shortcut menu. The Network and Dialup Connections window opens.

2. Right-click the **Local Area Connection** icon and select **Properties** on the shortcut menu. The Local Area Connection Properties dialog box opens.

3. Click **Install**. The Select Network Component Type dialog box opens.

4. Click **Protocol** and then click **Add**. The Select Network Protocol dialog box opens.

5. Click **TCP/IP Protocol** and then click **OK**. The Select Network Protocol and Select Network Component Type dialog boxes close.

6. The Local Network dialog box opens and informs you that you must restart the computer before the changes can take effect. Click **Yes** to restart the computer.

You've finished re-installing TCP/IP. Now you need to reconfigure the necessary TCP/IP settings. Follow these steps:

1. Right-click the **My Network Places** icon and select **Properties** on the shortcut menu. The Network and Dial-Up Connections window opens.

2. In the Network and Dialup Connections window, right-click the **Local Area Connection** icon and select **Properties** on the shortcut menu. The Local Area Connection Properties dialog box opens.

3. In the Local Area Connection Properties dialog box, click **Internet Protocol (TCP/IP)**, then click **Properties**. The Internet Protocol (TCP/IP) Properties dialog box opens.

4. In the Internet Protocol (TCP/IP) Properties dialog box, reconfigure the settings you recorded in Step 3 at the beginning of this lab.

5. Click **OK** to close the Internet Protocol (TCP/IP) Properties dialog box.

6. Click **OK** to close the Local Area Connection Properties dialog box and save your settings.

7. Test your settings by connecting to another computer or the Internet.

ADDITIONAL ACTIVITY (additional 20 minutes)

1. Install NetBEUI and remove TCP/IP on one more computer in your workgroup so that NetBEUI is the only network protocol installed on two computers.

2. Using NetBEUI, transfer files from one computer to the other.

3. Install TCP/IP and configure it and then remove NetBEUI as an installed networking protocol.

Review Questions

1. Is it possible to have more than one network protocol installed on the same network? Explain how you arrived at your answer.

   _____

   _____

   _____

2. If you had to access the Internet from your computer, which protocol would you use?

   _____

3. What features of NetBEUI make it appealing for a small network that does not need Internet access?

   _____

   _____

12

4. Of the two covered in this lab, which network protocol is better suited for troubleshooting problems? Why?

_____

_____

5. What type of computer name is used on a NetBEUI network?

_____

LAB 12.3 USE A PARALLEL PORT FOR DIRECT CABLE CONNECTION

Objectives

The goal of this lab is to help you use the Direct Cable Connection feature of Windows 98 to connect two computers via a parallel port. After completing this lab, you will be able to:

➤ Install Direct Cable Connection

➤ Link two computers with a parallel cable

➤ Transfer files

Materials Required

This lab will require the following:

➤ Windows 98 operating system

➤ Standard parallel cable with a DB 25-pin connection at both ends (or you can substitute a parallel printer cable with a 36-pin Centronics to DB 25-pin converter)

➤ Two computers that are not connected to the network

➤ Windows 98 installation CD or installation files stored in another location

➤ Workgroup of 2–4 students

Activity Background

Included with Windows 98, the Direct Cable Connection feature allows you to connect two computers without the benefit of a conventional network. Although slow in comparison to the typical LAN, this feature does allow you to transfer files via a serial null-modem or parallel cable. The only other requirement is that the computers share a common communications protocol. NetBEUI is ideal for this type of connection because it is easy to configure and is faster than other protocols. In this lab, you will connect two computers via the Direct Cable Connection feature.

Estimated completion time: **30 minutes**

ACTIVITY

First, you need to install the Direct Cable Connection feature on both computers. Follow these steps:

1. Click **Start** on the taskbar, point to **Settings**, click **Control Panel**, and then double-click **Add/Remove Programs**.

2. Click the **Windows Setup** tab.

3. Select **Communications** and then click **Details**. Select the **Direct Cable Connection** check box (if it is not already selected).

To use the Direct Cable Connection, work with at least one partner to follow these steps:

1. Shut both computers down, connect the parallel cable to each computer, and reboot both computers.

2. Decide which computer will be the "host" and which will be the "guest." The guest computer will have access to files on the host computer.

3. On both computers, click **Start**, point to **Programs**, point to **Accessories**, point to **Communications**, and then click **Direct Cable Connection**. The Direct Cable Connection dialog box opens.

4. On the host computer, select **Host** in the Direct Cable Connection dialog box. On the guest computer, select **Guest** on the Direct Cable Connection dialog box. On both computers click **Next**. If this is the first time that Direct Cable Connection has been used, the Configuring Ports dialog box will open and close, at which point you should continue with Step 5. If Direct Cable Connection has been run before, click **Change** in the Direct Cable Connection dialog box and then continue with Step 5.

5. The Direct Cable Connection dialog box presents a list of possible ports to use for the cable. In the "Select the port you want to use" list, select **Parallel cable on LPT1** and then click **Next** to continue.

6. On the host computer (not the guest computer), the Direct Cable Connection dialog box explains that it will have access to shared files and lists the steps required to share a folder. Summarize these steps below:

_____

_____

_____

_____

12

7. On the host computer click **Next** to continue. On the guest computer, wait until the host computer completes Steps 8 and 9 and your partner gives you the go-ahead, and then skip to Step 10.

8. On the host computer select the **Use Password Protection** check box and then click **Set Password**. The Direct Cable Connection Password dialog box opens.

9. Type **dcclab** in the Password text box and in the Confirm Password text box and then click **OK**. The Direct Cable Connection Password dialog box closes.

10. On the host computer, click **Finish**. The Direct Cable Connection dialog box displays "Status: Waiting to connect via parallel cable on LPT1." At this time the host team should signal the guest team to proceed. The guest team should then click **Finish**. The Direct Cable Connection dialog box appears on the guest computer.

11. On the guest computer, enter the password when prompted. Click **OK** to establish the connection.

12. On the guest computer, test the connection by browsing to the host in Network Neighborhood and transferring files from a shared folder.

Review Questions

1. What two kinds of cables could you use to implement a Direct Cable Connection?

_____

_____

2. In a direct cable connection, is it possible to share printers but not files? Is it possible to share files but not printers? Explain.

_____

_____

3. Would it make sense to use Direct Cable Connection to connect two computers that already have access to an existing network? Explain your answer.

_____

_____

_____

4. Why might you use Direct Cable Connection to connect two computers, even if one of the computers has access to a network?

_____

_____

_____

5. When using Direct Cable Connection to connect to computers via a printer cable, what must you use in addition to the printer cable? Why?

_____

_____

6. Of the two types of cables that can be used for Direct Cable Connection, which provides better transfer speeds?

_____

_____

LAB 12.4 INSTALL A NETWORK PRINTER

Objectives

The goal of this lab is to give you practice installing a local printer on a computer, sharing it and then installing it on a remote computer on the network. After completing this lab, you will be able to:

➤ Install a local printer

➤ Install a network printer

➤ Test the printer across the network

Materials Required

This lab will require the following:

➤ Windows 98, Windows 2000, or Windows XP operating system

➤ Printer, printer cable and printer driver files

➤ Functioning network

➤ Workgroup of 2–4 students

Activity Background

A local printer is one that is connected to a PC by way of a serial, parallel infrared or USB connection. A local printer is not usually available to the network for general printing jobs, but in some cases it may be useful to allow other computers to print from your local printer. (For example, suppose you have an expensive photo-quality printer installed locally on your computer. You might sometimes want to let users who need to print photos access your printer via the network.) In this lab you will install a local printer and test it. Then, as a challenge, you will determine for yourself how to install this printer as a network printer from a remote computer. Instructions in this lab are written for Windows 98, but work the same as for Windows 2000, or Windows XP, if you substitute My Network Places for Network Neighborhood.

Estimated completion time: 30 minutes

ACTIVITY

The following steps describe the default method for installing a printer in Windows. However, printer manufacturers often provide specialized steps for installing their devices. In that case, you should follow the steps prescribed by the manufacturer of your printer rather than the steps provided here.

1. With the computer off, attach the printer cable to the computer and the printer. Attach the power cable to the printer and then plug it in. Turn on the printer and then the computer. After the computer starts up, insert the installation disk if you have one.

2. Click **Start** on the taskbar, point to **Settings** and then click **Printers**. The Printers window opens, displaying any installed printers as well as the Add Printers icon.

3. Double-click the **Add Printers** icon to open the Add Printer wizard.

4. In the Add Printer wizard, click **Next** to begin the installation process.

5. What two options do you see in the Add Printer Wizard?

   _____

6. In the Add Printer Wizard, select the **Local Printer** option and then click **Next** to continue.

7. In the right pane of the Add Printers Wizard, select the manufacturer of your printer. A list of printers for that manufacturer is displayed in the left pane. Scroll down the list in the left pane to locate your printer.

8. If you can locate your printer, click it in the left pane of the Add Printer Wizard, click **Next**, and then skip to Step 11. If you cannot locate your printer in the list, click **Have Disk**. The Install From Disk dialog box opens.

9. In the Install From Disk dialog box, click **Browse**. Then locate and select the installation file for your operating system. This file will have an .inf file extension and most likely will be found in a folder that is named according to your operating system (such as \Win98\install.inf or \Windows98\oem.inf or something similar). Click **OK** to tell the wizard to use the selected file.

10. Click **OK** in the Install From Disk dialog box to close it. The Add Printer Wizard identifies your printer. Click **Next** to continue.

11. The Add Printer Wizard asks you to select the port you will use for the printer. In the Available Ports list box, select **LPT1: Printer Port**. This indicates that your printer is attached to the parallel port. Click **Next** to continue.

12. In the Printer name text box type a name for the printer (replacing the model name, which appears by default).

13. You are asked if you want this printer to be your Windows default printer. Click **Yes** and then click **Next**. When asked if you would like to print a test page, click **No** and then click **Finish**. The necessary files are copied to your computer and in some cases (if the printer has Fax capabilities for instance) a new wizard will launch. If this occurs, complete the wizard or follow instructions supplied by your instructor. When the installation process is complete, an icon for the newly installed printer appears in the Printers window.

Follow these steps to test the printer:

1. In the Printers window, right-click the icon for your printer and select **Properties** on the shortcut menu. The printer's Properties dialog box opens.

2. Click the **General** tab and then click **Print Test Page**. A test print job is sent to the printer and a dialog box opens asking you whether the page printed correctly.

3. Collect your test page and verify that it printed correctly (without any gibberish) then click **OK** to close the dialog box.

4. Open Windows Explorer and arrange it so that you can still see your printer's icon in the Printer's window. Using Windows Explorer, locate a .txt file or .bat file and drag-and-drop the file onto the printer's icon. What happens?

_____

_____

Now that you have tested your printer, share your printer (using Lab 12.1 as a guide). After you have shared your printer, go to the other computer and follow these steps to install a network printer:

1. Open the Printers window and launch the **Add Printer Wizard** as you did previously.

2. Click **Next**.

12

3. Select **Network Printer** and click **Next** to continue.

4. Click **Browse** to locate the printer that you will install. The Browse for Printer dialog box opens.

5. The Browse for Printer dialog box displays the network in a similar way to Windows Explorer. Locate your printer by expanding the computer on which you installed and shared it. When you have found the correct printer, click it (to select it) and then click **OK** to close the Browse for Printer dialog box.

6. In the Add Printer Wizard, verify that the path displayed is correct and click **Next** to continue.

7. In the Add Printer Wizard, as before, select the manufacturer and model or **Have Disk** as appropriate for your particular printer.

8. Complete the Add Printer Wizard as before.

9. Test your printer.

CRITICAL THINKING (additional 15 minutes)

You can use a shortcut method to install a remote printer on a computer without having to copy files from the installation disks. On a third computer on the network, try this method now:

1. Open **Network Neighborhood** and locate the printer shared on the network.

2. Right-click the printer and select **Install** on the shortcut menu. (For Windows 2000/XP, select **Connect**.)

3. Follow directions in the wizard to install the printer using the installation files stored on the computer that connects locally to the printer. If you have problems installing the printer, try this: Share the Windows folder on the local computer and then, once the printer is installed correctly on the remote computer, remove the sharing option on the local computer's Windows folder. (This will make that important folder more secure.)

Review Questions

1. A printer is connected to the parallel port on computer A, but is shared on the network. Computer B installs the shared computer and connects to it. Computer A considers it a _____ printer and computer B considers it a _____ printer.

2. If a manufacturer's prescribed method for installing its printer differs from the default Windows method, which method should you use?

3. When installing a local printer that is attached via a parallel cable, what port should you specify?

_____

4. Is it possible for a single printer to be both a local and a network printer? Why or why not?

_____

_____

_____

5. Explain how to print a document without opening it.

_____

_____

6. Describe a shortcut method of installing a network printer without having to access the printer's installation CD.

_____

_____

12

Lab 12.5 Configure and Use Dial-Up Server

Objectives

The goal of this lab is to give you practice using Dial-Up Server to allow dial-in access to a computer. After completing this lab, you will be able to:

> ➤ Install Dial-Up Server
> ➤ Configure Dial-Up Server
> ➤ Configure a Dial-Up Networking connection

Materials Required

This lab will require the following:

> ➤ Two Windows 98 computers
> ➤ Modem and telephone line for each computer
> ➤ Dial-Up Networking installed on both computers

➤ File and Print Sharing and Client for Microsoft Networks installed on both computers and at least one shared folder on the host computer

➤ Windows 98 installation CD or installation files stored in another location

➤ Workgroup of 2–4 students

Activity Background

You can set up your Windows computer to receive dial-in connections from other computers. You might wish to do this if you travel and want to be able to transfer files to and from your home computer while away. In Windows 95, you must install the Microsoft Plus utility; in Windows 98, you need to install the Dial-Up server component; and Windows NT requires the Remote Access Service (RAS). Windows 2000 and Windows XP have the ability to allow incoming calls by default. In this lab you will set up and use Dial-Up Server in Windows 98.

Estimated completion time: **45 minutes**

ACTIVITY

Follow these steps to install Dial-Up Server:

1. Open the **Control Panel**, double-click the **Add/Remove Programs** icon and then click the **Windows Setup** tab.

2. In the Components list box, double-click the **Communications** group. The Communications dialog box opens.

3. Select the **Dial-Up Server** checkbox and then click **OK**. The Communications dialog box closes and you return to the Add/Remove Programs dialog box.

4. Click **OK** to close the Add/Remove Programs dialog box. Supply Windows 98 installation files as necessary.

Follow these steps to configure Dial-Up Server:

1. In Windows Explorer or My Computer open **Dial-Up Networking**.

2. In Dial-Up Networking, click **Connections** on the menu bar, then click **Dial-Up Server**. The Dial-Up Server dialog box opens.

3. In the Dial-Up Server dialog box select the **Allow caller access** option button.

4. In the Dial-Up Server dialog box click **Change Password**. The Dial-Up Server Password dialog box opens.

5. In the Dial-Up Server Password dialog box, leave the Old password textbox blank. In the New password and Confirm new password text boxes type **test**. Click **OK** to close the Dial-Up Server Password dialog box.

6. In the Dial-Up Server dialog box, click **Server Type**. The Server Type dialog box opens.

7. In the Server Type dialog box, click the **Type of Dial-Up server** list arrow and then select **PPP: Internet**, **Windows NT Server**, **Windows 98**.

8. In the Advanced options section of the Server Type dialog box, make sure that the **Enable software compression** and the **Require encrypted password** check boxes are selected, then click **OK** to close the Server Type dialog box.

9. In the Dial-Up Server dialog box, click **OK**. The Dial-Up Server dialog box closes and a Dial-Up Server symbol appears in the system tray.

10. Double click the **Dial-Up Server** symbol in the system tray. The Dial-Up Server dialog box opens. Verify that the status of the Dial-Up Server is "Monitoring" (indicating that the system is ready to accept an incoming call). Close the Dial-Up Server dialog box and move to the second computer.

Follow these steps to set up a Dial-Up Networking connection to connect to your Dial-Up Server computer:

1. In Windows Explorer, double-click the **Dial-Up Networking** icon. The Dial-Up Networking window opens.

2. Double-click the **Make New Connection** icon. The Make New Connection dialog box opens.

3. Type **DISLAB** for the name of the connection, select the correct modem if necessary, and then click **Next** to continue.

4. The Made New Connection dialog box opens. Next, specify the number your computer will dial to complete the dial-up connection to the Dial-Up Server. Enter the Dial-Up Server computer's area code and phone number (as provided by your instructor), and select the country code from the drop-down menu. Click **Next** to continue.

5. The Make New Connection dialog box informs you that the connection icon was created successfully. Click **Finish** to close the Make New Connection dialog box. Your new connection appears in the Dial-Up Networking window.

Follow these steps to connect to the Dial-Up Server:

1. Following directions in Lab 12.2, install NetBEUI as the network protocol on both computers. When you are finished installing NetBEUI, you should see it associated with the dial-up adapter in Network Neighborhood.

2. Following directions in Lab 12.1, verify that both computers belong to the same workgroup.

3. To make the connection, double-click the connection icon in the Dial-Up Networking window.

4. The Connect To dialog box opens, showing the connection name. Enter **test** as the password and then click **Connect** to dial up the server.

5. Once the connection is made, verify that you are able to transfer files and then disconnect.

CRITICAL THINKING (additional 15 minutes)

Change the workgroup identity on one of the computers so that the two computers no longer belong to the same workgroup. Attempt to connect and transfer files. At what point did the process fail?

_____

_____

Review Questions

1. What Windows 98 component allows a computer to receive an incoming call?

_____

2. What dialog box includes the Identification tab, which allows you to make changes to the computer's network identity? How do you access that dialog box?

_____

3. Suppose the Dial-Up Server status for your computer is "monitoring." What is Dial-Up Server doing?

_____

_____

_____

4. How does each computer disconnect from a Dial-Up Server session?

_____

_____

_____

_____

13

WINDOWS ON THE INTERNET

Labs included in this chapter

➤ Lab 13.1 Install Software to Delete Cookies

➤ Lab 13.2 Use FTP to Download a Browser

➤ Lab 13.3 Download and Install Internet Explorer and Install Netscape

➤ Lab 13.4 Set Up NetMeeting

➤ Lab 13.5 Configure a Browser So It Doesn't Download Images

LAB 13.1 INSTALL SOFTWARE TO DELETE COOKIES

Objectives

The goal of this lab is to help you install software that will delete cookies each time you boot your computer. After completing this lab, you will be able to:

➤ Locate, download, and install the software

➤ Delete cookies using the software you downloaded

Materials Required

This lab will require the following:

➤ Internet access

➤ Windows 9x or higher

Activity Background

When you visit certain Web sites, cookies are placed on your system to collect information about you, including what Web sites you visit. Besides being an annoyance, cookies can also be a security risk, passing on information that you don't want to make accessible to others. For example, this information could be passed on to companies who might then sell it to someone else or use it for advertising purposes. Several utilities on the market will clean cookies from your computer. One of those is Webroot's Window Washer, which is available for trial download. In this lab, you will install Window Washer and use it to delete cookies.

Estimated completion time: **45 minutes**

ACTIVITY

Follow these steps to download Webroot's Window Washer software. As you are aware, Web sites change often so your steps might differ slightly from these.

1. Go to *www.webroot.com*.

2. Click the **Trial Downloads** link.

3. Scroll down until you see "Window Washer" and then click **Primary Download Site**. (If this download site does not work, you might have to use one of the alternate links listed below it.)

4. The File Download dialog box appears, indicating that you have chosen to download the installation file for Window Washer. Click the **Run this program from its current location** option button and click **OK**.

5. A dialog box appears indicating the progress of the installation. Select the **Close this dialog box when download completes** checkbox and wait for the download to finish. Depending on the speed of your connection, this could take a few minutes. While you are waiting, look on the Webroot site for information about the Window Washer and record a short description of what it does:

it clears (washes) cache, history, and instant message files.

6. When the download is finished, a Security Warning dialog box appears. Click **Yes** to verify that you want to install and run the trial version of Window Washer.

7. The Window Washer Setup dialog box appears. Click **Yes** to continue.

8. The Window Washer installation program launches. In the first dialog box, click **I Agree** to accept the license agreement.

9. The Installation Options dialog box opens. By default, the **Install to:** location is C:\Program Files\Washer, and the options for adding an icon to the desktop and a link to the Start menu are selected. If you wanted to find another location, you would click the Browse button. For this installation, click **Install** to accept the defaults and continue.

10. A message appears asking if, during a wash, you want Window Washer to delete data stored by a browser to be used when auto-completing data forms. Click **Yes**.

11. A message appears in the same dialog box informing you that the installation is complete. Deselect the **Run Window Washer Now** checkbox and the **View Release Notes** checkbox and then click **Exit**.

Follow these steps to use Window Washer to delete cookies:

1. Open Internet Explorer and browse the Web for a couple of minutes, visiting a variety of sites such as news sites and commercial sites. Click a few links and ads on those sites. Close Internet Explorer.

2. Open **Windows Explorer**, and then open the **Cookies** folder, which is usually located under C:\Windows. The cookies are stored as text files.

   - How many cookies are listed?

   4

13

- What sites appear to have stored cookies on your computer?

  expedia

  microsoft

  msn

3. On the Start menu, point to **Programs**, point to **Window Washer**, and then click **Window Washer**. A dialog box appears showing what information Window Washer is loading. When it finishes loading the required system information, Window Washer opens.

4. At the top of the Window Washer window you see a message indicating that this installation of Windows has never been washed. Click the **Standard Wash Items** button in the Washer Settings pane on the left (if this view is not already active), locate Internet Explorer on the list of Standard Wash items in the right pane, and then click the **Options** button. The Internet Explorer Wash Items dialog box opens. What other items are checked by default?

   auto complete.   _cookies._

   address bar   _history_

   cache.   _media bar_

5. Click **OK** to close the Internet Explorer Wash Items dialog box.

6. Click **Wash Now** in the Washer Controls pane to begin washing your system. Window Washer minimizes itself, and the icon in the system tray moves while the washer is working. Window Washer re-maximizes itself when the wash is complete. How has the message at the top of the window changed?

   washing complete.

7. Open the Cookies folder again to verify that the cookies are gone.

If you still see cookies in the Cookies folder after you run Window Washer, you might need to click **Change Wash Directories** in the Standard Wash Items list and then click **Redetect** to have Window Washer locate the folders containing the files you want to delete. You might also need to verify that you checked all the options indicating which files you want to delete before running Window Washer again.

Review Questions

1. What other items can Window Washer clean besides cookies?

2. List some reasons why you might not want cookies on your system and why you might want to clear Internet Explorer form data, as well as your document history.

_____

_____

_____

3. What information did the Webroot site provide about how Window Washer works?

_____

_____

4. Can you specify your own wash items—that is, items that are not already listed in Window Washer? Explain.

_____

_____

5. How might cookies be useful?

_____

_____

13

LAB 13.2 USE FTP TO DOWNLOAD A BROWSER

Objectives

The goal of this lab is to help you use FTP from the command prompt to download a browser. After completing this lab, you will be able to:

➤ Use common FTP commands from a command prompt

➤ Download a browser via FTP

Materials Required

This lab will require the following:

➤ Internet access

Activity Background

FTP (File Transfer Protocol) provides a quick and easy way to transfer files over the Internet without first converting them to ASCII text. One situation in which you might use FTP is when transmitting files that are too large to be sent as e-mail attachments. For this lab, imagine that your Web browser has been rendered inoperable, either by a virus or because you accidentally deleted some vital files. Suppose, however, that you can still connect to the Internet. How can you get your browser back? If you are using a network, it might be possible for you to go to another computer on the network, use that computer's browser to download a new browser, and then transfer the downloaded browser file to your computer. Another option is to reinstall Windows on your computer, a process that will install the Microsoft Internet Explorer browser. However, if none of these options are available or are practical, you can use FTP to download a browser. If you have no user-friendly GUI FTP software installed on your computer, you can use FTP from the command prompt. In this lab, you will use FTP commands from the command prompt to locate and download the latest version of Netscape.

Estimated completion time: **45 minutes**

ACTIVITY

Follow these steps to connect to the Netscape FTP site from a command prompt and download the latest version of the Netscape browser:

1. When you download the browser, you will want to store the file in a location on your hard drive that will be easy to find. In Windows Explorer, create a folder on your C: drive called **Downloads**.

2. Open a command prompt window.

3. When the command prompt window opens, the C:\Windows directory will probably be the active directory. When you use FTP, the files you download will be stored in whatever directory was active when you began the session. To change to the Downloads directory, type **cd c:\downloads** and press **Enter**.

4. Once the Downloads directory is active, type **ftp** and press **Enter**. How did the command prompt change?

   changed to FTP

5. To enter the Netscape FTP site, type **open ftp.netscape.com** and press **Enter**.

6. A message appears indicating that you are connected to the Netscape site and that the server is ready, followed by a User prompt. Many sites, including this one, allow limited access to the site via an anonymous login. Type **anonymous** at the user prompt and press **Enter**.

7. A message appears indicating that your guest logon is OK and requesting your complete e-mail address as a password. Type your e-mail address and press **Enter**. What message do you receive?

230 guest login ok, access restrictions apply

8. You now have access to certain files on the Netscape FTP site. Browse to the location of the latest version of the Netscape browser. Use the **dir** command to list the contents of the various directories and the **cd** command to change directories as necessary. At the time of this writing, Netscape 6.2.1 was located in the following path: ftp.netscape.com/pub/netscape6/english/6.2.1/windows/win32/N6Setup.exe. The names and locations of downloadable files can change as versions and site structure change, so you might find the file stored in a different directory. The exact name of the file might be different as well, depending on what the most current version of the browser is. If the location or name of the latest version of the browser setup file differs from the one mentioned earlier in this step, record the correct information here:

_its 7.1 version.   Pub/netscape7/english/7.1_bdp/ windows /win 3t._

9. Once you have located the file, type **bin** and press **Enter**. This sets the download mode to specify that you want the file downloaded as a binary (not ASCII) file.

10. To download the file, enter this command (substituting the correct file name if you noted a different one in Step 8): **get N6Setup.exe**. Remember that FTP commands are case-sensitive.

11. Press **Enter**. What messages appear?

Port command successful

opening Binary mode data connection for NSSetup.exe (217472 bytes)

Binary transfer complete.

12. Return to Windows Explorer, click **View** on the menu bar, click **Refresh**, then open the **Downloads** folder and verify that the file downloaded successfully.

13. To verify that the browser setup program you downloaded works, double-click the file you downloaded. The setup program opens.

14. Close the setup program, as you will not actually be installing the browser until the next lab.

15. Return to the command prompt window, type **bye** and then press **Enter** to close the FTP session.

Review Questions

1. List all the FTP commands you used in this lab, with a short description of each.

_____

_____

_____

_____

_____

_____

2. In what mode did you download the browser setup file? Why do you think this was necessary?

_____

_____

_____

3. For what other operating systems and in what other languages was Netscape available for download?

_____

_____

4. If you were using FTP to upload a text file that was too large to send as an e-mail attachment, which mode (ASCII or binary) would you choose to upload it and why?

_____

_____

5. Imagine that you are downloading FileABC.txt from the FTP site of CompanyXYZ.com. The file is located in the /pub/documentation/ folder of that site. Your FTP client defaults to binary mode for download. List in order all the commands you would use to open the FTP connection, download the file, and close the connection.

_____

_____

_____

LAB 13.3 DOWNLOAD AND INSTALL INTERNET EXPLORER AND INSTALL NETSCAPE

Objectives

The goal of this lab is to help you download and install the latest versions of Internet Explorer and Netscape. After completing this lab, you will be able to:

➤ Download the latest version of a browser from a company's Web site

➤ Install two downloaded browsers

Materials Required

This lab will require the following:

➤ Internet access

Activity Background

Companies that make Web browsers periodically offer new versions of their products that incorporate new features or fix known bugs. In this lab, you will install the Netscape browser that you downloaded in the previous lab, and you will also download and install an update for Microsoft Internet Explorer. Sometimes it can be helpful to have more than one browser on your machine, so that you can become familiar with, use the features of, and test software with each.

13

Estimated completion time: **30 minutes**

ACTIVITY

Follow these directions to download an update for Internet Explorer. As always, remember that Web sites change often, so your steps might differ slightly from these.

1. Go to ***www.microsoft.com***, and locate the link to download the latest version of Internet Explorer. At the time of this writing, the link for downloading the latest version was found at:

   www.microsoft.com/windows/ie/downloads/critical/ie6sp1/default.asp.

   If you find the link for the latest version at a different location, record that location here.

2. Select **English** and click **Go**. Click the link to begin downloading.

3. The File Download dialog box opens. Click the **Save this program to disk** option button and then click **OK**.

4. The Save As dialog box appears. Locate the C:\Downloads folder you created in the previous lab and click **Save** to save the Internet Explorer setup file (which is called ie6setup.exe or something similar) to that folder.

5. The File Download dialog box closes, and you see a dialog box indicating the progress of the download. Select the **Close this dialog box when download completes** check box. You will know that the download is finished when the File Download dialog box closes. If you did not select this option, the progress indicator and the messages in the File Download dialog box would change to indicate when the download was finished.

Follow these steps to install Netscape (which you downloaded in the Lab 13.2):

1. Open Windows Explorer, open the C:\Downloads folder, and double-click the setup file for Netscape.

2. Setup launches, showing the Welcome screen. Click **Next**.

3. The License Agreement screen appears. Click **Accept** to accept the license agreement.

4. The Setup Type screen appears. In this screen, you can choose Recommended, Full, or Custom Setup. For this installation, you will use the **Recommended** setup. Under what circumstances would you choose the Full installation option? The Custom installation?

   _____

   _____

   _____

5. Verify that the **Recommended** option button is selected, and then click **Next**.

6. A dialog box appears asking if you want to create the destination directory. Click **Yes** to continue.

7. The next screen gives you a chance to choose the Quick Launch option, which makes it possible to start Netscape faster by storing parts of the program in memory. Answer the questions below:

   ■ What type of user is this option designed for?

   _____

   ■ If a computer were configured for more than one user, why might you not want to select this option?

   _____

   _____

8. Verify that the **Use Quick Launch for faster startup times** check box is *not* selected, and then click **Next**.

9. The Download Options screen appears. What is one reason you might want to save the installer files rather than allowing the system to delete them from the temporary directory after installation?

_____

_____

10. Select the **Save installer files locally** check box, and then click **Next**.

11. The Start Install screen appears with a summary of options you selected. Scroll through the list to verify your choices, and then click **Install** to begin the installation. Use the space below to list the windows that appear on your screen as the installation progresses.

_____

_____

_____

_____

12. When the installation is complete, an Activation dialog box opens. Click the **I don't currently have a Netscape screen name** option button and then click **Activate**.

13. Fill in screen name, password, and Zip code fields; select a country and a language; uncheck the boxes next to the promotional offers if desired; and click **Activate**. (If the screen name you requested is not available, you will be given the chance to try another one.)

14. The Activation dialog box shows a message informing you of successful registration and lists your user name and the features you are configured to use. Click **OK** to close the window.

15. During installation, a window opened behind the Activation dialog box, showing the contents of the Netscape directory. In that window, double-click the **Netscape** icon to launch the browser.

16. A message appears, asking if you want to make Netscape your default browser. Click **No**. The Netscape browser opens.

Follow these directions to install the version of Internet Explorer you downloaded:

1. Close all Netscape windows.

2. Locate and double-click the **Internet Explorer** setup file in Windows Explorer in your C:\Downloads directory.

13

3. The Internet Explorer setup program opens, showing the license agreement screen. Click the **I accept the agreement** option button and then click **Next**.

4. In the next screen, you can choose a typical or custom installation. Verify that the **Install now** option is selected in order to proceed with a typical installation, and click **Next**.

5. A status screen appears, in which the progress of downloading and installing components is shown. This may take several minutes. When the status screen closes and a message appears prompting you to restart your computer, click **Finish** to restart your computer and complete the installation.

Review Questions

1. Which installation took longer, Internet Explorer or Netscape?

_____

2. Which installation required you to restart your computer? What message was displayed when you restarted?

_____

_____

3. Which installation offered more options for customization during the recommended/typical installation process?

_____

_____

4. List any other differences you noticed between the installation of Netscape and the installation of Internet Explorer.

_____

_____

_____

_____

5. List any differences you found between the procedures given in this lab and the actual steps required to download and install the most current versions of the two browsers.

_____

_____

_____

_____

LAB 13.4 SET UP NETMEETING

Objectives

The goal of this lab is to help you set up and use NetMeeting. After completing this lab, you will be able to:

➤ Install the NetMeeting component

➤ Configure NetMeeting

Materials Required

This lab will require the following:

➤ Windows 98 operating system

➤ Windows 98 installation CD or installation files stored in another location

➤ Computer with PC camera installed

➤ Sound card, speakers, and microphone (optional)

Note: You can substitute Windows 2000 or Windows XP for Windows 98.

Activity Background

NetMeeting is video conferencing software included with Windows 98 and Windows 2000/XP. One way to find others on a network or the Internet to join a conference is to use a directory service, an online database that NetMeeting uses to locate participants in a NetMeeting conference. One such directory service is Microsoft Internet Directory. When you install NetMeeting, you enter information about yourself, and can then be added to the Microsoft Internet Directory. The following steps ask you to use the Microsoft Internet Directory. Your instructor might tell you to use a different directory service. You can also use an IP address to locate someone for a conference, or you can use a computer name on the network. In this lab, you will install and configure NetMeeting. Instructions given are for Windows 98, but Windows 2000/XP works about the same way.

13

Estimated completion time: **45 minutes**

ACTIVITY

Follow these steps to install NetMeeting (if it is not already installed).

1. Open the Control Panel, open the **Add/Remove Programs** applet, and then click the **Windows Setup** tab. Windows searches for Windows Components.

2. Double-click the **Communications** group in the **Components** list box. The Communications dialog box opens.

3. Scroll down the Components list box, select the **Microsoft NetMeeting** checkbox, and then click **OK**. The Communications dialog box closes.

4. Click **OK** to close the Add/Remove Properties dialog box. The Copying Files dialog box appears. If prompted, supply the location of the Windows 98 installation files. When the files are copied, the Copying Files dialog box closes. Reboot your PC if prompted. (Note that for Windows 2000/XP, to install NetMeeting, in Windows Help, locate the topic Using NetMeeting, and follow the directions given.)

Now you will launch NetMeeting and configure it. Follow these steps:

1. Click **Start** on the taskbar, point to **Programs**, and then look for NetMeeting on one of the submenus. You might find it located under Internet Tools, or under **Accessories | Communications**.

2. Click **NetMeeting**.

3. Microsoft NetMeeting begins configuring your connection. Click **Next** to continue.

4. In the next NetMeeting dialog box, supply the requested identification information, and then click **Next** to continue. (Your identification information will be available to other NetMeeting users on the directory server.)

5. What you see on the next screen depends on the version of NetMeeting. You might see a screen asking you what category to use for your personal info. Select the category and click **Next**. For some versions of NetMeeting, you will have the option of selecting a directory server. The default is Microsoft Internet Directory. Leave the default selected and click **Next**.

6. You are asked to specify your connection speed. Select **Local Area Network** (or other speed as specified by your instructor) and then click **Next** to continue.

7. You are asked for permission to place a shortcut to NetMeeting on the desktop and the Quick Launch bar. Deselect both and click **Next**.

8. You are asked to specify your video capturing device. Select your camera on the drop-down menu, if it is not already selected, and then click **Next**.

9. NetMeeting informs you that it will help tune your audio settings. Click **Next**.

10. Set and test your audio settings. When they are satisfactory, click **Next**.

11. When the installation is complete, click **Finish**. NetMeeting launches.

12. Click **Place Call** and then click the **Start Video** button in the My Video frame. You should be able to see video supplied by your PC camera in the My Video screen.

CRITICAL THINKING (additional 20 minutes)

If others in the lab are connected to NetMeeting and you have access to a sound card, speakers, and microphone, join someone else in a video conference. If you don't have access to a directory server, you can make a connection with NetMeeting using IP addresses instead of a directory service. To find out your IP address:

1. Click **Start**, click **Run** type **Winipcfg** in the Run dialog box, and then press **Enter**. (For Windows 2000/XP, to find out your IP address, at a command prompt, enter the **Ipconfig/all** command.)

2. Select your NIC from the list of installed adapters on the resulting IP Configuration window.

3. Exchange IP addresses with others in the lab and make the NetMeeting call to another computer in the lab using that computer's IP address.

Figure 13-1 shows a full NetMeeting video conference complete with shared whiteboard, chat window and video.

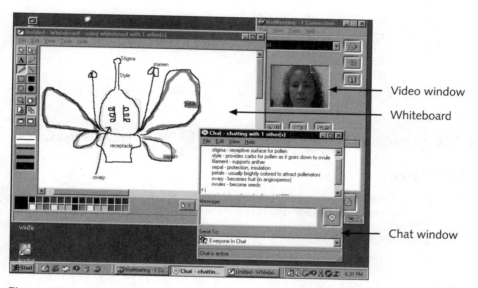

Video window

Whiteboard

Chat window

Figure 13-1   NetMeeting provides three windows during a session

Review Questions

1. What security risks are associated with NetMeeting?

2. Why might it be difficult to use NetMeeting over a 56.6K modem connection?

3. List at least two scenarios in which you might use NetMeeting.

4. What advantages does NetMeeting have over other methods of network communication, such as e-mail or instant messaging? Disadvantages?

_____

_____

5. List all the hardware required for a video conference with NetMeeting.

_____

_____

_____

LAB 13.5 CONFIGURE A BROWSER SO IT DOESN'T DOWNLOAD IMAGES

Objectives

The goal of this lab is to help you set up your browser so that it does not download images. After completing this lab, you will be able to:

➤ Configure Netscape so that it does not download images

➤ Configure Internet Explorer so that it does not download images

Materials Required

This lab will require the following:

➤ Netscape and Internet Explorer installed on the same computer (as specified in Lab 13.3)

Activity Background

Slow browser performance can be caused by factors such as a full cache, temporary files directory, or history file. It can also be caused by the content of the Web page you are viewing. You can set up your browser so it downloads only text and not images. In this lab, you will explore Netscape and Internet Explorer (which you installed in Lab 13.3) and find the options to allow you to select text-only downloads.

Estimated completion time: **30 minutes**

ACTIVITY

Follow these steps to configure Netscape and Internet Explorer so they don't download images:

1. Open Netscape and browse the Web, recording the URLs of the sites you visit. (You'll need these URLs later.)

   _____

   _____

   _____

2. Explore the menus on the menu bar, and then locate and click the command that allows you to change your preferences for Netscape. Use the space below to record the name of the menu on which you found the relevant command.

   _____

3. In the list box on the left side of the Preferences window you can select categories and subcategories of preferences you want to configure. Clicking the arrow to the left of a category expands the category so you can see its subcategories. Clicking the name of a category or subcategory displays associated settings to the right of the list box. Explore the categories and subcategories until you find the setting to allow you to configure Netscape so it does not download images. Record the location of that option here:

   _____

4. When you have located and displayed the image options, click the **Do not load any images** option button and then click **OK** to close the Preferences window.

5. Return to the Netscape browser window and click **Reload** on the View menu. How does the current Web page change?

   _____

6. Revisit the Web sites you recorded in Step 1. Are there any differences in how the pages display or how the browser performs? Why do you think this is?

   _____

   _____

   _____

13

7. Follow the same steps to configure Internet Explorer so it doesn't download images. Record the same information and answer the same questions for Internet Explorer as for Netscape, noting any differences in locations, names of menus, etc. HINT: You will have to *deselect* a checkbox to configure Internet Explorer not to download images.

_____

_____

_____

_____

Review Questions

1. Which browser was easier to configure? Explain your answer.

_____

_____

2. For both browsers, was the option for not downloading images located where you expected it to be? If not, where would you have expected to find it?

_____

_____

3. Did you notice any other similar options in either browser that might also improve browser performance? If so, list them.

_____

_____

4. Did you notice any difference in how the two browsers performed before you blocked downloading images? After you blocked downloading images? Explain.

_____

_____

_____

5. Under what circumstances might you want to block image downloads?

_____

_____

LINUX, MACS, AND NOTEBOOKS

LAB 14.1 EXAMINE A MACINTOSH

Objective

The objective of this lab is to help you become familiar with an Apple Macintosh computer. After completing this lab, you should be able to:

➤ Explain the differences between a Macintosh and a PC

➤ Identify differences between the Mac operating system and Windows

Materials Required

➤ Macintosh computer with OS 9 or OS X

➤ Workgroup of 2–4 students

Activity Background

In this lab you will take a look at a Macintosh computer. You will use the Mac's Graphical User Interface (GUI) to find files and launch applications, noting the main differences in the way a Mac and a Windows PC accomplish these tasks. You will also note the strengths and weaknesses of both operating systems.

As you know, a mouse on a Windows system has at least two buttons, and may include other features, such as wheels, that are devoted to specific tasks. If you prefer, you can use keystroke shortcuts in Windows to perform tasks via the keyboard instead of via the mouse. For some people, these keystrokes are more efficient than clicking a mouse. And even if you normally use the mouse, you can always use the keyboard shortcuts if the mouse happens to fail. By contrast, most Mac mouse devices have only one button. Others have no button at all (in which case pressing the entire mouse has the same effect as pressing a button). When using a Mac, then, you have to use the keyboard in combination with the mouse in order to perform tasks that could be performed using only the mouse in Windows. In this lab you will have a chance to experience these differences for yourself.

Estimated completion time: **45 minutes**

ACTIVITY

In Windows 9x and later, the quickest way to view the properties of an object is to open Windows Explorer, right-click the object and then click Properties in the shortcut menu. Alternately, you can highlight the object in My Computer and press Alt+F+R. A Macintosh mouse, however, has no right mouse button. Follow these instructions to view the properties of an object on a Mac:

1. Highlight a desktop icon using the arrow keys.

2. Press and hold the **Apple** key, press the **i** key and then release both keys. An Info window opens, giving information on that object. Close the window by clicking the box at the upper left-hand corner in OS 9 or the **X** box in OS X.

3. Use the mouse alone to highlight the same object on the desktop.

4. Click **File** on the menu bar at the top of the desktop and then click **Get Info** (in OS 9) or **Show Info** (in OS X). Close the window.

In Windows, each open window has its own menu bar. With a Mac, all open windows share the same menu bar at the top of the desktop. This menu bar changes its options according to which window is selected. When no applications are open, the Finder menu bar is displayed as shown in Figure 14-1.

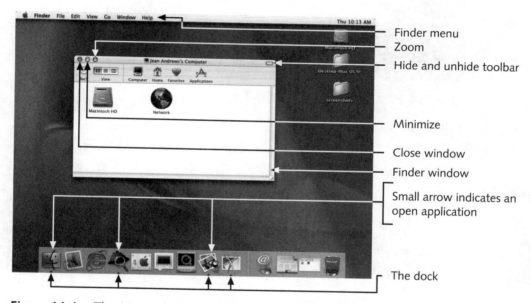

Figure 14-1   The Mac X desktop with a Finder window showing

Experiment with the Mac menu bar by following these steps:

1. Click **File** on the Finder menu and then click **Find**. This opens Sherlock, which is like the Windows Find or Search features.

2. Examine the menu bar, and notice that it has changed to display commands related to Sherlock.

The icons at the top of the Sherlock window indicate different places that Sherlock can look for information. By default, the hard drive is selected, indicating that Sherlock is ready to search for files or folders (see Figure 14-2). You'll use Sherlock now to search for a Web browser.

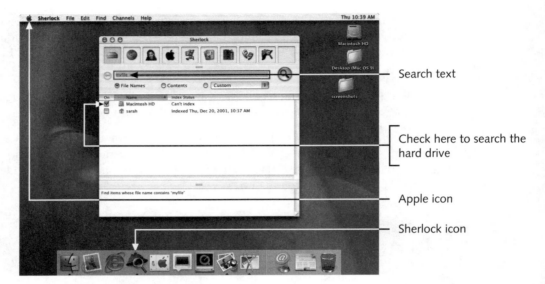

Figure 14-2   Use Sherlock to search for files and folders

Follow these steps:

1. In the field below the hard drive symbol, type **Explorer**. Make sure the **File Names** option button is selected, and check the box next to the hard drive in the field below.

2. Click the magnifying glass icon to start the search. The results are displayed in the same field where you checked the box next to the hard drive. (If you don't see "Explorer" in the list of results, begin again with Step 1, only this time type "Netscape".)

3. Double-click the **Internet Explorer** (or **Netscape**) icon to launch your browser and note that, once again, the menu bar has changed to offer options for the active application.

In Windows 9x and later, the taskbar displays buttons for all open applications. You can switch to an application by clicking its icon in the taskbar. Mac OS X has a feature called the Dock that functions much like the taskbar in Windows, which you can see at the bottom of the screen in Figure 14-1. (This feature is not included in Mac OS 9.) If you are working on a Mac OS X computer, you can experiment with the Dock feature by performing the following steps. If you are using a Mac OS 9 computer, simply read these steps instead.

1. Click the **Internet Explorer** (or **Netscape**) icon on the left side of the Dock. Internet Explorer opens, and the menu bar at the top of the screen changes to show options for this application. Record the options that the menu bar offers for Internet Explorer.

_____

_____

2. Click the **Sherlock** icon on the left side of the Dock. Sherlock is maximized, and the menu bar changes again. Record the options that the menu bar offers for Sherlock.

_____

_____

3. Minimize both Sherlock and the Web browser. Notice that these two icons on the right side of the Dock have small arrows pointing to them, indicating open applications. (These arrows are shown in Figure 14–2.) The menu bar should still reflect the last application that was active, not necessarily the last one you minimized.

4. Move your mouse over the icons on the Dock and use the space below to describe what happens.

_____

_____

5. Click the **Sherlock** icon on the right of the Dock. The Sherlock window and menu options are restored.

Review Questions

1. When using a Mac, why do you have to rely more on keyboard/mouse combinations than when using a PC?

_____

_____

2. What Mac feature is similar to the Find or Search feature of Windows?

_____

3. Does each window on a Mac include its own menu bar? Explain.

_____

_____

4. What Mac OS X feature performs much the same function as the Windows taskbar?

_____

14

5. What is the quickest way to view the properties of an object on a Mac?

_____

_____

LAB 14.2 DOWNLOAD AND INSTALL SHAREWARE ON A MAC

Objectives

The goal of this lab is to help you download and install a Shareware utility on a Mac. After completing this lab, you will be able to:

➤ Locate Shareware utilities for a Mac

➤ Download and install a utility

➤ Use the utility that you downloaded

Materials Required

This lab will require the following:

➤ Macintosh computer with OS 9 or OS X

➤ Internet access

Activity Background

Despite the similarities between the Macintosh and Windows environments, there are significant differences between the file structures and the interfaces. Thus, you can't always assume that just because you know how to perform a task on a PC that you also know how to perform it on a Macintosh. For example, installing a software program on a Mac is different from installing software on a Windows computer. In this lab, you will research available Shareware utilities for the Mac. Then you will download a program, install it on a Mac, and use it.

Estimated completion time: **30 minutes**

ACTIVITY

Follow these instructions to download and install a Shareware utility on a Mac:

1. Open Internet Explorer or another browser and go to *www.cnet.com.*

2. Click the **Downloads** link at the top of the page. (The same link is also included in the body of the page.)

3. The Downloads page opens, offering downloads for your operating system (Mac OS in this case). In the middle of the page, note the links for the categories of downloads available. List those categories here.

_____

_____

_____

_____

_____

4. Locate, download, and install one of the following:
   ■ Mac operating system update
   ■ Free browser
   ■ Game
   ■ Calendar for the Dock
   ■ Utility that allows you to read Microsoft Word documents on your Mac
   ■ Other (list here)

_____

_____

The following steps offer general instructions for downloading software on the Mac. The procedure may be slightly different on your Mac.

1. Navigate the categories and subcategories on the CNet site until you find the name of the utility you want to download.

2. Click the name of the utility you want to download.

3. The next Web page provides additional information about the selected utility.

4. Click **Download Now**.

5. You see a message indicating that the download site is being contacted. When your computer connects to the download site, the Mac's Download Manager launches, showing the progress of the download, including the estimated time that the download will take. When the download is complete, minimize the Download Manager and your Web browser.

Most installation files are downloaded to the Mac desktop by default. So now that the download is complete and you have minimized open windows, you should be able to see the program files you downloaded on the desktop. (Depending on the utility you downloaded, more than one file might have been installed.) You can move the file later by using

14

a Finder window to open the folder you want to store the downloaded file in and then dragging the installation file to that folder. For now, you will focus on installing the utility.

1. Double-click the installation file on your desktop and follow the directions to install the utility. (Depending on the size of the utility, it might have been downloaded as a compressed file. In that case, you will have to double-click the file to expand before the actual installation program appears on your desktop. Once the installation program appears, you can double-click it.)

2. After the program is installed, open it and verify that it is working.

3. Download and install additional utilities. Check with your instructor to see how many you should download and install.

4. Use Sherlock to search the hard drive for all files associated with the utilities you installed. Record the name of each utility, the names of files associated with the utilities, and their locations:

_____

_____

_____

_____

_____

Review Questions

1. What program or programs did you choose to install and why?

_____

_____

_____

_____

2. In labs in other chapters, you downloaded and installed utilities for Windows. What differences did you notice between that process and the process for downloading and installing a utility on a Mac?

_____

_____

_____

_____

3. Describe the differences between the general procedure given in this lab and the actual steps required to download and install the utility:

_____

_____

_____

_____

4. After you installed each utility, where was the shortcut for launching the utility located?

_____

5. What problems, if any, did you experience during the process of downloading and installing the program, and what did you do to solve them?

_____

_____

_____

_____

_____

LAB 14.3 EXPLORE THE GNOME ENVIRONMENT IN LINUX

14

Objectives

The goal of this lab is to help you become familiar with a Linux GUI operating environment. After completing this lab, you will be able to:

➤ Identify and use the main features of GNOME, a Linux GUI

➤ Describe differences between GNOME and Windows

Materials Required

This lab will require the following:

➤ Linux PC with GNOME installed (or another Linux GUI if necessary)

Activity Background

Linux and Unix rely more heavily on the command prompt than do Windows and the Mac OS. There are, however, several GUI operating environments available for Linux. One common Linux GUI is GNOME.

There are noticeable similarities between GNOME and Windows, such as the presence of menus and windows. However, while Windows 9x and later are true operating systems, GNOME is an operating environment that, in its relationship to the underlying OS, is closer to the earlier Windows 3.x. The menus and other features of the GNOME and the modern Windows interfaces also differ significantly. In this lab, you will explore the GNOME operating environment and note some of the differences between it and Windows. Note that if you don't have access to GNOME, you can perform this lab using another Linux GUI instead.

Estimated completion time: 30 minutes

ACTIVITY

1. Boot up your Linux computer. During the boot process, text on the screen shows which components are being loaded and whether each process succeeds or fails. Depending on your installation of Linux, whether or not other operating systems are installed on the machine, and which startup options are selected during installation, you may have to choose to launch GNOME from a startup menu. (This startup menu will look similar to the one you saw in Lab 10.4, where you installed Recovery Console on Windows XP.) If you encounter such a startup menu, record the options on that menu here.

   _____

   _____

   _____

   _____

2. The GUI begins to load, and a logon screen appears. Type **root**, press **Enter** and then enter the password if required. You are now logged on as the root user with administrative privileges. (You can also use the logon provided to you by your instructor.)

3. Wait for the GUI to load completely.

4. Before opening any programs, take a minute or two to familiarize yourself with the GUI's general appearance. List at least three similarities and three differences between GNOME and Windows.

_____

_____

_____

_____

_____

_____

5. In the bottom-left corner on the toolbar, look for a button labeled Start (or something similar). Click this button, explore the menus it offers. Find and open the following applications, taking notes below about how you opened each application.

- Word-processing program

_____

- Command prompt

_____

- A view that will allow you to explore the computer's file structure

_____

- A utility similar to Windows' Control Panel that allows you to change system settings and display properties

_____

- A game

_____

6. Once you have several windows open, practice using some of the applications and switching between them, making notes about similarities and differences with corresponding functions in Windows.

_____

_____

14

_____

_____

_____

_____

Review Questions

1. Which is more closely related to the underlying operating system, GNOME or the Windows GUI? Explain your answer.

_____

_____

2. Did your familiarity with Windows help you learn how to use GNOME? Why or why not?

_____

_____

3. How did the menus in GNOME work differently from the menus in Windows?

_____

_____

4. Do you find GNOME or Windows easier to use? Explain your answer.

_____

_____

5. Name at least three features of GNOME that offer functionality that is not included in Windows.

_____

_____

_____

Lab 14.4 Use the vi Editor in Linux

Objectives

The goal of this lab is to help you use the Linux vi editor. After completing this lab, you will be able to:

➤ Open the vi editor and create and save a memo

➤ Use commands from within the vi editor to manipulate text

Materials Required

This lab will require the following:

➤ A computer with Linux installed

Activity Background

Like Windows, most distributions of Linux offer at least one simple GUI word processing program. Linux also provides the vi editor that you can use to work with text documents in a command interface. The vi editor name comes from the fact that it is a visual text editor that was, at one time, the most popular Unix text editor. It is still used with shells that don't allow the use of the arrow, Delete, or Backspace keys. The vi editor can be used in insert mode, which allows you to enter text, or in command mode, which allows you to enter commands to perform editing tasks. In this lab, you will learn how to create and use commands on a text file in the vi editor. All of these commands are case-sensitive.

Estimated completion time: **30 minutes**

14

Activity

Follow these steps to open the vi editor and create a document:

1. Boot up your Linux computer. If you boot to a command prompt, skip to Step 3.

2. If you boot to a GUI, locate and open a terminal window. (This is similar to opening a command prompt window from within Windows.)

3. Type **vi mymemo** at the command prompt and press **Enter**. This command opens the vi editor and at the same time creates an empty text document called mymemo.

4. At this point, when you first open the vi editor, you are in command mode, which means that anything you type will be interpreted as a command by the vi editor. Type **i** to switch to insert mode. (You will not see the command on the screen, and you do not need to press Enter to execute it. The command automatically switches you to insert mode.) The word INSERT at the bottom of the screen indicates that you are now in Insert mode.

5. Type the first two sentences of Step 4 as the text for your memo. If your shell (the component of Linux that enables the user to interact with the OS) supports it, practice using the arrow keys to move the cursor through the text, up, down, left, and right, one character at a time. Table 14-1 shows the commands to use if your shell does not support the arrow keys, as well as other common vi editor commands.

Table 14-1   vi editor commands

Command	Alternate	Description
Ctrl+B	Pg up	Back one screen
Ctrl+F	Pg down	Forward one screen
Ctrl+U		Up half a screen
Ctrl+D		Down half a screen
k	Up arrow	Up one line
j	Down arrow	Down one line
h	Left arrow	Left one character
l	Right arrow	Right one character
w		Forward one word
b		Back one word
0 (zero)		Beginning of the current line
$		End of the current line
nG		Line specified by number n
H		Upper left corner of screen
L		Last line on the screen

6. To switch back to command mode, press the **Esc** key.

Now you are ready to enter commands to manipulate your text.

1. Type **H** to move the cursor to the upper-left corner of the screen. You must use an uppercase H, as all these commands are case-sensitive.

2. Type **w** repeatedly (make sure to use lowercase) until you reach the beginning of the word "first."

3. Type **dw** to delete the word "first." To delete one character at a time, you would use x; to delete an entire line, you would use dd.

4. Practice using some of the other commands listed in Table 14-1 that you have not already used in this lab. Switch between Insert and Command mode as necessary.

5. To save the file and exit the vi editor, type **:x** and press **Enter**. The file is saved and the vi editor closes.

Review Questions

1. Were any of the commands or keystrokes you tried to use within the vi editor not supported by your shell? If so, list them.

   _____

   _____

2. What do you see at the bottom of the screen when you are in insert mode? In command mode?

   _____

   _____

3. Assume that you are in insert mode in the vi editor. List in order the commands you would use to switch to command mode, move to the fourth word in the third line, type the text "new words," and move to the last line in the text.

   _____

   _____

   _____

   _____

4. Assume you are in the vi editor working with your document mymemo. List in order the commands you would use to exit the vi editor, save the document, and open the vi editor to work with a new document called mylist.

   _____

   _____

   _____

   _____

14

5. What are the advantages and disadvantages of working with text in the vi editor as opposed to a GUI word processing program?

_____

_____

_____

_____

LAB 14.5 USE LINUX COMMANDS

Objectives

The goal of this lab is to help you learn to use some Linux commands. After completing this lab, you will be able to:

➤ Use common Linux commands to work with files

Materials Required

This lab will require the following:

➤ A computer with Linux installed

Activity Background

In Lab 14.3, you learned about GNOME, which is a Linux GUI. When working with Linux or Unix, it is necessary to know how to use some common commands, as these operating systems rely heavily on the command prompt. In this lab, you will use the Linux command prompt to create and work with a file.

Estimated completion time: **30 minutes**

ACTIVITY

The shells file in the /etc directory contains a list of the shells available on a Linux system. Each shell incorporates slightly different support for programming and scripting languages, as well as keystrokes. The directions in this lab are for the bash shell. To determine whether you are using the bash shell (and to switch to it if necessary), do the following:

1. At a command prompt, type **echo $shell** and press **Enter**. If you see the output /bin/bash, you are using the bash shell.

2. If you are not using the bash shell, type **bash** and press **Enter** to change to the bash shell.

Follow these steps to view a list of available shells:

1. Type **cat /etc/shells** and press **Enter**.

2. A list of available shells appears. Notice that all these shells are stored in the /bin directory. Type **clear** and press **Enter**. What happens?

_____

_____

3. Type **cat –n /etc/shells** and press **Enter**. What happens?

_____

_____

Next, you will save the list of shells to a file. Follow these steps:

1. Go to the root directory by typing **cd /** and pressing **Enter**.

2. Type **cat /etc/shells > available_shells** and press **Enter**.

3. Notice that no command output appears on the screen, because the output has been saved to the new file available_shells. (The file is created when the command is entered.) To view the contents of the file, type **cat available_shells** and press **Enter**.

The file was saved in the root directory because that's the directory you were in when you created it. It is not a good idea to store data files in the root directory, so follow these steps to create a new directory and move the available_shells file to it:

1. Type **mkdir myfiles** and press **Enter**. This creates a new directory named myfiles under the current directory, which is root. (If you wanted to delete the directory later, you would use the command rmdir.)

2. Type **cd myfiles** to change from the current directory to the new directory.

3. Type **mv /available_shells .** and press **Enter**. (Don't overlook the period at the end of the command line; type it, too.) The period in the command line indicates that you mean the current directory. The complete command copies the file from the root directory to the current directory, which is /myfiles. The source directory is the root and the destination directory is /myfiles.

4. Type **ls** to see the contents of the myfiles directory. The available_shells file is listed.

Now that you have learned how to create a file and a directory and how to move a file, compose and execute commands that will do the following:

1. Make the root directory the current directory. What command did you use?

_____

14

2. Use the cat command to view the contents of the /bin directory. What command did you use?

_____

3. Use the cat command to send the output to a file. What command did you use?

_____

4. Move the file from the root directory to the /myfiles directory. What command did you use?

_____

5. You can also produce a list of the /bin directory in a file that is initially created in the /myfiles directory, eliminating the need to move the file. List below the commands required to do that and then execute the commands.

_____

_____

_____

_____

_____

6. Remove the /myfiles directory and all its contents. What command (or commands) did you use?

_____

_____

_____

Review Questions

1. What command would you use to create a file in the /myfiles directory that lists the contents of your user file, which is located in the home directory? (Assume that your user file is called yourname.)

_____

_____

2. What is the function of the clear command?

_____

_____

3. What is the function of the —n option that you used with the cat command, and how is it helpful?

_____

_____

4. From the root directory, what command would you use to create a directory called importantfiles? What command would you use to delete the directory?

_____

_____

LAB 14.6 BATTERY CALIBRATION AND POWER MANAGEMENT

Objectives

The goal of this lab is to demonstrate the affect battery calibration has on power management features of a laptop PC. After completing this lab, you will be able to:

➤ Explain the calibration process

➤ Discuss how a battery might drift from calibration

➤ Explain how battery calibration affects some power management features

14

Materials Required

This lab will require the following:

➤ Windows desktop computer

➤ Windows laptop computer

➤ Internet access

Activity Background

Many factors affect the battery life of a laptop PC. There are two common types of laptop batteries: NiMH or nickel metalhydride and LiION or lithium ion. LiION batteries are the more expensive and longer lasting type. Lithium ion batteries are more common. A fully charged LiION battery in good condition can provide about 2 ½ to 3 hours of normal use. By contrast, a healthy, fully charged Lithium battery can provide 1 ½ to 2 + hours of normal use.

As you might expect, though, "Normal use" is a rather subjective term. The actual way you use your laptop can greatly affect battery life. For instance, editing text in a word processor doesn't require much power compared to playing a DVD. The word processor uses only a little processor time and occasionally reads or writes to the hard drive. Playing a DVD is processor intensive and requires powering the laser in the drive, thus requiring even more power than the word processor.

What the laptop does when you stop using it for a time also affects battery life. For instance, if you do not use the laptop for 10 minutes, the laptop might or might not automatically go into hibernation to conserve power. In addition to the many power management features on desktop systems, laptops also employ a few additional features to extend battery life during inactivity and protect data when the battery charge becomes low. Some of these features depend on the laptop being able to accurately judge how much life is left in the battery. If the battery is accurately calibrated, the laptop can make better power management decisions. In this lab you will explore how power management and battery life are related.

Estimated completion time:	**30 minutes**

ACTIVITY

1. Examine your desktop computer's CMOS setup utility and the Power Management applet in Control Panel. Usually a computer's BIOS will offer a greater range of options for defining a power management profile than offered by Windows. Complete Table 14-2 to compare the power management options offered in BIOS and in Windows.

Table 14-2   Comparing power management options in BIOS and Windows

Power Management Options and Settings	Found in BIOS	Found in Windows

Although many times the two power management systems might work in conjunction, to avoid possible conflict, Microsoft recommends using the BIOS power management as the preferred method if the BIOS power management conforms to ACPI standards. These standards have been set by a group of manufacturers including Microsoft, Intel and Compaq.

In addition to the BIOS features just explored, laptops often have features or settings to allow the computer to shut down or suspend activity if the battery is about to run out of power. But how does the computer know when power is about to run out? In many batteries, an EPROM (Electronically Programmable Read-Only Memory) is included in the battery assembly to inform the computer about the remaining battery life. The steps below explain the basic procedure for calibrating a battery's EPROM. For specific steps, see your documentation or search the manufacturer's Web site.

1. Verify that your laptop has a fully charged battery that is attached to AC power.

2. Enter the CMOS setup utility and select the Power Management section.

3. In the Power Management section, disable the Power Savings option(s) so that the computer will not attempt to save power during the calibration process.

4. In the Power Management section, disable any Suspend on Low Battery options to prevent interference with calibration.

5. In the Power Management section, select the Battery Calibration option. A warning message appears that calibration should be carried out with a fully charged battery and prompting you to confirm that you wish to continue.

6. Remove the AC power and immediately press **Y** or **Enter**. A message appears with the estimated remaining battery life. In real life, when you actually needed to calibrate your laptop's battery, this information would likely be incorrect.

7. Wait for the battery to drain. It may take much more than an hour.

8. The manufacturer may specify that the battery should be left to cool for a period of time after the battery is drained and the laptop switches off. When appropriate, reattach AC power, boot up and enter CMOS setup.

9. Enter the Power Management section and select Battery Reset. This tells the EPROM that the battery is at (or near) zero charge and takes you back to the Power Management section of CMOS.

10. Reapply your preferred power management settings and save and exit CMOS setup. The battery is now calibrated so that the related power management and suspend features will work properly.

If you have access to a laptop and the permission of your instructor, do the following to calibrate the battery:

1. Locate documentation (in the user manual or on the Web) on how to calibrate the battery. Note how these steps differ from the ones listed above.

_____

_____

_____

_____

14

2. Follow the steps for your laptop to calibrate the battery. (Do *not* attempt this unless you have the specific steps for your laptop, as you might damage the laptop or battery.)

Some factors can also prevent power management from functioning as intended. For instance, word processing programs often include an auto-save feature that continuously saves changes to a document. This feature safeguards against lost work but tends to interfere with hard disk power-down settings. Many screen savers cause similar effects and can also prevent a computer from entering or exiting standby or suspend modes.

Review Questions

1. What types of activities might decrease the battery life of a fully charged battery more quickly than reading a document or spreadsheet? Give three examples.

_____

_____

_____

2. In your opinion, is aggressive power management more important on a desktop computer or a laptop computer? Explain why.

_____

_____

3. Should BIOS power management always be used in conjunction with Windows Power Management? Why or why not?

_____

_____

4. What types of programs might prevent a hard drive power-down setting from saving power as intended? Why?

_____

_____

_____

5. What are two possible consequences of an improperly calibrated battery? Explain.

_____

_____

_____

GLOSSARY

16-bit mode — *See* real mode.

32-bit flat memory mode — A protected processing mode used by Windows NT/2000/XP to process programs written in 32-bit code early in the boot process.

32-bit mode — *See* protected mode.

822 messages — Error messages that occur during e-mail transactions. 822 messages are named after RFC 822, which is the RFC that defines them.

ACPI (Advanced Configuration and Power Interface) — Specification developed by Intel, Compaq, Phoenix, Microsoft, and Toshiba to control power on notebooks and other devices. Windows 98 and Windows 2000/XP support ACPI.

Active Directory — A Windows 2000 and Windows .NET directory database service that allows for one point of administration for shared resources on a network, including files, peripheral devices, Web sites, users, and services.

active partition — The primary partition on the hard drive that boots the OS. Windows NT/2000/XP calls the active partition the system partition.

adapter address — *See* MAC address.

administrator account — In Windows NT/ 2000/XP, grants to the administrator(s) rights and permissions to hardware and software resources, such as the right to add, delete, and change accounts and to change hardware configurations.

Advanced Options menu — A Windows 2000/XP menu that appears when you press F8 when Windows starts. Can be used to troubleshoot problems when loading Windows 2000/XP.

AGP (Accelerated Graphics Port) bus — A bus or slot on the motherboard used for a single video card.

allocation blocks — Sets of hard drive sectors used by a Macintosh computer where the file system stores files.

answer file — A text file containing information Windows NT/2000/XP requires to do an unattended installation.

antivirus (AV) software — Utility programs that prevent infection or detect and remove viruses. McAfee Associates' VirusScan and Norton AntiVirus are two popular AV packages.

API (Application Program Interface) — A method used by an application program to call another program or the OS to perform a utility task.

Apple menu — The Mac OS menu accessed by an apple icon in the upper-right corner of the desktop. The Apple menu contains options that are always available.

Application layer — The OSI layer responsible for interfacing with the application using the network.

application program interface (API) call — A request from software to the OS to access hardware or other software using a previously defined procedure that both the software and the OS understand.

ARP (Address Resolution Protocol) — A protocol that TCP/IP uses to translate IP addresses into physical network addresses (MAC addresses).

Autoexec.bat — A startup text file once used by DOS and used by Windows 9x to provide backward-compatibility. It executes commands automatically during the boot process and is used to create a 16-bit environment.

Automated System Recovery (ASR) — The Windows XP process that allows you to restore an entire hard drive volume or logical drive to its state at the time the backup of the volume was made.

backup domain controller (BDC) — In Windows NT, a computer on a network that holds a read-only copy of the SAM (security accounts manager) database.

Backup Operator — A Windows 2000/XP user account that can back up and restore any files on the system regardless of its having access to these files.

backward-compatible — New hardware and software that is able to support older, existing technologies. This is a common choice of hardware and software manufacturers.

baseline — The level of performance expected from a system, which can be compared to current measurements to determine what needs upgrading or tuning.

basic disk — A way to partition a hard drive, used by DOS and Windows, that stores information about the drive in a partition table at the beginning of the drive. Compare to dynamic disk.

batch file — A text file containing a series of OS commands. Autoexec.bat is a batch file.

best-effort protocol — *See* connectionless protocol.

binding — Associating an OSI layer to a layer above it or below it, as when an IP address (Network layer) is associated with a network card and its MAC address (Data Link layer).

BIOS (basic input/output system) — Firmware that can control a computer's input/output functions, such as communication with the floppy drive and monitor. Also called ROM BIOS.

block — *See* allocation block.

321

blue screen — A Windows NT/2000/XP error that displays against a blue screen and causes the system to halt. Also called a stop error.

bootable disk — For DOS and Windows, a floppy disk that can upload the OS files necessary for computer startup. For DOS or Windows 9x, it must contain the files Io.sys, Msdos.sys and Command.com.

boot blocks — The first two allocation blocks on a Macintosh computer's hard drive. They are initially empty, but once a System folder is installed, they contain the location of the System folder so the system can find and load the OS.

booting — The process that a computer goes through when it is first turned on to get itself ready to receive commands.

boot loader menu — A startup menu that gives the user the choice of which operating system to load such as Windows 98 or Windows 2000 which are both installed on the same system creating a dual boot.

boot partition — The hard drive partition where the Windows NT/2000/XP OS is stored. The system partition and the boot partition may be different partitions.

boot record — The first sector of a floppy disk or logical drive in a partition; contains information about the disk or logical drive. On a hard drive, if the boot record is in the active partition, it is used to boot the OS. Also called boot sector.

boot sector — *See* boot record.

boot sector virus — An infectious program that can replace the bootstrap loader program with a modified, infected version, often causing boot and data retrieval problems.

bootstrap loader — A program at the end of the boot record used to boot an OS from the disk or logical drive.

bridging protocol — *See* line protocol.

Briefcase — A system folder in Windows 9x that is used to synchronize files between two computers.

buffer — A temporary memory area where data is kept before being written to a hard drive or sent to a printer, thus reducing the number of writes to the devices.

built-in user account — An administrator account and guest account set up when Windows NT/2000/XP is installed.

bus — Wires or printed circuits used to transmit electronic signals or voltage on the motherboard to other devices.

bus enumerator — A component of Windows Plug and Play that locates all devices on a particular bus and inventories the resource requirements for these devices.

cabinet file — A file with a .cab extension that contains one or more compressed files and is often used to distribute software on disk. The Extract command is used to extract files from the cabinet file.

cache — A location in memory or some other place used to store frequently used data.

catalog tree — A database of the folders and files on a Macintosh computer's hard drive, including information such as filenames and extensions, application used to open a file, creator of the file or folder, and date the file or folder was created. Works with the extents tree to allow the Mac to access hard drive data.

CD (change directory) command — A command given at the command prompt that changes the default directory, for example CD \Windows.

chain — A group of clusters used to hold a single file.

child directory — *See* subdirectory.

child, parent, grandparent backup method — Backing up and reusing tapes or removable disks by rotating them each day (child), week (parent), and month (grandparent).

clean install — Installing an OS on a new hard drive or a hard drive that has a previous OS installed, but without carrying forward settings kept by the old OS including information about hardware, software, or user preferences. A fresh installation.

client — A software program or computer that requests information from another software program on another computer.

client/server — One computer (the client) requests information from another computer (the server).

cluster — One or more sectors that constitute the smallest unit of space on a disk for storing data (also called file allocation unit).

Cmd.exe — The 32-bit program that provides a command window.

CMOS configuration chip — *See* CMOS setup chip.

CMOS RAM chip — *See* CMOS setup chip.

CMOS setup chip — A microchip on the motherboard that contains a small amount of RAM, enough to hold the configuration information for a motherboard. Also called CMOS configuration chip, CMOS RAM chip.

cold boot — *See* hard boot.

Command.com — Along with Msdos.sys and Io.sys, one of the three files that are the core components of the real-mode portion of Windows 9x. Command.com provides a command prompt and interprets commands.

command mode — The Linux vi editor mode in which you can type commands to manipulate text or to change the status of the editor.

comment — A line or part of a line in a program intended as a remark or comment and ignored when the program runs. A semicolon or an REM is often used to mark a line as a comment.

Compatibility mode — A Windows XP utility that provides an application with the older Microsoft OS environment it was designed to operate in.

compressed drive — A drive whose format has been reorganized to store more data. A compressed drive is not a drive at all; it's a type of file, typically with a host drive called H.

Config.sys — A text file used by DOS and supported by Windows 9x that lists device drivers to be loaded at startup. It can also set system variables used by DOS and Windows.

Configuration Manager — A component of Windows Plug and Play that controls the configuration process of devices and communicates configurations to the devices.

connectionless protocol — A protocol such as UDP that does not require a connection before sending a packet nor guarantees delivery. An example of a UDP transmission is streaming video over the Web. Also called a best-effort protocol.

connection-oriented protocol — A protocol that confirms a good connection has been made before transmitting data to the other end. An example of a connection-oriented protocol is TCP.

console — A centralized location from which to execute commonly used tools.

Control Panels folder — In Mac OS 9, a folder that contains control panels for system settings such as time and date, speaker volume, and the configuration of the Finder window and the desktop. In Mac OS X, control panels no longer exist; their functions are incorporated into the Library folder.

conventional memory — Memory addresses between 0 and 640K. Also called base memory.

cooperative multitasking — A type of pseudo-multitasking whereby the OS switches back and forth between programs loaded at the same time. One program sits in the background waiting for the other to relinquish control. Also called task switching.

CPU (central processing unit) — The heart and brain of the computer, which receives data input, processes information, and executes instructions. Also called a microprocessor.

cross-linked clusters — Errors caused when files appear to share the same disk space, according to the file allocation table.

CVF (compressed volume file) — The file on the host drive of a compressed drive that holds all compressed data.

data bus — See data path.

datagram — See packet.

Data Link layer — The OSI layer that disassembles packets and reassembles data into packets, preparing the packets to be passed on to the physical media.

data packet — See packet.

data path — That portion of a bus that carries data. A data bus is usually 32 or 64 bits wide. Also called a data bus.

default gateway — The gateway a computer on a network will use to access another network unless it knows to use another gateway for quicker access to that network.

default printer — The printer Windows prints to unless another printer is selected.

defragment — To "optimize" or rewrite a file to a disk in one contiguous chain of clusters, thus speeding up data retrieval.

desktop — The initial screen that is displayed when an OS has a GUI interface loaded.

device driver — A program stored on the hard drive that tells the computer how to communicate with an input/output device such as a printer or modem.

DHCP (Dynamic Host Configuration Protocol) server — A service that assigns dynamic IP addresses to computers when they first access a network.

dial-up networking — A Windows 9x and Windows NT/2000/XP utility that uses a modem and telephone line to connect to a network.

differential backup — Backup method that backs up only files that have changed or have been created since the last full backup. When recovering data, only two backups are needed: the full backup and the last differential backup.

digital certificate — See digital signature.

digital signature — Digital codes used to identify and authenticate the source of a file or document.

directory structure — Files created during formatting that allow a Macintosh computer to access its hard drive. Important directory include the boot blocks, the volume information block, the volume bit map, the catalog tree, and the extents tree.

directory table — An OS table that contains file information such as the name, size, time and date of last modification, and cluster number of the file's beginning location.

disk cache — Recently retrieved data and adjacent data are read into memory in advance, anticipating the next CPU request.

disk cloning — Making an exact image of a hard drive, including partition information, boot sectors, operating system installation, and application software to replicate the hard drive on another system or recover from a hard drive crash. Also called disk imaging.

disk compression — Compressing data on a hard drive to allow more data to be written to the drive.

Disk First Aid — A free Mac OS disk repair utility included with Mac OS 9. In Mac OS X, Disk First Aid and Drive Setup are combined into the single Disk Utility.

disk imaging — See disk cloning.

Disk Management — A Windows 2000/XP utility used to display and create and format partitions on basic disks and volumes on dynamic disks.

disk quota — A limit placed on the disk space available to users. Requires a Windows 2000/XP NTFS volume.

disk thrashing — Results when the hard drive is excessively used for virtual memory because RAM is full. It dramatically slows down processing and can cause premature hard drive failure.

Disk Utility — A Mac OS X utility that can be used to set up a drive, reformat a damaged drive, or detect and repair problems on it. It combines the functions of the Mac OS 9 tools Disk First Aid and Drive Setup.

distributions — Different versions of an OS by different vendors.

DLL (dynamic-link library) — A file with a .dll file extension that contains a library of programming routines used by programs to perform common tasks.

DMA (direct memory access) channel — Shortcut method whereby an I/O device can send data directly to memory, bypassing the CPU.

DNS (domain name service or domain name system) — A distributed pool of information (called the name space) that keeps track of assigned domain names and corresponding IP addresses, and the system that allows a host to locate information in the pool. Compare to WINS.

DNS server — A computer that can find an IP address for another computer when only the domain name is known.

dock — A new feature of the Mac OS X interface that consists of icons for frequently used and open applications on a bar at the bottom of the desktop.

docking station — A device that receives a notebook computer and provides additional secondary storage and easy connection to peripheral devices.

domain — In Windows NT/2000/XP, a logical group of networked computers that share a centralized directory database of user account information and security for the entire domain.

domain name — A unique, text-based name that identifies a network.

domain user account — An account for a user that has permission to access resources, folders, and files on a domain.

DOS box — A command window.

Dosstart.bat — A type of Autoexec.bat file that is executed by Windows 9x in two situations: when you select Restart the computer in MS-DOS mode from the shutdown menu or you run a program in MS-DOS mode.

Drive Setup — A Mac OS 9 tool that can be used to format a hard drive when it is initially installed or to reformat a damaged hard drive. In Mac OS X, Drive Setup and Disk First Aid are combined into the Disk Utility.

DriveSpace — A utility that compresses files so they take up less space on a disk drive, creating a single file on the disk to hold the compressed files.

Dr. Watson — A Windows utility that can record detailed information about the system, errors that occur, and the programs that caused them in a log file. Windows 9x names the log file \Windows\ Drwatson\WatsonXX.wlg, where XX is an incrementing number. Windows 2000 names the file \Documents and Settings\user\Documents\ DrWatson\Drwtsn32.log.

Drwatson.log — The log file for the Dr. Watson utility in Windows XP.

dual boot — The ability to boot using either of two different OSs, such as Windows 98 and Windows 2000.

dump file — A file that contains information captured from memory at the time a stop error occurred.

dynamic disk — A way to partition one or more hard drives, introduced with Windows 2000. Information about the drive is stored in a database at the end of the drive. Compare to basic disk.

dynamic IP address — An assigned IP address used for the current session only. When the session is terminated, the IP address is returned to the list of available addresses.

dynamic volume — A volume type used with dynamic disks for which you can change the size of the volume after you have created it.

dynamic VxD — A VxD that is loaded and unloaded from memory as needed.

EFS (Encrypted File System) — A way to use a key to encode a file or folder to protect sensitive data. Because it is an integrated system service, EFS is transparent to users and applications and is difficult to attack.

EIDE (Enhanced Integrated Drive Electronics) — A standard for managing the interface between secondary storage devices and a computer system. A system can support up to four IDE devices such as hard drives, CD-ROM drives, and Zip drives.

Emergency Repair Disk (ERD) — A Windows NT record of critical information about your system that can be used to fix a problem with the OS. The ERD enables restoration of the Windows NT registry on your hard drive.

Emergency Repair Process — A Windows 2000 process that restores the OS to its state at the completion of a successful installation.

emergency startup disk (ESD) — *See* rescue disk.

Emm386.exe — A DOS and Windows 9x utility that provides access to upper memory for 16-bit device drivers and other software.

enabler file — A file included with Macintosh hardware that is released before the instructions to control it are incorporated into the Mac OS. Enabler files allow a device to function with the version of Mac OS being used on the computer.

encrypting virus — A type of virus that transforms itself into a nonreplicating program to avoid detection. It transforms itself back into a replicating program to spread.

encryption — The process of putting readable data into an encoded form that can only be decoded (or decrypted) through use of a key.

enhanced metafile format (EMF) — A format used to print a document that contains embedded print commands. When printing in Windows 9x, EMF information is generated by the GDI portion of the Windows kernel.

environment — As related to OSs, the overall support that an OS provides to applications software.

executive services — In Windows NT/2000/XP, a group of components running in kernel mode that interfaces between the subsystems in user mode and the HAL.

extended memory — Memory above 1024K used in a DOS or Windows 9x system.

extended partition — The hard drive partition that can contain more than one logical drive.

Extensions folder — A Mac OS 9 folder that contains add-ons to provide new features to a Mac, as well as shared libraries and icons. Extensions no longer exist in Mac OS X; their functions are incorporated into the Library folder.

extents — On a Mac, the pieces into which a file is broken when it is larger than one allocation block.

extents tree — A Mac directory structure that contains information about where the allocation blocks are located for files that take up more than one allocation block.

external command — Commands that have their own program files.

FAT (file allocation table) — A table on a hard drive or floppy disk that tracks the clusters used to contain a file.

FAT12 — A file system used on floppy disks in which the width of each entry in the one-column table used to track clusters on the disk is 12 bits.

fatal system error — An error that prevents Windows from loading. An example is a damaged registry.

fault tolerance — The degree to which a system can tolerate failures. Adding redundant components, such as disk mirroring, is a way to build in fault tolerance.

file extension — A three-character portion of the name of a file used to identify the file type. In command lines, the file extension follows the filename and is separated from it by a period. For example, Msd.exe, where exe is the file extension.

filename — The first part of the name assigned to a file. In DOS, the filename can be no more than 8 characters and is followed by the file extension. In Windows, a filename can be up to 255 characters.

file system — The overall structure that an OS uses to name, store, and organize files on a disk. Examples of file systems are FAT16 and FAT32.

file virus — A virus that inserts virus code into an executable program and can spread wherever that program is accessed.

Finder window — A type of Mac window that allows a user to navigate the Mac OS hierarchical file structure. It functions like My Computer or Explorer in Windows and includes buttons similar to those on a Web browser.

firmware — Programs permanently embedded on a microchip. The BIOS on a motherboard is an example of firmware.

folder — *See* subdirectory.

forgotten password floppy disk — A Windows XP disk created in case the user forgets the user account password to the system.

fragmentation — The distribution of data files such that they are stored in noncontiguous clusters.

fragmented file — A file that has been written to different portions of the disk so that it is not in contiguous clusters.

frame — The header and trailer information added to data to form a data packet to be sent over a network.

front-side bus — *See* system bus.

FTP (File Transfer Protocol) — The protocol used to transfer files over a TCP/IP network so the file does not need to be converted to ASCII format before transferring.

full backup — A complete backup. All the files on the hard drive are backed up each time the backup procedure is performed. It is the safest backup method, but takes the most time.

fully qualified domain name (FQDN) — A host name and a domain name such as jsmith.amazon.com. Sometimes loosely referred to as a domain name.

gateway — A computer or other device that connects networks.

GDI (Graphics Device Interface) — A Windows 9x component that controls screens, graphics, and printing.

global user account — Sometimes called a domain user account, the account is used at the domain level, created by an administrator, and stored in the SAM (security accounts manager) database on a domain controller.

group files — Windows 3.x files with the .grp file extension that contain information about a program group of Program Manager.

group profile — A group of user profiles. All profiles in the group can be changed by changing the group profile.

Guest user — A user who has limited permissions on a system and cannot make changes to it. Guest user accounts are intended for one-time or infrequent users of a workstation.

GUI (graphical user interface) — A user interface, such as the Windows interface, that uses graphics or icons on the screen for running programs and entering information.

HAL (hardware abstraction layer) — The low-level part of Windows NT/2000/XP, written specifically for each CPU technology, so that only the HAL must change when platform components change.

hard boot — Restart the computer by turning off the power or by pressing the Reset button. Also called a cold boot.

hardware address — *See* MAC address.

hardware cache — A disk cache that is contained in RAM chips built right on the disk controller.

hardware interrupt — An event caused by a hardware device signaling the CPU that it requires service.

hardware profile — Hardware configuration information that Windows keeps in the registry. Windows can maintain more than one hardware profile for the same PC.

hardware tree — A database built each time Windows 9x starts up that contains a list of installed components and the resources they use.

HCL (hardware compatibility list) — The list of all computers and peripheral devices that have been tested and are officially supported by Windows NT/2000/XP. (See *www.microsoft.com/hcl.*)

HFS (Hierarchical File System) — The file system used for Macintosh computer disks before 1998, when drives larger than 1 GB became common. HFS limited the number of allocation units on a disk to 65,536. Also known as Mac OS standard format.

HFS+ — The file system used for Mac disks since the release of Mac OS 8.1 in 1998. HFS+ is an update of HFS, and can format drives up to 2,048 GB. Also called Mac OS extended format.

hidden file — A file that is not displayed in a directory list. Whether to hide or display a file is indicated by one of the file's attributes kept by the OS.

Himem.sys — The DOS and Windows 9x memory manager extension that allowed access to memory addresses above 1 MB.

hive — Physical segments of the Windows NT/ 2000/XP registry that is stored in a file.

HMA (high memory area) — The first 64K of extended memory.

host — Any computer or other device on a network that has been assigned an IP address.

host drive — Typically drive H on a compressed drive. *See* compressed drive.

host name — A name that identifies a computer, printer, or other device on a network.

Hosts — A text file located in the Windows folder that contains host names and their associated IP addresses. This file is used for name resolution for a TCP/IP network using DNS.

HTML (HyperText Markup Language) — A markup language used for hypertext documents on the World Wide Web. This language uses tags to format the document, create hyperlinks, and mark locations for graphics.

HTTP (HyperText Transfer Protocol) — The protocol used by the World Wide Web.

HTTPS (HTTP secure) — A version of the HTTP protocol that includes data encryption for security.

hub — A network device or box that provides a central location to connect cables.

hypertext — Text that contains links to points in the document or other files, documents, or graphics. Hypertext is created using HTML and is commonly distributed from Web sites.

I/O addresses — Numbers used by devices and the CPU to manage communication between them. Also called ports or port addresses.

ICMP (Internet Control Message Protocol) — Part of the IP layer that is used to transmit error messages and other control messages to hosts and routers.

IDE (Integrated Drive Electronics) — A standard governing hard drive technology and how secondary storage devices, such as hard drives and Zip drives, relate to a system.

IEEE (Institute of Electrical and Electronics Engineers) — A nonprofit organization that develops standards for the computer and electronics industries.

IMAP4 (Internet Message Access Protocol version 4) — Version 4 of the IMAP protocol, an e-mail protocol that has more functionality than its predecessor, POP. IMAP can archive messages in folders on the e-mail server and allow the user to choose not to download attachments to messages.

incremental backup — A time-saving backup method that only backs up files changed or newly created since the last full or incremental backup. Multiple incremental backups might be required when recovering lost data.

infestation — Any unwanted program transmitted to a computer without the user's knowledge and designed to do damage to data and software. There are different types of infestations, including viruses, Trojan horses, worms, and logic bombs.

information (.inf) file — Text file with an .inf file extension, such as Msbatch.inf, that contains information about a hardware or software installation.

initialization files — Configuration information files for Windows. System.ini is one of the most important Windows initialization files.

insert mode — A Linux vi editor mode in which you can type text into the editor.

Installable File System (IFS) — A Windows 9x Plug and Play component that is responsible for all disk access.

internal command — Commands that are embedded in the Command.com file.

Internet Connection Firewall (ICF) — Windows XP software designed to protect a PC from unauthorized access from the Internet.

interrupt handler — A program (either BIOS or a device driver), used by the CPU to process a hardware interrupt. Also called request handler.

interrupt vector table — A table that stores the memory addresses assigned to interrupt handlers so the CPU can find one when needed. Also called a vector table.

intranet — A private network that uses the TCP/IP protocols.

Io.sys — Along with Msdos.sys and Command.com, one of the three files that are the core components of the real mode portion of Windows 9x. The first program file of the OS.

IP (Internet Protocol) — The rules of communication in the TCP/IP stack that control segmenting data into packets, routing those packets across networks, and then reassembling the packets once they reach their destination.

IP address — A 32-bit address consisting of four numbers separated by periods, used to uniquely identify a device on a network that uses TCP/IP protocols. The first numbers identify the network; the last numbers identify a host. An example of an IP address is 206.96.103.114.

IPX/SPX (Internetwork Packet Exchange/Sequenced Packet Exchange) — A networking protocol suite first used by Novell NetWare, which corresponds to the TCP/IP protocols.

IRQ (interrupt request number) — A line on a bus that is assigned to a device and is used to signal the CPU for servicing. These lines are assigned a reference number (for example, the normal IRQ for a printer is IRQ 7).

ISA (Industry Standard Architecture) — An 8-bit or 16-bit slot first used in the 1980s on motherboards and sometimes still used today.

ISO (International Organization for Standardization) — A standards organization composed of standards bodies from several countries. The ISO developed the OSI model.

ISP (Internet service provider) — A commercial group that provides Internet access for a monthly fee. AOL, Earthlink, and CompuServe are large ISPs.

kernel — The portion of an OS that is responsible for interacting with the hardware.

kernel mode — A Windows NT/2000/XP "privileged" processing mode that has access to hardware components.

key — (1) In encryption, a secret number or code used to encode and decode data. (2) In Windows, a section name of the Windows registry.

LAN (local area network) — A computer network that covers only a small area, usually within one building.

laptop — *See* notebook.

legacy — A term used to refer to older computer devices or software that does not use the most current technologies.

Library — The Mac OS X folder that takes over the functions of the Mac OS 9 control panels and extensions, which do not exist in Mac OS X. System settings and add-ons are controlled from the Library folder.

Limited user — Windows XP user accounts known as Users in Windows NT/2000, which have limited access to other users' data.

line protocol — A protocol used to send data packets destined for a network over telephone lines. PPP and SLIP are examples of line protocols.

LMHosts — A text file in the Windows folder that contains NetBIOS names and their associated IP addresses. Used for name resolution for a NetBEUI network.

local bus — A bus that runs synchronized with the system bus and CPU.

local printer — A printer connected to a computer by way of a port on the computer.

local profile — User profile stored on a local computer and cannot be accessed from another computer on the network.

local user account — A user account that applies only to a local computer and cannot be used to access resources from other computers on the network.

logic bomb — Dormant code added to software that is triggered by a predetermined time or event.

loopback device — A virtual device, which consists of the local system and has the IP address 127.x.x.x. It is used to test the TCP/IP configuration on a computer.

lost allocation units — *See* lost clusters.

lost clusters — Lost file fragments that, according to the file allocation table, contain data that does not belong to any file. The command Chkdsk/F can free these fragments.

MAC address — A 6-byte hexadecimal hardware address unique to each NIC card and assigned by the manufacturer. The address is often printed on the adapter. An example is 00 00 0C 08 2F 35. Also called a physical address, an adapter address, or a hardware address.

Mac OS extended format — *See* HFS+.

Mac OS ROM file — The first item that the Mac loads into memory from the System folder during the startup process. This file contains commands required for interaction with hardware and the lower levels of the Mac OS.

Mac OS standard format — *See* HFS.

macro — A small sequence of commands, contained within a document, that can be automatically executed when the document is loaded, or executed later by using a predetermined keystroke.

macro virus — A virus that can hide in the macros of a document file. Typically, viruses do not reside in data or document files.

mandatory user profile — A roaming user profile that applies to all users in a group, and individual users cannot change that profile.

master file table (MFT) — The database used by the NTFS file system to track the contents of a logical drive.

MBR (Master Boot Record) — The first sector on a hard drive, which contains the partition table and a program the BIOS uses to boot an OS from the drive.

memory address — A number assigned to each byte in memory. The CPU can use memory addresses to track where information is stored in RAM. Memory addresses are usually displayed as hexadecimal numbers in segment/offset form.

memory bus — *See* system bus.

memory dump — The contents of memory saved to a file when an event halted the system. Support technicians can analyze the dump file to understand the source of the problem.

memory extender — For DOS and Windows 9x, a device driver named Himem.sys that manages RAM giving access to memory addresses above 1 MB.

memory leak — When software unloads from memory but does not release the memory addresses used for its data back to the OS.

memory paging — In Windows, swapping blocks of RAM memory to an area of the hard drive to serve as virtual memory when RAM is low.

memory-resident virus — A virus that can stay lurking in memory even after its host program is terminated.

microprocessor — *See* CPU.

Microsoft Management Console (MMC) — A utility to build customized consoles. These consoles can be saved to a file with a .msc file extension.

minifile system — In Windows NT/2000/XP, a simplified file system that is started so that Ntldr (NT Loader) can read files from any file system the OS supports.

mixed mode — A Windows 2000 mode for domain controllers used when there is at least one Windows NT domain controller on the network.

motherboard — The largest circuit board inside the computer; it holds the CPU, slots, connections, and ports for other devices and wires for communication called a bus. Also called system board.

Msdos.sys — In Windows 9x, a text file that contains settings used by Io.sys during booting. In DOS, the Msdos.sys file was a program file that contained part of the DOS core.

multicasting — A process in which a message is sent by one host to multiple hosts, such as when a video conference is broadcasted to several hosts on the Internet.

multipartite virus — A combination of a boot sector virus and a file virus. It can hide in either type of program.

multiprocessing — Having two or more CPUs in a system.

multitasking — Doing more than one thing at a time. A true multitasking system requires two or more CPUs, each processing a different thread at the same time. Compare to cooperative multitasking and preemptive multitasking.

multithreading — The ability to pass more than one function (thread) to the OS kernel at the same time, such as when one thread is performing a print job while another reads a file.

name resolution — The process of associating a NetBIOS name or host name to an IP address.

NAT (Network Address Translation) — Converts private IP addresses on a LAN to the proxy server's IP address before a data packet is sent over the Internet.

native mode — A Windows 2000 mode used by domain controllers when there are no Windows NT domain controllers present on the network.

NetBEUI (NetBIOS Extended User Interface) — A fast, proprietary Microsoft networking protocol used only by Windows-based systems, and limited to LANs because it does not support routing.

NetBIOS (Network Basic Input/Output System) — An API protocol used by some applications to communicate over a NetBEUI network. NetBIOS has largely been replaced by Windows Sockets over a TCP/IP network.

network drive map — Mounting a drive to a computer, such as drive E, that is actually hard drive space on another host computer on the network.

Network layer — The OSI layer responsible for routing packets.

network printer — A printer that is available to users on a network.

NIC (network interface card) — A expansion card that plugs into a computer's motherboard and provides a port on the back of the card to connect a PC to a network. Also called a network adapter.

NNTP (Network News Transfer Protocol) — The protocol used by newsgroup server and client software.

non-memory-resident virus — A virus that is terminated when the host program is closed. Compare to memory-resident virus.

NOS (network operating system) — An operating system on the controlling computer in the network. The NOS controls what software, data, and devices a user on the network can access.

notebook — A portable computer designed for travel and mobility. Notebooks use the same technology as desktop PCs, with modifications for conserving voltage, taking up less space, and operating on the move. Also called a laptop computer.

NTFS (NT file system) — The file system for the Windows NT/2000/XP operating systems. NTFS cannot be accessed by other operating systems such as DOS. It provides increased reliability and security in comparison to other methods of organizing files. There are several versions of NTFS that might or might not be compatible.

NTHQ (NT Hardware Qualifier) — A utility found on the Windows NT installation CD-ROM that examines your system to determine if all hardware present qualifies for NT.

Ntldr (NT Loader) — In Windows NT/2000/XP, the OS loader used on Intel systems.

NTVDM (NT virtual DOS machine) — An emulated environment in which a 16-bit DOS application resides within Windows NT/2000/XP with its own memory space or WOW (Win16 on Win32).

octet — Term for each of the four 8-bit numbers that make up an IP address. For example, the IP address 206.96.103.114 has four octets.

operating system — Software that controls a computer. An operating system controls how system resources are used and provides a user interface, a way of managing hardware and software, and ways to work with files.

OSI (Open Systems Interconnect) reference model — A network communication model that provides a universally accepted reference that illustrates how data is transmitted on a network or between two or more networked devices. This model separates communication into seven layers.

packet — Segment of network data that also include header, destination address, and trailer information that is sent as a unit. Also called data packet or datagram.

page fault — An OS interrupt that occurs when the OS is forced to access the hard drive to satisfy the demands for virtual memory.

page file — *See* swap file.

Pagefile.sys — The Windows NT/2000/XP swap file.

page-in — The process in which the memory manager goes to the hard drive to return the data from a swap file to RAM.

page-out — The process in which, when RAM is full, the memory manager takes a page and moves it to the swap file.

pages — 4K segments in which Windows NT/2000/XP allocates memory.

parallel port — A 25-pin female port on a computer that can transmit data in parallel, 8 bits at a time, and is usually used by a printer. Sometimes configured as LPT1 or LPT2.

partition table — A table at the beginning of the hard drive that contains information about each partition on the drive. The partition table is contained in the master boot record.

patch — An update to software that corrects an error, adds a feature, or addresses security issues. Also called an update or service pack.

path — (1) A drive and list of directories pointing to a file such as C:\Windows\command. (2) The OS command to provide a list of paths to the system for finding program files to execute.

PCI (Peripheral Component Interconnect) bus — A bus common on Pentium computers that runs at speeds of up to 33 MHz or 66 MHz, with a 32-bit-wide or 64-bit-wide data path. PCI-X, released in September 1999, enables PCI to run at 133 MHz. For some chip sets, it serves as the middle layer between the memory bus and expansion buses.

peer-to-peer network — A network of computers that are all equals, or peers. Each computer has the same amount of authority, and can act as a server to the other computers.

physical address — *See* MAC address.

Physical layer — The OSI layer responsible for interfacing with the network media (cabling).

PIF (program information file) — A file used by Windows to describe the environment for a DOS program to use.

Ping — A program that allows one computer to send a packet to another computer and then receive a reply. Used as a method of testing connectivity.

pixel — Small spots on a fine horizontal scan line that are illuminated to create an image on a monitor.

Plug and Play (PnP) — A standard designed to make the installation of new hardware devices easier by automatically configuring devices to eliminate system resource conflicts (such as IRQ or I/O address conflicts). PnP is supported by Windows 9x, Windows 2000 and Windows XP.

Plug and Play BIOS — System BIOS that supports the Plug and Play standards and is designed to automatically recognize new devices when they are installed.

polling — The CPU checks the status of connected devices to determine if they are ready to send or receive data.

polymorphic virus — A virus that changes its distinguishing characteristics as it replicates itself. Mutating in this way makes it more difficult for AV software to recognize its presence.

POP (Post Office Protocol) — The protocol that an e-mail server and client use when the client requests the downloading of e-mail messages. The most recent version is POP3. POP is slowly being replaced by IMAP.

port — (1) For services running on a computer, a number assigned to a process on a computer so the process can be found by TCP/IP. Also called a port address or port number. (2) Another name for an I/O address. *See also* I/O address.

port address — *See* I/O address.

port number — *See* port.

port replicator — A device designed to connect to a notebook computer to make it easy to connect the notebook to peripheral devices.

POSIX (Portable Operating System Interface) — A set of standards for Unix and similar operating systems used to create applications to comply with standards used by federal agencies for their software.

POST (power-on self test) — A self-diagnostic program used to perform a simple test of the CPU, RAM, and various I/O devices. The POST is performed by startup BIOS when the computer is first turned on and is stored in ROM-BIOS.

power scheme — A feature of Windows XP support for notebooks that allows the user to create groups of power settings for specific sets of conditions.

Power User — *See* standard user.

PPP (Point-to-Point Protocol) — A protocol that governs the methods for communicating via modems and dial-up telephone lines. The Windows Dial-up Networking utility uses PPP.

PRAM (parameter RAM) — A small amount of RAM on a Mac that contains configuration information for the Mac.

preemptive multitasking — A type of pseudo-multitasking whereby the CPU allows an application a specified period of time and then preempts the processing to give time to another application.

Presentation layer — The OSI layer that compresses and decompresses data and interfaces with the Application layer and the Session layer.

primary domain controller (PDC) — In a Windows NT network, the computer that controls the directory database of user accounts, group accounts, and computer accounts on a domain. Also see backup domain controller.

primary partition — A hard disk partition that can contain only one logical drive.

primary storage — Temporary storage on the motherboard used by the CPU to process data and instructions. Memory is considered primary storage.

private IP address — An IP address that is used on a private TCP/IP network that is isolated from the Internet.

process — An executing instance of a program together with the program resources. There can be more than one process running for a program at the same time. One process for a program happens each time the program is loaded into memory or executed.

product activation — The process that Microsoft uses to prevent software piracy. Once Windows XP is activated for a computer, it cannot be installed on another computer.

program file — A file that contains instructions designed to be executed by the CPU.

protected mode — An operating mode that supports preemptive multitasking, the OS manages memory and other hardware devices, and programs can use a 32-bit data path. Also called 32-bit mode.

Protocol.ini — A Windows initialization file that contains network configuration information.

proxy server — A server that acts as an intermediary between another computer and the Internet. The proxy server substitutes its own IP address for the IP address of the computer on the network making a request, so that all traffic over the Internet appears to be coming from only the IP address of the proxy server.

public IP address — An IP address available to the Internet.

RAID (redundant array of inexpensive disks or redundant array of independent disks) — Several methods of configuring multiple hard drives to store data to increase logical volume size and improve performance, and to ensure that if one hard drive fails, the data is still available from another hard drive.

RAM (random access memory) — Memory modules on the motherboard containing microchips used to temporarily hold data and programs while the CPU processes both. Information in RAM is lost when the PC is turned off.

RAM drive — An area of memory treated as though it were a hard drive, but that works much faster than a hard drive. The Windows 98 startup disk uses a RAM drive. Compare to virtual memory.

RARP (Reverse Address Resolution Protocol) — A protocol used to translate the unique hardware NIC addresses (MAC addresses) into IP addresses (the reverse of ARP).

real mode — A single-tasking operating mode whereby a program has 1024K of memory addresses, has direct access to RAM, and uses a 16-bit data path. Using a memory extender (Himem.sys) a program in real mode can access memory above 1024K. Also called 16-bit mode.

Recovery Console — A Windows 2000/XP command interface utility and OS that can be used to solve problems when the Windows cannot load from the hard drive.

redirection symbol — The greater than (>) symbol used in OS commands to redirect output to a file or printer instead of to a screen.

registry — A database that Windows uses to store hardware and software configuration information, user preferences, and setup information.

Remote Access Service (RAS) — The Windows NT service used to configure a computer to allow inbound calls.

Remote Assistance — A Windows XP feature that allows a support technician at a remote location to have full access to the Windows XP desktop.

request handler — See interrupt handler.

rescue disk — A floppy disk that can be used to start up a computer when the hard drive fails to boot. Also called ESD or startup disk.

resolution — The number of pixels on a monitor screen that are addressable by software, such as 1024 × 768.

resource arbitrator — A Plug and Play component that decides which resources are assigned to which devices.

resource management — The process of allocating resources to devices at startup.

restore point — A snapshot of the Windows Me/XP system state, usually made before installation of new hardware or applications.

restricted user — See user.

RFC (Request for Comments) — A document that proposes a change in standards for the communications industry. An RFC can be presented by different organizations but is managed under the guidance of the Internet Architecture Board (IAB).

roaming user profile — A user profile for a roaming user. Roaming user profiles are stored on a server so that the user can access the profile from anywhere on the network.

roaming users — Users who can move from PC to PC within a network, with their profiles following them.

root account — The principal user account in Linux, accessible by the system administrator. Only the owner of the root account has the ability to make certain alterations to the system and perform certain system tasks.

root directory — The main directory created when a hard drive or disk is first formatted. In Linux, indicated by a forward slash. In DOS and Windows, indicated by a backward slash.

root privileges — The privileges that the system administrator has on a Linux system, which allow the system administrator full access to the system.

run-time configuration — An ongoing Plug and Play process that monitors changes in system devices, such as the removal of a PC card on a notebook computer.

secondary storage — Storage remote to the CPU that permanently holds data, even when the PC is turned off, such as a hard drive.

sector — On a disk surface one segment of a track, which almost always contains 512 bytes of data.

security accounts manager (SAM) — A portion of the Windows NT/2000/XP registry that manages the account database that contains accounts, policies, and other pertinent information about local accounts.

serial port — A male 9-pin or 25-pin port on a computer system used by slower I/O devices such as a mouse or modem. Data travels serially, one bit at a time, through the port. Serial ports are sometimes configured as COM1, COM2, COM3, or COM4.

server — (1) A software program that interacts with client software in a client/server environment. (2) A computer that runs server software and responds to requests for information from client computers.

service pack — *See* patch.

session — An established communication link between two software programs. On the Internet, a session is created by TCP.

Session layer — The OSI layer that makes and manages an extended connection between two hosts on a network.

SFC (System File Checker) — A Windows tool that checks that Windows is using the correct versions of system files.

shell — The portion of an OS that relates to the user and to applications.

shortcut — An icon on the desktop that points to a program that can be executed or to a file or folder.

Sigverif.exe — A Windows 2000/XP utility that allows you to search for digital signatures.

simple volume — A type of dynamic volume used on a single hard drive that corresponds to a primary partition on a basic disk.

single-tasking — When only one program is running at a time.

SLIP (Serial Line Internet Protocol) — A line protocol used by regular telephone lines that has largely been replaced by PPP.

SMARTDrive — A hard drive cache program that came with Windows 3.x and DOS and can be executed as a TSR from the Autoexec.bat file (for example, Device=Smartdrv.sys 2048).

SMTP (Simple Mail Transfer Protocol) — The protocol used by e-mail clients and servers to send e-mail messages over the Internet. *See* POP and IMAP.

snap-ins — Components added to a console using the Microsoft Management Console.

SNMP (Simple Network Management Protocol) — A protocol used to monitor and manage network traffic on a workstation. SNMP works with TCP/IP and IPX/SPX networks.

socket — *See* session.

soft boot — To restart a PC without turning off the power, for example, by pressing three keys at the same time (Ctrl, Alt, and Del). Also called warm boot.

software cache — Cache controlled by software whereby the cache is stored in RAM.

software interrupt — An event caused by a program currently being executed by the CPU signaling the CPU that it requires the use of a hardware device.

spanned volume — A type of dynamic volume used on two or more hard drives that fills up the space allotted on one physical disk before moving to the next.

spooling — Placing print jobs in a print queue so that an application can be released from the printing process before printing is completed. Spooling is an acronym for simultaneous peripheral operations online.

standard user — Also called power user. Standard users can read from and write to parts of the system other than their own local drive, install applications, and perform limited administrative tasks.

startup BIOS — Part of system BIOS that is responsible for controlling the PC when it is first turned on. Startup BIOS gives control over to the OS once it is loaded.

startup disk — *See* rescue disk.

static IP address — An IP address permanently assigned to a workstation.

Static VxD — A VxD that is loaded into memory at startup and remains there for the entire OS session.

stealth virus — A virus that conceals itself by temporarily removing itself from an infected file about to be examined, and then hiding a copy of itself elsewhere on the drive.

stop error — An error severe enough to cause the operating system to stop all processes.

striped volume — A type of dynamic volume used for two or more hard drives that writes to the disks evenly rather than filling up allotted space on one and then moving on to the next. Compare to spanned volume.

subdirectory — A directory or folder contained in another directory or folder. Also called a child directory or folder.

subnet mask — A subnet mask is a group of four numbers (dotted decimal numbers) that tell TCP/IP if a remote computer is on the same or a different network.

subsystems — The different modules into which the Windows NT/2000/XP user mode is divided.

swap file — A file on the hard drive that is used by the OS for virtual memory. Also called page file.

Sysedit — The Windows System Configuration Editor, which is a text editor generally used to edit system files.

system BIOS — BIOS located on the motherboard.

system bus — The bus between the CPU and memory on the motherboard. The bus frequency in documentation is called the system speed such as 200 MHz. Also called the memory bus, front-side bus, local bus, or host bus.

system disk — Windows terminology for a bootable disk.

System file — The Mac OS file that contains the libraries and commands that make up the core of the OS.

System File Protection — A Windows Me feature that prevents system files from being deleted.

System folder — The folder that a Mac system designates as the one from which the OS is to be loaded.

System.ini — A text configuration file used by Windows 3.x and supported by Windows 9x for backward-compatibility.

system partition — The active partition of the hard drive containing the boot record and the specific files required to load Windows NT/2000/XP.

System Restore — A Windows Me/XP utility, similar to the ScanReg tool in earlier versions of Windows, used to restore the system to a restore point. Unlike ScanReg, System Restore cannot be executed from a command prompt.

system state data — In Windows 2000/XP, files that are necessary for a successful load of the operating system.

System Tray — An area to the right of the taskbar that holds the icons of small applets launched at startup.

task switching — See cooperative multitasking.

TCP (Transmission Control Protocol) — Part of the TCP/IP protocol suite. TCP guarantees delivery of data for application protocols and establishes a session before it begins transmitting data.

TCP/IP (Transmission Control Protocol/Internet Protocol) — The suite of protocols that supports communication on the Internet. TCP is responsible for error checking, and IP is responsible for routing.

Terminate-and-stay-resident (TSR) — A program that is loaded into memory and remains dormant until called on, such as a memory-resident antivirus program.

thread — Each process that the CPU is aware of; a single task that is part of a longer task or program.

top-level domain — The highest level of domain names, indicated by a suffix that tells something about the host. For example, .com is for commercial use and .edu is for educational institutions.

track — One of many concentric circles on the surface of a hard drive or floppy disk.

Transport layer — The OSI layer that verifies data and requests a resend when the data is corrupted.

Trojan horse — A type of infestation that disguises itself as a useful program, yet is designed to cause damage later.

UDP (User Datagram Protocol) — A connectionless protocol that does not require a connection to send a packet and does not guarantee that the packet arrives at its destination. UDP works at the Transport layer and is faster than TCP because TCP takes the time to make a connection and guarantee delivery.

UMB (upper memory block) — In DOS and Windows 9x, a group of consecutive memory addresses in RAM from 640K to 1MB that can be used by 16-bit device drivers and TSRs.

unattended installation — A Windows NT/ 2000/XP installation that is done by storing the answers to installation questions in a text file or script that Windows NT/2000/XP calls an answer file so that the answers do not have to be typed in during the installation.

upgrade install — The installation of an OS on a hard drive that already has an OS installed so that settings kept by the old OS are carried into the upgrade, including information about hardware, software, and user preferences.

upper memory — In DOS and Windows 9x, the memory addresses from 640K up to 1024K, originally reserved for BIOS, device drivers, and TSRs.

URL (Uniform Resource Locator) — An address for a resource on the Internet. A URL can contain the protocol used by the resource, the name of the computer and its network, and the path and name of a file on the computer.

USB (universal serial bus) — A bus that is expected to eventually replace serial and parallel ports. USB is designed to make installation and configuration of I/O devices easy, providing room for as many as 127 devices daisy-chained together. The USB uses only a single set of resources for all devices on the bus.

user — In Windows NT/2000/XP permissions, a restricted user who has read-write access only on his or her own folders, read-only access to most system folders, and no access to other users' data.

user account — The information, stored in the SAM database, that defines a Windows NT/ 2000/XP user, including username, password, memberships, and rights.

user component — A Windows 9x component that controls the mouse, keyboard, ports and desktop.

user mode — In Windows NT/2000/XP, a mode that provides an interface between an application and the OS, and only has access to hardware resources through the code running in kernel mode.

user profile — A personal profile about a user that enables the user's desktop settings and other operating parameters to be retained from one session to another.

User State Migration Tool (USMT) — A Windows XP utility that helps migrate user files and preferences from one computer to another to help make a smooth transition from one computer to another.

value data — In Windows, the name and value of a setting in the registry.

VCACHE — A built-in Windows 9x 32-bit software cache that doesn't take up conventional memory space or upper memory space as SMARTDrive did.

VDM (virtual DOS machine) — An environment that a 32-bit protected-mode OS provides for a real-mode program to operate in.

vector table — *See* interrupt vector table.

VFAT (virtual file allocation table) — A variation of the original DOS 16-bit FAT that allows for long filenames and 32-bit disk access.

vi editor — A text editor in Linux that operates in two modes: insert mode, in which you can type text into the editor, and command mode, in which you can enter commands to work with the text or change the status of the editor.

virtual device driver (VxD or VDD) — A Windows device driver that may or may not have direct access to a device. It might depend on a Windows component to communicate with the device itself.

virtual DOS machine (VDM) — Environment in which Windows runs a 16-bit DOS application. In a VDM, the application "thinks" it is running in real mode, but the OS is managing hardware resources using 32-bit drivers and providing virtual memory to the application.

virtual machine — One or more logical machines created within one physical machine by Windows, allowing applications to make serious errors within one logical machine without disturbing other programs and parts of the system.

Virtual Machine Manager (VMM) — A Windows 9x program that controls virtual machines and the resources they use including memory. The VMM manages the page table used to access memory.

virtual memory — A method whereby the OS uses the hard drive as though it were RAM. Compare to RAM drive.

virtual real mode — An operating mode that works similarly to real mode provided by a 32-bit OS for a 16-bit program to work.

virus — A program that often has an incubation period, is infectious, and is meant to cause damage. A virus program might destroy data and programs or damage a disk drive's boot sector.

virus signature — A set of distinguishing characteristics of a virus used by antivirus software to identify the virus.

volume bit map — On a Macintosh computer, a map of the allocation blocks on a hard drive. It uses a 1 to indicate that a block is storing files and a 0 to indicate that it is empty.

volume information block — On a Macintosh computer, the directory structure that comes right after the boot blocks on a hard drive. It holds information about the drive, including its format, name, number of files and folders, and allocation block size.

VxD — *See* virtual device driver.

warm boot — *See* soft boot.

WDM (Win32 Driver Model) — The only Windows 9x Plug and Play component that is found in Windows 98 but not Windows 95. WDM is the component responsible for managing device drivers that work under a driver model new to Windows 98.

WFP (Windows File Protection) — A Windows 2000/XP tool that protects system files from modification.

Win.ini — The Windows initialization file that contains program configuration information for running the Windows operating environment. Its functions were replaced by the registry with Windows 9x, which still supports it for backward compatibility with Windows 3.x.

Win386.swp — The Windows 9x swap file. Its default location is C:\Windows.

window manager — A graphical user interface for a Linux computer. A popular window manager is GNOME.

WINS (Windows Internet Naming Service) — A Microsoft resolution service with a distributed database that tracks relationships between NetBIOS names and IP addresses. Compare to DNS.

WinSock (Windows Sockets) — A part of the TCP/IP utility software that manages API calls from applications to other computers on a TCP/IP network.

WIS (Windows Installer Service) — A feature new to Windows 2000 that standardizes the installation process for applications.

workgroup — In Windows, a logical group of computers and users in which administration, resources, and security are distributed throughout the network, without centralized management or security.

worm — An infestation designed to copy itself repeatedly to memory, on drive space or on a network, until little memory or disk space remains.

WOW (Win16 on Win32) — A group of programs provided by Windows NT/2000/XP to create a virtual DOS environment that emulates a 16-bit Windows environment, protecting the rest of the OS from 16-bit applications.

THOMSON
COURSE TECHNOLOGY ™

A+ PC Repair
Total Solution

URSE TECHNOLOGY offers *everything* you need to prepare CompTIA's 2003 A+ Certification Exams and embark on a ccessful career as a computer technician.

books are written by best-selling author and instructor Jean Andrews.

MPREHENSIVE TEXTS

Guide to Managing and Maintaining
r PC, Comprehensive,
urth Edition
N: 0-619-18617-8

A+ Guide to Hardware: Managing,
Maintaining, and Troubleshooting,
Second Edition
ISBN: 0-619-18624-0

A+ Guide to Software: Managing,
Maintaining, and Troubleshooting,
Second Edition
ISBN: 0-619-18627-5

ANDS-ON PRACTICE

b Manual for A+ Guide to Managing
d Maintaining Your PC,
urth Edition
3N: 0-619-18619-4

Lab Manual for A+ Guide to Hardware:
Managing, Maintaining, and
Troubleshooting, Second Edition
ISBN: 0-619-18626-7

Lab Manual for A+ Guide to Software:
Managing, Maintaining, and
Troubleshooting, Second Edition
ISBN: 0-619-18629-1

DDITIONAL PRACTICAL EXPERIENCE

Computer-Based Training (CBT),
ird Edition
InfoSource
3N: 0-619-18621-6

PC Troubleshooting Pocket Guide,
Third Edition
ISBN: 0-619-18620-8

KAM PREPARATION

CoursePrep StudyGuide,
cond Edition
3N: 0-619-18622-4

A+ CoursePrep ExamGuide,
Second Edition
ISBN: 0-619-18623-2

A+ Hardware CourseCard
ISBN: 0-619-20362-5

A+ Software CourseCard
ISBN: 0-619-20363-3

N THE JOB

-Piece Toolset with ESD Strap
3N: 0-619-01655-8

Digital Multimeter
ISBN: 0-619-13101-2

or more information visit **www.course.com/pcrepair** or call 800-648-7450